Through a lens all of us can understand ........ daughters and granddaughters—Dale H....... ...... ...... focus the hardships, obstacles, and threats faced by girls growing up in resource-poor communities around the world. Some of what she shares is heartbreaking, but much of it is filled with hope. Progress is being made, and Dale points us to practical actions we can take to help lift up a generation of strong girls who will make the world stronger. With more children in crisis in the world today than ever before, Dale's message is one we need now.

MICHAEL J. NYENHUIS, president and CEO, UNICEF USA

As I've traveled the world I've seen over and over again that girls face tremendous disadvantages, but manage to overcome them in amazing ways. So often they need just a little help. This inspiring and practical book gives us all the opportunity to invest in the future of girls.

PATRICIA HEATON, actress and advocate

Dale Hanson Bourke approaches the challenging issues facing girls today with the skill of an experienced author, the passion of an activist, the grace of a person of faith, and the heart of a grandmother. If you agree with Dale and me that the disadvantages and burdens on girls around the world are unacceptable, please read this book to find out exactly how we can help girls soar.

EDGAR SANDOVAL SR., president and CEO of World Vision

*Strong Girls, Strong World* is an important book about a simple truth: Girls face monumental challenges around the world just because they're girls. Yet, we don't have to sit idly by—we all have the ability to change the world if we choose to act. Dale Hanson Bourke has created an easy-to-read guide to learn more about the issues affecting girls and discover practical ways to make an effective difference today.

**MARGO DAY**, CEO and cofounder, Mekuno Project;
former vice president, US Education, Microsoft

In my travels around the world, I have seen that girls often suffer the most. And yet, when given the opportunity, they are the first to give back to others and make their communities stronger. In *Strong Girls, Strong World*, Dale Hanson Bourke offers a clear explanation of how change can happen, then presents often simple ways we can each make a difference. Her personal stories and practical solutions make this a hopeful and important book.

**STEVE STIRLING**, president and CEO, MAP International

When we think of the plight of girls globally, it is easy to become overwhelmed by the lack of progress toward equality and access to resources to meet basic needs. What can one do? Why should we care? My organization works to address these very concerns, but we need other truth-tellers to amplify a collective, urgent voice that this work is far from done. With compelling statistics as well as stories from her own personal life and from girls overcoming challenging circumstances, Dale gives us all the right reasons for why we should care—and why investing in a better future for girls around the world improves life for us all.

**MARTHA HOLLEY NEWSOME**, president and CEO, Medical Teams International

What would it take to create a better, safer, and stronger world for our children and grandchildren? I have come to believe that their future well-being may depend on one simple commitment: to help girls and women realize their full God-given potential and to make them equal partners in leading our communities, institutions, and governments. Regrettably, since the Garden of Eden, we have left fully half of our most creative, gifted, and capable leaders sitting on the bench. But what if we committed to correcting that by investing in girls and women—in their education, their health, their safety, and their opportunities? Dale Hanson Bourke believes that girls can change the world, and so do I. This is a book you need to read and then buy extras to give copies to your friends.

RICHARD STEARNS, president emeritus of World Vision US; author of *The Hole in Our Gospel* and *Lead Like It Matters to God*

Girls around the world deserve the opportunity to put their God-given talents to full use, no matter what their birth circumstances. Dale Hanson Bourke's thoughtful book guides us all in how we can be part of creating those opportunities, thus creating a better world for us all.

ATUL TANDON, CEO, Opportunity International

Dale Hanson Bourke is well known as a lifelong advocate for women and girls. In *Strong Girls, Strong World* Dale makes the case that we must all act now to do our part to help girls reach their full God-given potential. In this beautifully written book, she also gives us practical ways to support girls and the organizations committed to making sure girls are included in every aspect of their work. This is a call to action for all of us to recommit our efforts to women and girls and thus ensure a better future for everyone.

SCOTT JACKSON, president and CEO, Global Impact

# STRONG GIRLS, STRONG WORLD

*A Practical Guide to Helping Them Soar—*
*and Creating a Better Future for Us All*

## DALE HANSON BOURKE

**TYNDALE**
REFRESH™

*Think Well. Live Well. Be Well.*

Visit Tyndale online at tyndale.com.

Visit stronggirlsstrongworld.com.

*Tyndale* and Tyndale's quill logo are registered trademarks of Tyndale House Ministries. *Tyndale Refresh* and the Tyndale Refresh logo are trademarks of Tyndale House Ministries. Tyndale Momentum is a nonfiction imprint of Tyndale House Publishers, Carol Stream, Illinois.

Strong Women Strong World is a registered trademark of World Vision. *Strong Girls, Strong World* used with permission.

*Strong Girls, Strong World: A Practical Guide to Helping Them Soar—and Creating a Better Future for Us All*

Designed by Lindsey Bergsma

Published in association with The Steve Laube Agency.

The names of some people have been changed for the privacy of the individuals.

For information about special discounts for bulk purchases, please contact Tyndale House Publishers at csresponse@tyndale.com, or call 1-855-277-9400.

**Library of Congress Cataloging-in-Publication Data**

A catalog record for this book is available from the Library of Congress.

ISBN 978-1-4964-5232-0 (hc)
ISBN 978-1-4964-5233-7 (sc)

Printed in United States of America

29  28  27  26  25  24  23
7   6   5   4   3   2   1

*For Genevieve Elizabeth, who is loved and adored,*
*and for all the other girls in the world*
*who deserve the same opportunities to soar.*

# Contents

# Introduction

. . . . . . . . . . . . . .

# IT'S PERSONAL

SHE WAS THE MOST BEAUTIFUL BABY my husband, Tom, and I had ever seen. From the first image we saw of our granddaughter, we were smitten. Separated by 3,000 miles and pandemic restrictions, we carefully studied every photo and video our son and daughter-in-law sent of our first grandchild.

Her fingers moved so gracefully, we noted. Perhaps she would be an artist. Her feet kept finding their way out of every blanket. Maybe she would be an athlete. Was she smiling already? Certainly that was a sign that she was very advanced. Within weeks we had imagined various scenarios for little Genevieve's ("Evie's") future.

Our friends indulged us. We'd been through this with many of them already. Stern, no-nonsense men who had turned into cooing fools. Hard-charging women who neglected their careers so they could babysit their grandchild. We'd shaken our heads until it happened to us. Then we happily joined the club of doting, goofy grandparents.

In her book *Becoming Grandma*, Lesley Stahl says it well: "Becoming a grandmother turns the page. Line by line you are rewritten. You are tilted off your old center, spun onto new turf."[1] Even before we met her in person, little Evie had rocked our world.

The fact is, our granddaughter *is* special. Of the approximately 385,000 babies born on the same day worldwide,[2] little Evie was already in the top third of her class just by the circumstances of her birth. She was born in a well-equipped hospital in the United States, attended by doctors and nurses, with loving, healthy parents waiting to embrace her. Her mother had taken vitamins, eaten carefully, avoided alcohol, done prenatal yoga, and regularly saw her obstetrician for checkups. Both parents had completed birthing classes, outfitted a safe nursery, and equipped their car with a crash-tested infant seat. Evie had already won the birth lottery.

But despite my new-grandmother euphoria, I was aware of a different reality. My years of traveling overseas while serving on the boards of international development organizations, writing about global issues, and running an international foundation had opened my eyes to the brutal reality that so many babies born on the same day as Evie would face. I had just written an article that included a sobering statistic: In 2020 nearly 14,000 children under five died every single day from preventable causes.[3] The reality was that a tragic number of Evie's birth cohorts would already be gone by the time she celebrated her one-month birthday.

And there was something else. I had seen how vulnerable girls are in particular. My son, a lawyer who has served as a prosecutor, confided a similar fear early in his days of being a new father. "Mom, I'm so happy we have a little girl, but I'm also worried. Girls are so vulnerable," he said. Because of his work, he'd seen too many disturbing cases of child abuse and violence against women to ignore the harsh reality.

He was right. Girls are more vulnerable than boys. Girls are at a disadvantage on almost every measure in almost every part of the world. Even in relatively rich countries, girls still face more challenges, are more subject to abuse, are less likely to thrive. "Gender inequality cuts across every single country on Earth. No matter where you are born, your life will be harder if you are born a girl. If you are born in a poor country or district, it will be even harder," according to the Bill and Melinda Gates Foundation.[4]

And yet, in some ways there has never been a better time to be a girl. Girls play every sport, set new records, and win Olympic medals. Evie will grow up seeing women lead corporations, win Nobel Prizes, and run for president. Women lead more than two dozen countries in the world, many the first female to hold the position. It's easy to tell ourselves that girls have come a long way, because in many ways they have. But for too many girls, life is brutally difficult.

## WHY SHOULD WE CARE?

A few months after Evie's birth I was attending World Vision's Strong Women, Strong World virtual conference. We were learning about some of the challenges girls face and the organization's work to improve their lives when a video came on of a little girl name Shemema.[5] Just ten years old, the beautiful little girl glowed with confidence as she began to recite a poem called "I Want to Marry." She spoke of wanting to marry someday but not before she enjoyed her childhood and finished school. She said she wanted to wear a graduation gown before a wedding gown. "Someday, I want to marry," she concluded. "But most definitely I'm not in a hurry."

Little Shemema was everything

> *It's easy to tell ourselves that girls have come a long way, because in many ways they have. But for too many girls, life is brutally difficult.*

I hoped Evie would be as she grew up—strong, confident, creative. She was simply extraordinary. But she lived in rural Ghana, and her poem was recited in the context of a society that—because she was a girl—was more likely to expect little Shemema to marry early, to drop out of school and have her first child while she was still a child herself.[6] Shemema's reality was very different than Evie's would be.

Like most of the people watching the video, I applauded Shemema. She couldn't hear us, of course, but I was acutely aware that this little girl deserved no less than my own beautiful granddaughter did. Shemema's poem was a work of art; her delivery breathtaking. She was clearly a talented girl who could go far in the world—if she was given a chance. But girls like Shemema face struggles Evie will never know.

This is a book about the challenges girls like Shemema are confronted with in the world, but it is also about how the decision to make the world a better place can have a profound impact. I hope this book helps educate us all about the simple, sometimes systemic obstacles girls face globally. But it also sheds light on individuals, communities, and organizations that have made a difference—and how all of us can effectively make a difference too.

Musimbi Kanyoro is a Kenyan human rights activist who has served as CEO of the Global Fund for Women. In a TED Talk she describes a principle that her mother taught her when she was growing up in a Kenyan village. She calls it *isirika* and explains that it is a word that embraces charity and service to one another. Simply put, she says, "You're your sister's keeper." Kanyoro emphasizes the mutual responsibility we all share to care for one another. As her mother taught her, "Those who have more really enjoy the *privilege* of giving more."[7]

If you are reading this book, you are probably privileged by global standards. You are not wondering where you will find food to eat or shelter for the night. Day-to-day survival is not an aching concern. Of course, you have worries and wish you had more money. But the simple truth is that you have the ability to change the world. Indeed, you have the *privilege* of helping others. I hope this book will show you how.

## WE ARE ALL CONNECTED

Evie was born during a global pandemic, a time of profound connection and disconnection. Because of COVID-19 restrictions we couldn't visit her in person for months. But also because of the pandemic, we watched footage from around the world of people struggling with the disease. The butterfly effect[8] (the theory that a butterfly flapping its wings in one part of the world can cause a tornado somewhere else) was suddenly demonstrated in real time. A localized disease could become a pandemic in months. When it came to a highly communicable disease, the world seemed suddenly very small.

The interconnectedness of the world was on display from the first days of my granddaughter's life.

> *The simple truth is you have the ability to change the world.*

The problems of the other 140 million babies born in the same year as Evie[9] will affect her life one way or another. How she—and the rest of us—relates to those other children will have a profound impact on her life.

And yet I knew something else from my international work and travels. The actions of one person can change the world. Evie would not just be affected by events elsewhere. She could effect change, become someone who could improve the world. Part of loving Evie is helping her grow up in a better world. And I believe that her life will be better if the lives of other girls are also better.

I am not a development professional. I've had the honor of spending more than two decades on the boards of some wonderful humanitarian organizations, including World Vision, Opportunity International, MAP International, and the Center for Interfaith Action on Global Poverty. I ran a foundation that supported health care for women and children in Zambia. I have written articles for various publications about these and other groups and the people they serve. Mostly I'm a wife, mother, and businessperson, who, over the years, has become increasingly aware of the gaps between my life and those I've met in many of the countries I visited.

I wish I could say I have always been so concerned about the lives of those less fortunate. The fact is, it took a tragedy in my own life to open my eyes to the pain of the world. In my early thirties I learned I was pregnant for the second time. Our son was four, and we were thrilled to be adding to our family. Then we learned I was pregnant with twins—a boy and a girl. It was a wonderful surprise, and we went about preparing ourselves for not one but two babies. My doctor monitored me carefully. I spent time on bed rest as a precaution, took vitamins, went for regular ultrasounds, had blood tests.

All was fine—until it wasn't. A routine visit in my eighth month revealed only one heartbeat. *Our daughter was gone.* The doctors had no idea what had happened. I had done everything possible to have a healthy pregnancy, but it wasn't enough. I delivered our son—Evie's father—and our stillborn little girl. It was a time of great joy and profound heartbreak.

Months later I was still coping. We were so grateful to have our son and his older brother. But our devasting loss was still acutely painful. I kept trying to "snap out of it" without much success.

Then a strange thing changed my life. Not the kind word of a friend or the therapy of a professional. It was a cold, hard statistic. A number I may have heard before but never truly absorbed. A number that now felt personal and represented unimaginable loss and pain: *Thirty-five thousand children under the age of five died every single day, most from preventable causes.*[10] Suddenly I realized that 35,000 other mothers felt the same pain I did. And even more tragic, something could have been done to save many of those precious little lives. I knew I couldn't do anything to bring back my daughter. But that day I vowed to do everything possible to save the lives of other babies.

I began to read, to study, to listen. I opened my mind and heart to the needs of the world and was astounded by what happened. The simple thought that I didn't want other women to feel the pain I had experienced helped guide me. And as I write this book, one of the things that gives me the most hope is that the very statistic that changed my life has decreased year by year. Through the work of individuals, communities, and organizations, the number of babies dying each year is one-third of what it was when I lost my own baby. In Evie's lifetime it is possible that the number will be reduced to hundreds, not thousands.

*Through the work of individuals, communities, and organizations, the number of babies dying each year is one-third of what it was when I lost my own baby.*

The number of preventable deaths—especially of baby girls—must continue to drop. So must the number of child brides, adolescent pregnancies, school dropouts, and other circumstances affecting too many girls in the world. It will take the will of governments, organizations, communities, and individuals to make it a reality.

This is a book about the challenges facing girls, but it is also about how the decision to make the world a better place can have a profound impact. It is meant to help us understand some of the obstacles they encounter. It is a basic road map toward finding ways to exhibit *isirika* in our actions, whether we get personally involved, support a charity, or become advocates. I hope it will make us all smarter about what works and what doesn't, how we can help girls, and when we need to ask more questions on their behalf. It is a starting point for further exploration.

## TAKING A FIRST STEP

One of the first times I visited a developing country, I was overwhelmed. Shocked by the needs, my first instinct was to take all the money I had in my wallet and give it to a woman who was telling us her story. I was visiting a Compassion International site, and one of the staff members kindly stopped me and explained the problems I would cause by doing so. The fact was, I felt sorry for the people I met and wanted to make myself feel better by giving them money. It never occurred to me that I might embarrass that person, cause jealousy in the community, or create more problems. I just wanted to do something—anything—to "fix" what I saw as a problem. It is a typical American response, and I was—and continue to be—a typical American.

*This is a book about the challenges facing girls, but it is also about how the decision to make the world a better place can have a profound impact.*

At times I have been overwhelmed not only by the harsh realities of poverty but also by my own inadequacy. It is tempting to delegate the problems of the world to the professionals. There was a time when I believed in making as much money as possible and then giving generously to those who knew best how to help. But I have also been convicted by people like Rich Stearns, who left his lucrative corporate job to become president of World Vision from 1998 to 2018.

"One of the most common mistakes we can make is to believe that we have nothing of significance to offer—that we're not rich enough, smart enough, skilled enough, or spiritual enough to make much difference at all, especially in the face of huge global problems."[11]

> *At times I have been overwhelmed not only by the harsh realities of poverty but also by my own inadequacy.*

We may not be able to fix all the world's problems, but we can begin by understanding more about what they are and why they exist.

When Evie was thirteen months old, I offered to babysit for a weekend while her parents took a much-needed break. She had just begun to walk and resembled a mechanical windup toy, putting one foot forward and then the other as she lurched along. She didn't want help. She wanted to walk on her own. But she also didn't have enough control to change direction once she started moving forward. I soon learned to clear the path of toys and other obstacles so Evie could walk as far as possible before she fell. It was a comical scene as I rushed forward moving things out of the way while Evie marched along. But what I was doing for Evie is not unlike what I believe all girls deserve. The world needs more advocates for girls, people who will simply help clear the way for girls who want to move forward on their own.

As much as my grandmother heart wants to believe that little Evie is the most amazing little girl and will one day change the world, I know that so many incredibly talented, wise, brilliant girls will never have that chance because of something so simple as the lack of access to vitamins or a basic education or the safety net of health insurance. I am sorry for them, but I am also sorry for the rest of us. The world is a poorer place because some of the world's most amazing girls lack simple resources that would allow them to thrive. And when I think of the contemporaries of my granddaughter around the world, I know that many were also born with talent, intellect, and drive. But for too many, life will present more obstacles than opportunities. Those living in poverty will have to be extraordinarily resourceful, determined, and fortunate to live up to their potential.

> *Those living in poverty will have to be extraordinarily resourceful, determined, and fortunate to live up to their potential.*

Over the years I have gathered insights by visiting projects, attending conferences, reading books, and interviewing experts. I have been honored to serve on the boards of worthy organizations and have even worked for some of them. I helped guide the work of a foundation benefiting those living with HIV/AIDS in Zambia. But I have learned the most by listening to those often called the world's poor.

I once heard the life of those living in poverty described as a constant game of Chutes and Ladders.[12] Every time they start to make progress, another event undermines them. Without access to savings, investments, insurance, or legal protection, they are always one event away from losing everything they've gained. This was one of the hardest things for me to understand when I began to listen to the stories of people living in poverty. Because I lived in a society where hard work and determination was enough to move one forward, I had made assumptions that those who didn't move out of poverty simply weren't working hard enough or didn't have enough determination. I couldn't have been more mistaken.

Once I began to meet people who worked every single day from before sunup until they fell into bed just to make a pittance, I was shocked and ashamed. *"But it's not fair!"* I wanted to yell. Over and over again I have had to learn that life isn't fair if you are living in poverty. Even families who love their daughters and want the best for them often have few options when they lack resources. It is possible to love a little girl just as much as we love Evie but not be able to give her the benefits of health, education, and safety.

## OFFERING CHOICES

Evie likes to make decisions. Now two, she already has strong feelings about what she wears each day, which toy travels with her, even what banana she will eat out of the bunch. I love that her parents give her so much space to make decisions about her life while still setting boundaries. They're not "anything goes" parents, but they are raising a girl who is already confident and has learned to trust her own choices. Sometimes when I'm with Evie I forget and "helpfully" try to pick out a shirt I think is right or a toy that is easier to carry just to hurry us along. Occasionally she'll consider my choice and agree. But often she politely says, "No, Gaga," and proceeds to make her own choice that seems very clear to her. It is a trait that will serve her well in life.

One of the more memorable programs I've seen for empowering girls was in Zambia several years ago. Adolescent girls were experiencing harassment from boys and even older men as they walked to school. The girls felt unsafe, and some had even dropped out of school. An NGO (nongovernmental organization) had brought in a karate teacher who offered free instruction to any girl interested. Classes were held outside after school in full view of passersby, and the girls soon progressed enough to chop boards in half with their bare hands. The boys looked on in fascination and then fear as the girls perfected their technique.

I saw the girls after class one day laughing at the boys' response. I asked them if the boys bothered them on the way to and from school anymore. "No way," one of the girls said, smiling. "They run away from us now." I asked if they'd ever had to use their karate training on the boys, and none had. "The most important thing is that they know we're not afraid. We can take care of ourselves now." I'll always remember the beaming faces of those confident girls who now had the power to walk freely to school.

"Our goal needs to be that every girl can see what's possible and can imagine living her life to its full potential. Because once girls see what's possible, they will rise up and there will be no stopping them," says my friend, business owner Gina Wright Buser,[13] a member of World Vision's Strong Women Strong World advisory council and a powerful advocate for women and girls. It is a goal to have for every girl in the world.

## FINDING BALANCE

The old woman was sitting in the dirt outside her hut, the relentless Mozambican sun beating down as she sought shade in the shadows. She slowly looked up as we approached, and her wrinkled face and clouded eyes showed no surprise, just exhaustion.

It was 2001, and the AIDS pandemic had devastated Mozambique, wiping out many of the young adults. In this culture, the elderly were traditionally cared for by their children. But here, too many of the adult children were gone, leaving the oldest villagers to fend for themselves.

I was with workers who were assessing the needs of the local villages after recent drought conditions had devastated the meager food supply. When our translator asked the woman how she was, she explained that she had found a few weeds early that morning and was cooking them in some water. It was all she had to eat.

Suddenly we heard whispers and looked up to see small faces peering out from the hut. "Those are my grandchildren," she explained. "My children have all died, so I must care for their children." We then realized that the woman was hoping to feed all the children with her weed soup, doing what she could to fill their empty, aching bellies.

The worker promised to come back with an emergency food supply for her and the children, and she thanked us, then stopped and grabbed the translator's hand, saying something urgently as he nodded his head and spoke to her. Stepping back, he said, "She asked us to pray for her. She asked us to pray that she would live long enough to raise the children." The pastor in our group knelt and prayed with her as I brushed tears away.

Evie does not need me to survive into the future, but I hope and pray I live long enough to see her soar in all the ways she chooses. My early dreams for her have been overtaken by the fact that she is her own remarkable person. When she decides it's time for a "dance party," she turns on the music herself and dances with remarkable rhythm and abandon. When she is done, she says, "All right!" and throws up her hands. My role is simply to applaud.

I want to imagine other girls all over the world dancing like Evie—healthy, happy, free, and safe. Some of them need help, not because they are weak or in need of our sympathy but because there is no music in their lives. It is drowned out by violence or illness or the relentlessness grind of poverty. They need all of us to come together and fight for the simple goal of letting girls be girls—of giving them the chance to turn on the music and dance.

> *I want to imagine other girls all over the world dancing like Evie—healthy, happy, free, and safe.*

# 1

. . . . . . . . . . . . . . . .

# HELPING
# GIRLS SOAR

MY FRIEND AND I were reflecting over coffee. She had run a successful business, and I knew she had been generous in supporting both her church and other charities. As she considered retirement, she asked me, in light of my international travel and board experience, to give her my best ideas for changing the world. "If you could invest in anything that would be world changing, what would it be?"

I had just returned from Kenya where I had seen clean water transform the health of a village and provide sanitation for a school. I had seen a small clinic offering lifesaving interventions to babies. Agricultural training was helping farmers produce more crops. I had observed faith leaders' training sessions that were helping change long-held beliefs about gender roles. It had been an amazing trip, and I had seen many interventions that were helping Kenyans overcome challenges and take advantage of opportunities. There were many right answers to her question. But I surprised myself by saying what I had begun to understand during this and other times in the developing world.

"Girls," I said. She looked at me, perplexed, and I realized it was a confusing answer. But as I witnessed all the good things that had been done, I had also recognized how many times girls had stood out to me. They were the ones articulating what sanitation had meant to them and why it now gave them the opportunity to go to school. They were the ones who had come back to their village to serve as health workers. They were the ones who—given a chance—seemed to not only succeed, but also to give back to their communities.

So I started again. "There are many great organizations in the world investing in important work: clean water, access to health care, improving education, offering microloans. But in every case, it seems to me that girls are the ones who not only benefit the most from this work, but also time and time again, I see them giving back. They are the ones who so often come back to their homes after receiving an education and training."

My friend and I talked for a few more minutes and then went back to our lives. But I realized that I had just made an observation that was becoming a conviction to me. Girls held the key to changing the world. This belief had grown in part from seeing how often girls were disadvantaged in the world.

*An observation was becoming a conviction to me. Girls held the key to changing the world.*

I had seen little girls around the world lose their childhoods because of poverty, disease, war, displacement, and lack of protections that most of us consider fundamental. Children the world over suffer, but girls suffer even more. We often talk about gender inequality in terms of how it affects women, but little girls face double discrimination in many parts of the world as female children.

As the mother of two boys, I used to wonder why international development experts emphasized specifically helping girls. But then I began to see that from the time of their birth, in almost every way, girls suffer more than boys. They are more vulnerable, more subject to violence, less likely to receive an education, more likely to be married off at an early age, more often give birth long before their bodies are mature.

"It's important that we empower girls," said Rotary International's president, Shekhar Mehta, "as we all find that more often than not, the girl is disadvantaged. We will serve all children, but our laser focus will be specially on the girl."[1] Mehta's speech, in June 2021, signaled a shift of emphasis for the international service organization.

Here's something I had seen clearly: Strong girls make the world stronger. When we give them opportunities, they soar—and they take those around them along. Changing the circumstances for girls is one of the best ways to change the world.

> *Strong girls make the world stronger. When we give them opportunities, they soar—and they take those around them along.*

According to the UN Foundation, "Investing in girls is one of the smartest things we can do to promote a healthier, more prosperous world. More importantly, it's the right thing to do. Every girl has the right to be in charge of her future and her fate, and we have the collective obligation to protect her rights and promote her wellbeing."[2]

The World Bank sees educating girls as one of the best ways to lift countries out of poverty. It seems amazing that this sophisticated institution analyzing economic trends has concluded that simply educating girls can be one of the most powerful and world-changing investments.

> A recent World Bank study estimates that the "limited educational opportunities for girls, and barriers to completing 12 years of education, cost countries between US $15 trillion and $30 trillion in lost lifetime productivity and earnings." All these factors combined can help lift households, communities, and countries out of poverty.[3]

When the Nike Foundation began to look for the best ways to solve the global poverty issue, they discovered that girls were the key. Talking about girls who reach adolescence, the foundation president, Maria Eitel, said, "We realized to solve poverty, we'd have to get to her before she arrived at that intersection; we had to figure out how to get her on the first path. And if we could do that, it wouldn't just be an investment in her, but an investment in everyone around her."[4] Because of those findings, the foundation launched The Girl Effect campaign.[5] "The one thing that never changes is girls' potential," said Eitel. "Wherever you are, whatever the context, girls prove that they have the potential to rebuild their families, communities, and countries."[6]

*Girls are the leverage point for the world's future. Simply put, interventions and opportunities offered to girls help create long-term solutions and avoid long-term problems.*

Girls are the leverage point for the world's future. Simply put, interventions and opportunities offered to girls help create long-term solutions and avoid long-term problems. Because my granddaughter has been vaccinated, she won't be debilitated by polio, diphtheria, measles, or other diseases that could derail her life and drain her family financially. Already in preschool, she will happily continue her schooling as long as she wants and use her education to contribute to society. Because laws protect her and her family loves her, she will enjoy her childhood and have a better chance of becoming a well-adjusted adult. If she chooses, she will marry and have children of her own. The investments made in Evie's childhood offer proven rewards in the future for her, her family, and the society in which she will contribute. And such is the case for other girls in the world. Contributing to health, education, clean water, safety, legal protections, and other measures for girls isn't just right, it's smart. What we invest in girls today will reap rewards for the entire world in the future.

## IT'S A GIRL!

The crowd stood in a field looking up at the sky. Family and friends of the expectant couple had gathered for an elaborate "gender reveal" near an airfield. As the airplane flew over, a cloud of pink smoke filled the sky. "It's a girl," they screamed, jumping up and down and hugging.[7] Living in our society, we can't imagine someone seeing a cloud of pink smoke and expressing sadness or condolences to the expectant mom. But news of a girl's birth is not greeted in the same way in many parts of the world.

Issues of inequality start at birth. You might expect that of the approximately 385,000 babies born the same day as my granddaughter, half would be boys and half girls. Actually, the ratio is generally skewed a bit more toward boys than girls naturally, but in recent years, and especially in some parts of the world, the ratio has become quite imbalanced toward boys. Known as the "son prefer-ence," it means that a baby boy gets the cheers and a baby girl may be abandoned or killed. In Chinese society, son preference is deeply rooted, including in traditionally held Confucian values, which are strongly patrilineal.[8] Patrilinealism is, of course, found not just in Confucianism. In the Bible, tribal membership was passed through the father, and the twelve tribes of Israel were identified as sons of Jacob.

## DID YOU KNOW?

**PATRILINEAL CULTURE**
Patrilineal cultures use the father's line as a way to define inheritance of property, privileges, titles, and social position. In patrilineal family systems, children and wives take the father's surname, the patronym. Family property often follows the patrilineal line of descent as well. Sons inherit property from their fathers, but daughters, who marry outside the family, often inherit nothing.

The degree to which newborn girls are considered a burden—even to the point of infanticide—was shocking to me. We will dis-cuss in later chapters how girl babies are often neglected from birth. But girls continue to have to fight for their very lives in many coun-tries. The term *missing girls* is used to indicate an abnormal male-to-female sex ratio. "In the early 1990s, the widespread use of prenatal ultrasound scanning, coupled with a strong cultural preference for sons and policies to reduce fertility levels, increased the abortion of female fetuses in some countries. The result was highly skewed sex ratios at birth, or missing girls, something that had not happened before in human history.

"Today, five countries with highly skewed sex ratios at birth show the highest numbers of missing girls, with a ratio of 113 males to 100 females in China and Azerbaijan, followed by Vietnam (112), Armenia (111), and India (110). Over time, skewed sex ratios produce abnormal gender imbalances."[9]

Why are boys preferred? In some cases, especially in rural societies, boys can simply do more manual labor, affecting both the family's livelihood and their survival. In other societies in which a dowry is expected when a girl is married, a family incurs an economic burden with every daughter. In China, the one-child policy (1980–2016) created such a strong preference for boys that the recent official numbers show China has 723.34 million men and 688.44 million women, accounting for 51.24 percent and 48.76 percent of the population, respectively. It means there are 34.9 million more men than women.[10]

While girls in many developed countries may fight stereotypes, being born a girl is actually a health threat in too many countries. The birth of a boy brings congratulations. A newborn girl is greeted with "maybe next time" or "try again." A woman who gives birth to sons is considered blessed. A woman who has only girls is considered cursed.

In her book *Home Is Us*, Kenyan Jackie Ogega tells the story of her mother, who was harassed and threatened because she had given birth to three daughters and no sons. Her own mother-in-law cursed her and urged her son to leave her for another woman who would have a better chance of producing a boy. When Jackie fell ill as a child, her grandmother urged her mother to let Jackie die.

> *While girls in many developed countries may fight stereotypes, being born a girl in too many countries is actually a health threat.*

The physical and mental harassment went on until Jackie's mother was forced to take her girls and flee to her own mother's home for safety. Sadly, Jackie's story is not all that rare.[11]

"The status of girls is significantly less than that of boys in some countries. This makes girls more vulnerable to discrimination and neglect," says Robin Haarr, an expert on violence against women and children. "Available indicators reveal that girls are discriminated against from the earliest stages of life in the areas of nutrition, health care, education, family care, and protection. Girls are often fed less, particularly when there are diminished food resources. A diet low in calories, protein, and nutrients negatively affects girls' growth and development. Less likely to receive basic health care, they are at increased risk of childhood mortality."[12]

In their book *Half the Sky*, authors Nicholas Kristof and Sheryl WuDunn put it even more starkly. "It appears that more girls have been killed in the last fifty years, precisely because they were girls, than men were killed in all the battles of the twentieth century."[13]

## DID YOU KNOW?

### INTERNATIONAL DAY OF THE GIRL CHILD

The United Nations, in an effort to increase awareness of the inequality faced by girls worldwide, established the International Day of the Girl Child in 2012. It is observed each year on October 11 and helps support more opportunity for girls while raising awareness of inequality in areas such as access to education, nutrition, legal rights, medical care, and protection from discrimination, violence against women, and forced child marriage.[14]

These few facts show the huge divide between boys and girls and the incredible challenges girls face during childhood:

- Girls under five years old are three times more likely to suffer malnutrition than boys under five.
- In developing countries, one in three girls do not finish primary education, most often because they spend eight times longer carrying out household tasks. Consequently, there are 96 million illiterate girls aged between 15 and 24, compared to 57 million illiterate boys.
- Every day 25,000 girls are victims of forced marriage. This can mean that they are forced to leave school. Pregnancy is the number one cause of death among 15- to 19-year-old girls.
- 50 percent of sexual assaults in the world involve girls under 16 years old.[15]

It's easy to get lost in the statistics, but stop for a minute and think about little girls under the age of five. They are precious, playful, creative, and full of wonder. Most of us instinctively want to protect them and help them grow up. But in societies where poverty is extreme, childhood is lost. There is no time to play and no margin to spend protecting innocence. Both mothers and fathers work long hours just to survive. They are often malnourished themselves or suffering from untreated illness. As soon as a little girl can walk, she must help contribute to the household. Making the choice to send a girl to school can mean a family will eat less in order to pay the small school fee or to buy her a uniform. And when disruptions

*In societies where poverty is extreme, childhood is lost for little girls.*

> *Most of the people I have met in the world want a better life for their children.*

occur—drought, floods, hurricanes, war—families living in poverty sink even further.

Poverty is a powerful force. It has taken me years to understand how few choices people living in poverty really have and to understand that if I were facing the same challenges, I might make the very same choices. Most of the people I have met in the world want a better life for their children. Faced with limited options, they do what they can to help their children.

Such was the case with Jackie Ogega's mother, who left her husband and returned to her own family to protect her girls. While it took courage to leave her situation, her desire to offer her daughters more opportunities motivated her. Jackie didn't just survive because of her mother's sacrifice, she thrived, receiving an education and going on to earn a PhD. Today she is senior director for Gender Equality and Social Inclusion at World Vision, where she makes sure all girls have the opportunities she fought so hard to achieve.

## THE DANGER OF ADOLESCENCE

Girls who survive the first five years of life hit another dangerous point when they become adolescents, starting at age ten. In all parts of the world—including highly developed countries like the United States—adolescence is fraught with challenges for girls.

Once a girl begins to menstruate, her childhood is considered over in much of the world. Menstruation is difficult to manage in many settings where personal hygiene products don't exist or are too expensive, so girls must stay at home during their period. Many miss so much school that they drop out. This issue is discussed more in later chapters.

In some countries, from the time a girl menstruates (and even younger in some societies), she is considered ready to marry and have children. For families living in poverty, especially where there is a bride price—a common custom in Africa in which the groom and his family pay the bride's family—marrying off a daughter can bring much-needed financial relief. It means there is one less mouth to feed because their daughter is now the responsibility of another family. The family is paid either in money or goods, such as livestock, which is often a huge help to a struggling family. In most cases it means the girl drops out of school and begins to care for her new home and family. Even if she does not have children right away, she is now expected to care for her in-laws and other members of her husband's household.

## LIKE A GIRL

When Edgar Sandoval Sr. was in charge of overseeing the feminine hygiene product line at Procter & Gamble, he learned some startling statistics: Girls' self-esteem drops twice as much as boys' during puberty. Moreover, women never regain the prepuberty level of self-esteem. According to a study by the American Psychological Association, this is true for girls everywhere in the world. Sadly, one of the leading causes of death in adolescents worldwide is suicide, according to the World Health Organization (WHO).

Digging deeper into the causes of the drop in confidence, Edgar and his team realized that gender stereotypes have a big impact on girls during puberty, when young womanhood comes to be defined by certain standards of beauty and submissiveness. Society constantly dwells on gender differences, sending out the message that leadership, power, and strength are for men, not for women. Subtle and not-so-subtle messages often communicate that being a girl is not as good as being a boy. Learning this was troubling both professionally and personally for Edgar, who has three daughters.

P & G did video interviews with boys, girls, men, and women, and asked them a series of questions such as, "What does it mean to run like a girl? Fight like a girl? Throw like a girl?" When they asked girls ten years old and under, they got a positive, enthusiastic response. When they asked older girls, boys, and men, they got a stereotypical inept version.[16]

> *Gender stereotypes have a big impact on girls during puberty, when womanhood comes to be defined by certain standards of beauty and submissiveness.*

The video became the basis of a social media campaign launched in 2014, #LikeAGirl.[17] It was viewed more than 90 million times and shared by more than a million viewers. Men and women all over the world joined the movement to help reclaim "like a girl" as a positive statement. Before the campaign, the expression was mostly used in a derogatory way. Since the launch, it's been attached to overwhelmingly positive sentiment, becoming a symbol of female empowerment around the globe. The UN acknowledged the power of #LikeAGirl in March 2015, awarding P & G's campaign for the impact it had on female empowerment around the world.[18]

When Edgar Sandoval left P & G, he didn't head to another corporate post. Instead, he transitioned to World Vision, where he first served as COO before being named president in 2018. His commitment to girls remains strong:

I feel a deep, personal commitment to empowering women and girls. Not just because I'm the dad of three daughters. You see, among vulnerable children living in the world's poorest places, girls are *even more* vulnerable. This fact continues to strike me as one of the most under-addressed issues in our world. It was the inspiration that fueled my desire, when I was a vice president at P & G, to launch the breakthrough "Like a Girl" campaign in 2014. And it's the inspiration that fuels my desire, as World Vision president, to achieve gender equality everywhere we work.[19]

## FINDING SOLUTIONS

How do we make the world better for girls?

What I have learned is that some of the solutions require systemic change and take years to accomplish. But some solutions are surprisingly simple and inexpensive. It wasn't costly to have a karate teacher show girls how to defend themselves in Zambia. In chapter 7 you'll read about a woman who developed a way for girls to make a living by using discarded plastic bags to weave beautiful purses. And I continue to be inspired by a group of women in Burkina Faso who, without spending any money, set up listening posts, places where women could confidentially seek help and advice. A small investment has supported a movement of private schools that helps meet the needs of children who lack access to education. And just a few dollars can provide lifesaving oral rehydration therapy to children suffering from diarrhea.

All of the amazing people you'll read about have simply chosen to make a difference. In almost every case, solutions were found by first listening and learning.

That's the principle Margo Day used when she took a leave of absence from her job as vice president at Microsoft and spent time in Kenya, listening to girls who had run away to escape female genital mutilation (FGM) and early marriage. She said, "Standing at the rescue center talking with the girls blew open my heart and mind to the simple fact that every human has potential, but sadly the opportunity to realize it is not available for millions of girls simply by virtue of being born a girl, where you're born and your family's resources. I felt called to be part of changing that dynamic however I could."[20]

An open heart and mind was the first step for me, Margo, and many of the people I interviewed over the years who went on to make a difference.

After reading *Strong Girls, Strong World*, perhaps you'll choose to support one of the many worthy organizations mentioned.[21] Maybe you'll decide to visit a country yourself and see what life is like there. Maybe one particular issue will break your heart or spur you to act and learn more.

## WHAT YOU CAN DO

### START A STUDY GROUP
The best way to start investing in the lives of girls is to understand more about their challenges and opportunities. The sidebars in this book contain suggested resources that can help explain what life is like for girls and what they face. Consider using some of these resources in a book club or Sunday school class.

## SETTING GOALS

Who decides what's right for girls? Even in American society, families vary greatly in their standards for discipline, education, and even health.

In 2000, the United Nations set goals that all 191 member countries agreed to as a way to focus on the most pressing international

## DID YOU KNOW?

**MILLENNIUM DEVELOPMENT GOALS**

The eight Millennium Development Goals to achieve by 2015 included:

1. To eradicate extreme poverty and hunger
2. To achieve universal primary education
3. To promote gender equality and empower women
4. To reduce child mortality
5. To improve maternal health
6. To combat HIV/AIDS, malaria, and other diseases
7. To ensure environmental sustainability
8. To develop a global partnership for development

Each goal had subcategories and specific targets to help focus efforts.[22]

development problems. They called them the Millennium Development Goals (MDGs). By focusing on these specific issues and establishing targets to achieve by 2015, the goal was to bring governments, funding organizations, international humanitarian groups, local communities, and individuals to a consensus about how best to solve the world's most pressing issues.

Although some countries made great progress in achieving the goals, others fell behind. And even though the third goal emphasized gender equality, it became clear that achieving all the goals was more difficult for girls than for boys.

After evaluating the progress on the MDGs, new goals were set for subsequent years. Called the Sustainable Development Goals (SDGs), they established a course of action to be achieved by 2030. The seventeen SDGs are:

1. No poverty
2. Zero hunger
3. Good health and well-being
4. Quality education
5. Gender equality
6. Clean water and sanitation
7. Affordable and clean energy
8. Decent work and economic growth
9. Industry, innovation, and infrastructure
10. Reduced inequality
11. Sustainable cities and communities
12. Responsible consumption and production
13. Climate action
14. Life below water
15. Life on land
16. Peace, justice, and strong institutions
17. Partnerships to achieve the goals for sustainable development.

These goals each have additional subcategories and many of those contain specific goals relating to girls.[23]

The next chapters highlight specific ways girls can be empowered in many of these key areas and how you can be involved. Besides introducing people who have made a difference, there are also specific actions to take, organizations to support, and ideas to ponder.

What I've found barely scratches the surface of these important topics. But it is a first step in understanding the challenges and opportunities facing girls and the ways in which many of us can contribute to their future.

# 2

KEEPING GIRLS
HEALTHY

THE SHADE OF THE ENORMOUS BAOBAB TREE provided a perfect setting for the pop-up pediatric clinic in rural Malawi. Health workers were examining children from nearby villages for signs of illness and malnutrition and providing instructions to their parents. Many families carried health cards issued by the government so that their child's progress could be noted. I was traveling with World Relief, documenting their health work through local churches in rural areas of the beautiful but resource-poor country.

A thin woman stood waiting in line, holding a bundle in her arms that I assumed was a baby. When it was finally her turn, the woman unwrapped the child, who was clearly very ill. The nurse couldn't hide her shock as she took the tiny girl in her arms. As she talked quietly to the woman, a translator listening to the conversation told me that this was not a baby; the child was three years old. You could see the distinct outline of bones under her skin as she barely moved in the nurse's arms.

The nurse immediately arranged for the girl to be taken to a nearby hospital. When I interviewed the nurse later, I asked if she thought the little girl would recover.

"It's difficult to say," she admitted. "Sometimes when a child has gone that long without food her body can no longer take anything in. We have to very slowly give her water and nutrients."

That night I went to bed in a comfortable guesthouse and prayed for the little girl. The next day, when our group returned to the same location, I asked the nurse if the girl was improving. She shook her head. "We lost her last night. There was nothing we could do."

"What was wrong?" I asked.

The nurse shrugged, then said, "Children die every day here. Look at her mother. She was probably ill herself. The girl might have had malaria or chronic diarrhea and was too ill to eat or drink. The mother walked two days to bring her to us. Maybe if she'd reached us sooner . . ." Her voice trailed off, indicating how exhausted she was.

The death of that little Malawian girl haunted me for days. I never learned her name because I didn't want to disturb her mother with my questions. I wanted to treat her with dignity and commemorate her child's death as I would any tragic loss. And yet, in this setting, she was simply one of the thousands of children who die before their fifth birthday. Her mother was probably on her way back to her village already to bury her daughter. I felt compelled to tell the three-year-old's story, but I also realized that I seemed to be the only one surprised by her death.

*The harsh reality is that living to the age of five in many parts of the world is a milestone to be celebrated.*

The harsh reality is that living to the age of five is a milestone to be celebrated in many parts of the world. Deaths of infants and toddlers are all too common. Approximately *14,000 children under the age of five die every day.*[1] It is a staggering statistic that hardly does justice to the pain and suffering of thousands of families. Although the number rarely makes headlines, it is equivalent to twenty-eight jumbo jets with every seat occupied by a child crashing each day. Even more

> *Approximately 14,000 children under the age of five die every day.*

heartbreaking, most of the deaths are from preventable causes. And sadly, girls are often more vulnerable simply because of their gender.[2]

Many of the health challenges facing children affect both girls and boys. But in some parts of the world the cultural preference for sons over daughters directly threatens the health and survival of girls even before birth. With the increased availability of ultrasounds, some couples seek abortions when they learn they are expecting a girl. Although abortions for gender preference are now illegal in many countries, the practice continues. The UN Human Rights Council says that more than 117 million girls are "missing" in Asia due to sex-selective abortions. Normal sex ratios at birth are not equal. There are typically 102 to 106 males to 100 female births. But because of selective abortions, the male ratio is much higher in some countries.[3]

As mentioned, this attitude may account for some early deaths in baby girls who tend to be nurtured less and even abandoned in some countries. According to Ranjani Iyer Mohanty, writing in the *The Atlantic*,

> *Health challenges affect both girls and boys. But in some parts of the world the cultural preference for sons over daughters directly threatens the health and survival of girls even before birth.*

Thousands of baby girls are abandoned each year, an

extension of sex selection practices that, according to a 2011 study in *The Lancet*, include half a million abortions in India every year. Most abandoned babies die, but a few are rescued. While the statistics on the number of babies killed or abandoned at birth are murky—the vast majority go unreported—the radically skewed sex ratio of children under six years of age is an inescapable indication.[4]

Once a girl is born, the struggle to survive does not stop. There are myriad health issues that she will face, a picture I paint in broad strokes in this chapter. Many experts prefer to look at women and girls' health issues together, but that tends to place a great deal of emphasis on reproductive health. While that is an important aspect of female health issues which sadly does directly affect girls in some countries, we are looking here primarily at the issues that affect younger girls.

## THE FIRST MOMENTS OF BIRTH

There is some encouraging news. According to the World Health Organization (WHO), "Deaths among children aged one month to five years old have fallen dramatically in recent decades. That's wonderful and encouraging news. But progress in reducing the deaths of newborn babies—those aged less than one month—has been less impressive, *with 7,000 newborns still dying every day*."[5]

Often in less-developed countries, mothers have no help in giving birth, so newborns die from asphyxia due to long labor or being in a breach position. Sometimes babies born in rural settings are literally delivered in a field or on a dirt floor, and the umbilical cord cut with a rock or dirty implement. Sepsis can easily set in.

## WHAT YOU CAN DO

### BIRTHING KITS

Birthing kits are one of the simplest ways to save newborns in developing countries, where pregnant women too often give birth in unsanitary conditions. Many organizations raise funds for such kits, and some organizations also encourage groups to create kits on their own. Birthing kits typically include:

- A bar of **soap** or hand sanitizer for the person assisting the birth.
- One or two pairs of **plastic gloves**.
- Squares of **gauze** to wipe the mother's perineum and the baby's eyes.
- A disposable **scalpel** or sanitized single edge razor blade to cut the umbilical cord.
- Pieces of **soft**, 10-inch-long cotton **string** for tying the umbilical cord at both ends or umbilical tape or clamp.
- One **plastic sheet** for a clean birthing surface.
- One **gallon-size freezer bag** (11 × 11 inches) to pack the contents of the kit and for cleanup after the birth.
- One flannel **receiving blanket**. Some people also include a diaper and stocking hat for the baby and a feminine pad and undergarment for the mother.

Various organizations such as Love a Child (loveachild .com) accept kit donations directly. Others, such as MedShare (medshare.org), have a list of supplies on their website and information about how to host a birthing kit party. You can purchase birthing kits via the Medical Teams International online giving catalog at medicalteams.org/catalog. Food for the Poor is an organization that supplies birthing kits primarily in Latin America and the Caribbean. For information, go to foodforthepoor.org/gift-catalog/ and click on Birthing Kits.

According to the Center for Global Health and Development,

> In many parts of the world, even if a pregnant woman
> can convince her husband or family that she needs
> medical care, she faces difficulties in getting to the
> hospital. Once she gets there, there may not be
> electricity, essential supplies, or trained health workers.
> More than a third of women in developing countries
> are not assisted by skilled health workers while giving
> birth. Young women are especially at risk: adolescents
> 15–19 are twice as likely to die in childbirth as women
> in their twenties, and pregnancy and childbirth-related
> deaths are one of the leading causes of death for
> adolescent girls.[6]

Whenever I visited Zambia, I always took with me a box of
rubber surgical gloves. On one of my first visits, I heard a heartbreaking story at one hospital. Because medical supplies were
severely limited, pregnant women were required to bring surgical
gloves with them. In this instance, when a pregnant woman arrived
at this hospital without gloves, the medical staff's supply had run
out. Because of the fear of HIV transmission, the staff wouldn't
help the mother deliver and her baby died. That is why so many
nonprofit organizations specifically ask for surgical gloves in their
gift catalogs.

## MALNUTRITION

Unfortunately, women in low-income countries often enter pregnancy malnourished, and the demands of pregnancy can create
negative health consequences for both the mother and baby.

# INNOVATIONS THAT MAKE A DIFFERENCE

## SAVING PREMATURE AND LOW-BIRTH-WEIGHT BABIES

Low-birth-weight babies born in developing countries often lack access to incubators or other support to get them through their earliest days. Medical Teams International tells the story of a woman in the Nyarugusu Refugee Camp in Tanzania who delivered twin girls. Both newborns had very low birth weight, and the mother didn't have access to a hospital with an incubator. The Medical Teams staff taught the new mother something called "kangaroo mother care," holding her twins close to her chest with skin-to-skin contact.[7]

"For premature and low-birth-weight infants, being held against a parent's bare chest for a continuous length of time each day is a high-impact intervention. This special hold reduces mortality rates for premature infants. It helps regulate a newborn's temperature, breathing, and heart rate. It also prevents hypothermia and severe infection, and promotes healthy weight gain," said Martha Holley Newsome, president of Medical Teams International.[8]

This simple solution is one of the innovations developed by those experts who work in countries where health infrastructure is poor and not readily available to the average person. It is a practical way to provide for the needs of premature babies without making mothers travel long distances to hospitals.

Specific deficiencies, such as folic acid (vitamin $B_9$), vitamin D, zinc, and iodine can affect the development and birth weight of the baby. Some women are still nursing one child when their next baby is born. They continue nursing two and even three children, all the while suffering from their own nutritional deficits.

Some of the most common vitamin deficiencies can have devastating consequences for newborns:

**Iodine** deficiency is the primary cause of preventable brain damage in children. Its worst impacts occur in utero and in the first few years of a child's life. "Globally, 30 percent of the world's population live in areas with iodine deficiencies."[9]

> Women in low-income countries often enter pregnancy malnourished, creating negative health consequences for both the mother and baby.

**Vitamin A** deficiency affects about one-third of children living in low- and middle-income settings, mainly in sub-Saharan Africa and South Asia.[10] Vitamin A deficiency weakens the immune system and increases a child's risk of contracting and dying from infections.

**Iron** deficiency can lead to anemia, which increases the risk of hemorrhage and bacterial infection during childbirth and is implicated in maternal deaths. Babies may be born prematurely and suffer from infections, learning disabilities, and delayed development. According to the *Journal of Nutrition*, more than 50 percent of women in developing countries suffer from iron deficiency and anemia.[11]

**Zinc** deficiency impairs immune functions and is associated with an increased risk of gastrointestinal infections. Zinc deficiency is especially common in lower income countries due to a poor diet lacking in protein and other zinc-rich food.

**Calcium, vitamin D, and folate** deficiencies are a particular concern during pregnancy, and can lead to a number of health complications for both the mother and growing baby.[12]

## WHAT YOU CAN DO

### WHERE THERE IS NO DOCTOR

For more than fifty years *Where There Is No Doctor: A Village Health Care Handbook* has been a resource for communities and individuals where health care is not readily available. Written for lay people and using simple diagrams, it demonstrates how to respond to medical emergencies, ways to improve hygiene and health, how to deliver a baby or set a broken limb, and when more advanced medical attention is needed.

Published by the Hesperian Foundation, the handbook is a valuable resource with more than one million copies sold in a hundred languages. It is also available as a free download for people with no means to purchase it. The foundation also publishes *Where There Is No Dentist* and *A Book for Midwives*, among many other helpful books available on their website at hesperian.org. You can support their work at that site.

# FOOD INSECURITY

For many families living in poverty, nutritious foods are simply not available, or they live off a diet of nutritionally poor crops. One of the most pervasive nutritional problems in the world is iron deficiency. Most of us have a diet that includes iron-rich meat, eggs, fish, beans, and enriched bread and cereal. But for much of the world, people subsist on starches such as rice, noodles, maize, or baked flour because they are an inexpensive and available way to fill empty stomachs.

In many cultures, cornmeal is a staple that is used to make *mealie meal* or *nshima*. In Zambia, nearly every meal is based around nshima, a thick, starchy food usually eaten with your hands. The first time I tried to eat it with a fork everyone began to laugh. As someone explained, "Nshima *is* the fork!" You use it to mop up sauces and wrap around meat and vegetables. Nshima is filling but not particularly nutritious. But for people with few resources, nshima, a few vegetables, and some sauce makes up the majority of their diet. Other developing countries use starchy fruits or vegetables such as cassava to produce a flour.

*For many families living in poverty, nutritious foods are simply not available, or they live off a diet of nutritionally poor crops.*

Even in developed countries, pregnant women with access to good, nutritious diets are still prescribed prenatal vitamins to make up for any deficits and to help supply the needs of a growing baby. Increasingly, access to prenatal vitamins for women living in poverty is becoming a high priority. The cost is low, and the benefits to mother and baby are high.

## CHILDREN UNDER FIVE

I was interviewing a group of women in Guatemala about their lives and families when I posed what I considered a simple question: "How many children do you have?" When my translator asked the women in Spanish, most of them held up fingers on two hands. One mother had ten children, while another woman held up two hands and then one finger, indicating eleven.

Then the translator turned to me and asked me if I wanted to know how many children were still alive. I was momentarily confused, until I realized that she had literally asked each woman the number of children to whom she had given birth.

"Yes," I answered. "Please ask how many children each woman still has."

## WHAT YOU CAN DO

### PROVIDE VITAMINS

Vitamin Angels is dedicated to providing pregnant women and young children in low-resource settings with critically needed vitamins and other nutritional supplements, working with such suppliers as Walgreens, Goli, SmartyPants Vitamins, Bayer, and others. You can help Vitamin Angels by supporting one of their partners:

- For every bottle of SmartyPants Vitamins sold, a one-for-one grant is made to Vitamin Angels to provide vitamins and nutrients to moms in need.
- Every purchase of Goli Vitamins equals a six-month supply of donated essential vitamins to Vitamin Angels for a child in need.
- Walgreens donates one percent of the retail sales of Walgreens brand and other vitamins to Vitamin Angels. See walgreens.com and search for Vitamin Angels.

In both the United States and other countries around the world, Vitamin Angels provides vitamins and nutritional supplements critical to the development of healthy babies and children and supports the needs of pregnant women. For more information or to donate directly to the organization, go to vitaminangels.org.

The women listened politely to the translator and then held up fingers again. This time fewer of them held up two hands. The woman who had previously indicated eleven children now only held up eight fingers. One woman had lost more than half of her children.

I stopped writing and looked at each woman. Some had tears in their eyes. "I'm so sorry," I blurted in English, then, remembering my meager Spanish, "*Lo siento*." Later I asked the translator if it was all right that I had asked the question.

"Yes, it's a good thing that you did. Women here lose children too often. But that doesn't mean they don't mourn each one. Every woman who loses a baby or a child still has a hole in her heart."

With my translator beside me, I asked one woman how she had lost her three children. She shook her head sadly, not sure how to explain. Then she began talking softly. The translator explained that one child was healthy but suddenly got sick with a fever and terrible diarrhea. She died less than a week later. Another died soon after birth, and the third child had cut his leg and it became extremely infected. The closest clinic was more than two hours away, and by the time the woman was able to find someone to take them, her son had become too sick and died. I hugged the woman and cried with her.

> *The loss of a child is heartbreaking to every mother.*

What was especially sad about the woman's story was that each of her children had probably died from preventable and treatable causes. As I spent more time in the developing world, I was horrified to realize how small the margin was between life and death for many children. And I was reminded over and over again that the loss of a child is heartbreaking to every mother.

Let's look at the most common causes of childhood death.

## DIARRHEA

More than 2,000 children die daily from complications caused by diarrhea, according to the CDC.[13] That's more than 800,000 deaths each year.

Parents know that children often suffer from diarrhea, but it is easily treated in the developed world with Pedialyte or other available fluids. This widely available formula provides sodium, potassium, and glucose to keep a child from becoming dehydrated. Pedialyte is a branded version of an oral rehydration therapy (ORT), also known as Oral Rehydration

*A ten-cent packet of oral rehydration therapy formula mixed with a liter of water is one of the most cost-effective and important interventions available in poor countries.*

Solution (ORS). If a baby or small child becomes dehydrated, she can experience severe complications or even death in just days.

Oral rehydration therapy is very inexpensive. A ten-cent packet of formula mixed with a liter of water is one of the most cost-effective and important interventions available in poor countries.[14] And yet rural clinics often run out. When I served on the board of MAP International, I learned that health-care workers on medical missions requested ORTs more than any other treatment because it was so often needed in clinics.[15]

## WHAT YOU CAN DO

### DONATE ORAL REHYDRATION SOLUTIONS

Dehydration is a leading cause of death in developing countries for children and adults who are suffering from diarrhea. The longer the condition persists, the weaker a person becomes. Oral rehydration solution (ORS) given daily immediately begins to stabilize and rehydrate a person. A full course of treatment (about ten packets) costs only a dollar. For more information, go to map.org/catalog.

## INNOVATIONS THAT MAKE A DIFFERENCE

### READY TO USE THERAPEUTIC FOOD

Ready-to-use therapeutic food (RUTF) has made an enormous difference in treating malnutrition in children since it was introduced twenty-five years ago. The peanut-based paste comes in individual packets that don't require refrigeration and last up to two years. In African countries the most popular brand of RUTF is Nutriset's Plumpy'Nut.[16]

Nutriset, the French company that makes Plumpy'Nut, lists the ingredients as "peanut paste fortified with milk, vegetable fat, sugar, vitamins and micronutrients."[17] Children seem to love its taste, and it can be used in a home setting. It is also used in mass famine situations for children and adults who need a quick and efficient way to receive nutrition.

While it is not to be used routinely, it can treat children over six months of age who are suffering from acute malnutrition. UNICEF is one of the largest distributors of Plumpy'Nut to young children. To support their efforts, go to unicef.org .au/give-a-gift/choose/clean-water-nutrition/126-sachets-of -peanut-butter.

While most babies, even in wealthy countries, may experience diarrhea from time to time, it is mostly preventable with proper sanitation and handwashing and by vaccinating against rotavirus, one of the most common viruses in children. My granddaughter received her rotavirus immunization when she was two months old. Now there is an effort to provide this cost-effective vaccine to children throughout the world to prevent a deadly problem.

When diarrhea does occur, ORT saves lives. One of the World Health Organization's "essential medicines,"[18] it should be stocked in every clinic in the world and available to community health workers who often travel to rural areas. When I travel in the developing world, I often carry ORT with me in case I get "traveler's diarrhea." The packets are available in drugstores or on Amazon.[19] I try to always leave packets behind and am surprised by how grateful people are to receive them. When friends tell me they are going on a mission trip I always urge them to include packets of ORT in their suitcases, not only for themselves but also to give this lifesaving formula to people who can't easily access it.

## PNEUMONIA

All children get sniffles from time to time. I remember many instances of using the dreaded infant syringe to open up my sons' stuffy noses and help them breathe. Fortunately, I also had access to over-the-counter cough syrups and decongestants as well as an attentive pediatrician. When a cold lingered too long and an infection set in, a prescription for antibiotics helped my sons recover.

But for most mothers living in the developing world, there is often no medicine available, or it is prohibitively expensive. Children become congested from colds that linger for weeks or even months. These children often live in small homes that use indoor fires for heat and cooking. Smoke accumulating in these enclosed areas irritates little lungs, making the children more vulnerable to infection.

*Childhood pneumonia is blamed for many of the heart problems adults experience in the developing world.*

When I traveled to Guatemala with MAP International in 2019, I heard numerous stories of children who had been ill for months or even years with untreated pneumonia. One of the doctors explained that untreated pneumonia can have long-term effects on the lungs (such as asthma) and the heart. Childhood pneumonia is blamed for many of the heart problems adults experience in the developing world. Because of that, MAP and other organizations work to provide specially formulated pediatric antibiotics so children will receive the proper dosage to completely clear their infections.[20]

According to the World Health Organization, pneumonia accounts for 14 percent of all deaths of children under five years old, killing 740,180 children in 2019.[21]

Pneumonia can be caused by viruses, bacteria, or fungi and can be prevented by immunization, adequate nutrition, and addressing environmental factors. Pneumonia caused by bacteria can be treated with antibiotics, but only a third of children with pneumonia receive the antibiotics they need.

## WHAT YOU CAN DO

### DONATE A MOSQUITO BED NET

Diseases like malaria, the Zika virus, and dengue fever can lead to missed school, hospital stays, and in extreme cases, death. However, they are all preventable and treatable. Your gift of an insecticide-treated bed net also includes training to help children and their families avoid the mosquito bites that cause these deadly diseases. For just eighteen dollars, you can donate a bed net through Compassion International. See compassion.com/catalog/donate-mosquito-net-charity-gift.htm.

# MALARIA

After diarrhea and pneumonia, malaria is the third largest killer of children under the age of five. According to the 2021 World Malaria Report, there were an estimated 241 million malaria cases in 2020,

95 percent of them in Africa. An estimated 627,000 people died from malaria in 2020, mostly children under age five.[22] According to UNICEF, every two minutes a child dies of malaria.[23]

Malaria is caused by parasites transmitted by mosquitoes. Even in relatively mild cases, it can cause a high fever, chills, flu-like symptoms, and severe anemia. These symptoms can be especially dangerous for pregnant women and young children and can cause lifelong intellectual disabilities. It is most deadly for young children.

Over the last twenty years, many organizations have made a concerted effort to stop the spread of malaria and to provide treatment for those infected. The use of insecticide-treated bed nets (ITNs) has helped protect many children from mosquito bites. Better diagnostic tests have made it possible to identify and treat malaria (usually with antibiotics). And research continues to find ways to attack malaria-carrying mosquitoes, with the goal of using genetic or other technology to make malaria-carrying mosquitoes extinct.[24]

## INNOVATIONS THAT MAKE A DIFFERENCE

### DEWORM THE WORLD

The nonprofit Evidence Action helps provide free deworming treatments to children at their schools. Working in partnerships with local governments, the group treats all children in settings with infection rates of at least 20 percent rather than simply treating children who are showing signs of infection. School-based deworming programs are effective because they treat children where they are attending classes, helping improve their overall health as well as school attendance. Find out more at evidenceaction.org.

## WHAT YOU CAN DO

### BE A MEDICAL VOLUNTEER

Do you have medical, dental, or nursing experience? Several organizations offer short-term opportunities to use your medical skills.

Medical Teams International places volunteers with a variety of medical and dental experience in both domestic and international response teams for short- and longer-term assignments (usually one to two months).

They also use lay volunteers, such as individuals with communication and financial skills, to support the response teams, who are often working in international disaster settings. You can apply on their website at MedicalTeams.org/volunteer.

CURE International operates hospitals around the world that offer lifesaving and life-changing surgeries for children in need. In addition to surgeons, nurses, and anesthesiologists, they need support staff to help at each hospital. Find out more at cure.org/cure-global-outreach/.

World Medical Mission (part of Samaritan's Purse) also offers short-term medical assignments for people with nursing, medical, or dental experience. For more information, go to samaritanspurse.org/medical/world-medical-mission/#serve.

Other medical volunteer opportunities exist at Operation Smile (operationsmile.org/medical-volunteers), Doctors Without Borders (doctorswithoutborders.org/careers/work -field), and Project HOPE (projecthope.org/volunteer/).

Even without a medical background, you can help volunteer to pack medicines for shipments overseas at Medical Teams International offices in Oregon (medicalteams. org/volunteer), at MAP International offices in Georgia (map .org/volunteer), or at Food for the Poor in Florida (volunteer .foodforthepoor.org).

## PARASITES

Some of the most common infections in children living in resource-poor countries are caused by parasitic worms, including roundworms, hookworms, and whipworms. Officially called soil-transmitted helminth infections, they are contracted in soil where sanitation is poor. Children can experience internal bleeding, diarrhea, anemia, and malnutrition because the worms impair digestion and absorption of nutrients. Although the infections don't necessarily lead to death, they impair the health of children in many ways and make them vulnerable. In *Half the Sky* the authors contend, "One of the most cost-effective ways to increase school attendance is to deworm students."[25]

According to the WHO, more than 1.5 billion people, or 24 percent of the world's population, are infected worldwide. Infections mostly occur in sub-Saharan Africa, the Americas, China, and East Asia.[26]

More than 267 million preschool-age children and over 568 million school-age children live in areas where these parasites are readily transmitted and are in need of treatment and preventive interventions. Many live in homes with dirt floors or routinely play in soil that has been contaminated by poor sanitation.[27]

In some parts of the world where there is a high incidence of infection, the World Health Organization recommends periodic deworming treatment for all children.

## HIV/AIDS

Once a major cause of death for newborns and young children, HIV/AIDs has been successfully treated both in pregnant mothers and children through a concerted effort to prevent mother-to-child transmission (MTCT). Women who are infected with HIV can be treated with antiretroviral drugs (called antiretroviral therapy or ART) during

*AIDS remains one of the leading causes of death among adolescents in Africa and where the majority of HIV infections occur in children.*

pregnancy, decreasing the likelihood of their child being born HIV positive. But in order to be treated, women must first be tested.

Sadly, in parts of Africa, AIDS is still a leading cause of death among adolescents.[28] Some became HIV positive through mother-to-child transmission and have not been treated with ART. Others were raped or given in child marriage and contracted the virus from their husband. According to a UNICEF report, at least 300,000 children were newly infected with HIV in 2020, or one child every two minutes. Another 120,000 children died from AIDS-related causes during the same period, or one child every five minutes.[29]

"Globally, 28.7 million people living with HIV were receiving ART in 2021. Global ART coverage was 75% [66–85%] in 2021. However, more efforts are needed to scale up treatment, particularly for children and adolescents. Only 52% [42–65%] of children (0–14 years old) were receiving ART at the end of 2021," according to the WHO.[30]

## WHAT YOU CAN DO

### HELP A PREGNANT WOMAN GET TESTED

The cost of testing a pregnant woman for HIV so she can then receive drugs that will stop the transmission to her baby is just twenty dollars. One of the most respected organizations working to stop the spread of HIV, especially in children, is the Elizabeth Glaser Pediatric AIDS Foundation (EGPAF). To learn more about EGPAF or to support their work in testing pregnant moms, go to act.pedaids.org/a/donate.

The majority of children living with HIV live in Africa, where AIDS remains one of the leading causes of death among all adolescents. Sadly, the COVID-19 pandemic disrupted both HIV testing and treatment and early studies indicate that those who are HIV positive are more vulnerable to dying from other infections, including COVID.[31]

## OTHER INFECTIOUS DISEASES

By the time my granddaughter was two months old, she was already immunized against some of the deadliest illnesses for children: pneumonia, diphtheria, meningitis, polio, tetanus, and rotavirus. Such immunizations are routine for babies in the United States and most developed countries. But for children in many parts of the world, vaccines are either not widely available or are difficult to obtain, especially for those living in remote areas. Sadly, lack of immunizations costs millions of lives.[32]

Measles, whooping cough, and meningitis still kill far too many children.

While immunization is one of the best ways to prevent disease and save children's lives, the WHO reported that the COVID-19 pandemic and other disruptions strained health systems, causing 23 million children to miss out on vaccinations in 2020. Over 1.5 million people die annually from diseases that can be prevented by vaccination.

Some key facts:

- Global coverage dropped from 86 percent in 2019 to 81 percent in 2021. An estimated 25 million children under the age of one year did not receive basic vaccines, the highest number since 2009.

- In 2021, the number of completely unvaccinated children increased by five million.[33]

Here is how specific vaccinations help:[34]

**Haemophilus influenzae type b (Hib)** causes meningitis and pneumonia, and left unchecked could potentially lead to deadly brain infections. By the end of 2021, the Hib vaccine had been introduced in 192 countries. Global coverage with three doses of Hib vaccine is estimated at 71 percent but varies by region.

> *The lack of immunizations costs millions of lives.*

**Hepatitis B** is a viral infection that attacks the liver. By the end of 2021, the hepatitis B vaccine for infants has been introduced in 190 countries. Global coverage with three doses of hepatitis B vaccine is estimated at 80 percent.

**Human papillomavirus (HPV)** is the most common viral infection of the reproductive tract and can cause cervical cancer in women as well as other types of cancer and genital warts in both men and women. The HPV vaccine is recommended for eleven- or twelve-year-old children, but can be given as early as nine. Global coverage of the first dose of HPV vaccine is estimated at just 15 percent.

**Meningitis A** is an infection that is often deadly and leaves one in five affected individuals with long-term devastating effects such as blindness, hearing loss, and even paralysis. By the end of 2021, 350 million people in 24 out of the 26 countries in the meningitis belt had been vaccinated.

**Measles** is a highly contagious disease usually resulting in a high fever and rash. It can lead to blindness, encephalitis, or death. By the end of 2021, 81 percent of children worldwide had received one dose of measles-containing vaccine by their second birthday. In developed countries, the measles vaccine is first given to babies around a year old as part of a three-part MMR vaccine (measles, mumps, rubella).

**Mumps** is a highly contagious virus that causes painful swelling at the side of the face under the ears (the parotid glands), fever, headache, and muscle aches. It can lead to viral meningitis. A spike in mumps infections occurred in 2021, blamed on delays in immunizations due to COVID-19.

**Pneumococcal vaccine** prevents pneumonia, meningitis, and febrile bacteremia, as well as otitis media, sinusitis, and bronchitis. In 2021, pneumococcal vaccine had an estimated global coverage of just 51 percent.

**Polio** is a highly infectious viral disease that can cause irreversible paralysis. Targeted for global eradication, polio had been eradicated in all countries except for Afghanistan and Pakistan, primarily through the work of groups like Rotary International, UNICEF, and the Gates Foundation. Sadly, the Taliban has prevented the polio campaign from continuing in Afghanistan, and in February of 2022, eight polio vaccination workers were killed in Afghanistan.[35]

Ukraine, despite being a developed country, has been found to have one of the lower rates of polio vaccination in the world. As of October 2021, only 53 percent of one-year-olds were vaccinated for polio in Ukraine, according to the National Center for Public Health in Ukraine. That same month, twenty-two cases of polio were reported, triggering what the Ministry of Health called a "biological emergency on a regional scale," sparking a coordinated effort with the WHO to begin a vaccination campaign. But when Russia invaded Ukraine in February 2022 and hospitals were bombed and the welfare of health workers was put at risk, the polio vaccinations were halted.[36]

**Rotavirus vaccine** became available in the United States in 2006 and is now distributed in more than 100 countries. It helps prevent severe diarrhea in young children throughout the world and is estimated to save the lives of 228,000 children annually.

**Rubella** is a viral disease that is usually mild in children, but infection during early pregnancy may cause fetal death or congenital rubella syndrome, which can lead to defects of the brain, heart, eyes, and ears. Rubella vaccine is part of the MMR vaccine given in the developed world. Globally, approximately 66 percent of children receive it.

**Tetanus** is caused by bacteria that grow in dirty wounds or the umbilical cord if it is not kept clean, resulting in serious complications such as breathing problems or even death. According to the *Lancet*, an estimated 30 million children missed completing their three doses of the tetanus vaccine in 2020.[37]

**Yellow fever** is an acute viral disease transmitted by infected mosquitoes. As of 2019, yellow fever vaccine had been introduced in routine infant immunization programs in 36 of the 40 countries and territories at risk in Africa and the Americas. In these 40 countries and territories, coverage is estimated at 47 percent.[38]

## ADOLESCENTS

Pregnancy is the number one cause of death among fifteen- to nineteen-year-old girls globally.[39] Both the girls' lives and the lives of their babies are at risk because the girls' bodies are not mature enough to safely carry a child, and they often do not have access to medical care during the pregnancy, birth, or postnatal period.

Each year, 70,000 teenagers die in developing countries due to complications related to childbirth or pregnancy.[40]

*Pregnancy is the number one cause of death among fifteen- to nineteen-year-old girls globally.*

Several factors contribute to adolescent pregnancies and births. In many societies, girls are under pressure to marry and bear children early. According to the UN Population Fund, in the least developed countries, at least 36 percent of girls marry before they are eighteen and 10 percent before they are fifteen years old.[41]

A cause of unintended pregnancy is widespread sexual violence, with more than a third of girls in some countries reporting that their first sexual encounter was coerced.[42]

According to the WHO, adolescent mothers aged ten to nineteen face higher risks of eclampsia, puerperal endometritis, and systemic infections than women aged twenty to twenty-four.

Dr. Ashok Dyalchand, who heads a public health organization in India and has worked with pregnant adolescent girls in low-income communities for more than forty years, explains that a child's pelvis is too small for childbirth.

"They have long labor, obstructed labor, the fetus bears down on the bladder and on the urethra, sometimes causing pelvic inflammatory disease and the rupture of tissue between the vagina and the bladder and rectum."[43]

When the pressure of childbirth is too great, it can cause a hole between the wall of the bladder or rectum and the vagina called a fistula, a painful condition and the source of shame and rejection for many girls and women in the developing world. "Women who experience obstetric fistula suffer constant incontinence, shame, social segregation, and health problems. It is estimated that more than 2 million young women live with untreated obstetric fistula in Asia and sub-Saharan Africa," according to the World Health Organization.[44]

Early childbearing can increase risks for newborns as well as young mothers. Babies born to mothers under twenty years of age face higher risks of low birth weight, preterm delivery, and severe neonatal conditions.[45]

## DID YOU KNOW?

**SINGLE-FOCUSED CARE**

Addis Ababa Fistula Hospital is the only hospital in the world dedicated exclusively to women with obstetric fistula. The hospital was created in 1974 by Australian obstetricians and gynecologists Catherine Hamlin and her husband, Reginald Hamlin, to care for women with childbirth injuries free of charge. Patients undergo surgical repair by Ethiopian and expatriate surgeons trained at the hospital's main facility in Addis Ababa. Dr. Catherine Hamlin has written an inspiring book about the work called *The Hospital by the River*. To learn more about the hospital and support the work, go to hamlinfistula.org/donate/.

# FEMALE GENITAL MUTILATION

Female genital mutilation (FGM) is a procedure that involves partial or total removal of the external female genitalia for nonmedical reasons. Practiced in some parts of Africa, the Middle East, and Asia, it is mostly carried out by traditional practitioners, often women in the village who have learned the practice from their mothers. The cutting, performed on girls from infancy to age fifteen, is often done with a razor blade or knife in nonsterile conditions and without anesthesia.

While there are cultural and legal issues related to FGM that are discussed in later chapters, the health implications for girls are often devastating.

The WHO explains, "FGM has no health benefits, and it harms girls and women in many ways. It involves removing and damaging healthy and normal female genital tissue, and interferes with the natural functions of girls' and women's bodies. Although all forms of FGM are associated with increased risk of health complications, the risk is greater with more severe forms of FGM."[46]

Immediate complications can include severe pain, excessive bleeding, infections, shock, and death. Long-term complications can include urinary tract infections, vaginal infections, difficulty in passing menstrual blood, and increased risk of childbirth complications.[47]

## CLOSING THOUGHTS

In order for girls to receive an education, to live full lives, and to flourish, they first need to have the obstacles to health removed. Simple interventions like deworming, oral rehydration therapy, bed nets to prevent malaria, and other low-cost, high-impact health interventions have made and are making a difference.

As I watch Evie grow up and thrive, I also mourn for the girls who are not receiving vaccinations, regular checkups, and nutritious food. I watch her play and think of the many little girls who are playing on dirt floors, too close to open fires, and being subjected to unthinkable violence.

Every little girl deserves to enjoy a healthy childhood. Making that possible is within our reach.

# 3

## CLEAN WATER, SANITATION, AND HYGIENE FOR GIRLS

WE HAD DRIVEN FOR HOURS through the desert landscape of Mauritania, the two-lane road soon disappearing into the sand that blew and shifted continuously. I had no idea how our driver knew where to go. There were no landmarks and nothing to break up the horizon except a few wild camels and an occasional barren tree. We were heading to the town of Kiffa, several hours from the capital city of Nouakchott, along a road that was marked on the map but in reality looked no different from the acres of sand that surrounded us.

On top of our Land Rover, jerry cans held gallons of water. After more than an hour of seeing no other cars or humans, I realized how essential the contents of those containers were in case we broke down and were stranded. Never before in my life had I been in a situation where saying, "I could die of thirst!" was actually a possibility. It was a stunning realization.

After several hours, we crested a mountainous sand dune and came upon a valley where a few sparse trees were growing and a few thin cows had gathered. As we came closer, I saw women as well, many with buckets on their heads, all surrounding a fetid green pond. Several of the cows were standing in the water as women dipped their buckets in. My stomach turned at the thought of them using that water to cook or drink.

Our driver explained that the pond was all that was left of the water that collected here during the rainy season. It had mostly evaporated, and now the small pond was all the nearby villagers had left for drinking, cooking, and bathing. He explained that the women would walk as much as an hour with the bucket of water on their heads so that their families had water for the day. That one bucket was all an entire family used for their daily water needs.

While the situation in the desert of Mauritania is extreme, an estimated 785 million people around the world do not have easy access to basic, clean drinking water, according to the UN, and 2.2 billion lack access to water that is clean, reliable, and available in their own home.[1] For those of us who routinely turn on a faucet to drink or bathe, it's hard to understand what a challenge the lack of clean water is. Not only is it a health threat, but it generally falls on the women and girls of a household to search for water and then bring it back to the family. The walk to the water source exposes them to being assaulted or attacked by animals. In some cases, the work of gathering water can take hours each day, leaving little time for school or other tasks. And the water most of them carry home will be contaminated, becoming a source of disease and long-term health issues.[2]

> *An estimated 785 million people around the world do not have easy access to basic, clean drinking water.*

Water, sanitation, and hygiene are all closely related and collectively are known as WASH by development professionals. Although they are separate fields, each is dependent on the other so they tend to be grouped together when discussing the needs of a community. Without a good water source, it is hard to have good hygiene. And if proper sanitation practices are ignored, what water source there is can easily become contaminated.

According to the Gates Foundation, "Poor sanitation, which is widely accepted as a chief contributor to waterborne diseases, causes the deaths of more than 1,200 children under age 5 every day—more than from AIDS, measles, and tuberculosis combined. Inadequate sanitation and hygiene caused more than half a million deaths from diarrhea alone in 2016."[3]

The United Nation's Sustainable Development Goals emphasize the need for bringing clean water and sanitation to the developing world, primarily as a way to support better health. And recognizing that the burden of gathering water falls primarily on women and girls, access to water is considered an important part of improving their health and well-being. In addition, girls who are burdened with carrying water each day often don't have time to go to school, so accessible water often means increased school enrollment.

WASH is especially critical in times of disaster, when people are displaced and infrastructure is destroyed. Setting up shelter for refugees means not just housing but also creating sources of clean water and safe waste disposal.

> *Girls who are burdened with carrying water each day often don't have time to go to school.*

Some organizations—for instance, charity: water, Lifewater, and Blood:Water—concentrate primarily on this issue, bringing clean water to communities through local organizations using various methods, while improving sanitation and hygiene. Their methodology is to support whatever approach is most appropriate to the community.

Other major international development organizations, including

**DID YOU KNOW?**

**UN SUSTAINABLE DEVELOPMENT GOAL #6:
TO ENSURE ACCESS TO SAFE WATER SOURCES
AND SANITATION FOR ALL.**
"Access to water, sanitation and hygiene is a human right.
The demand for water has outpaced population growth, and
half the world's population is already experiencing severe
water scarcity at least one month a year. Water is essential not
only to health, but also to poverty reduction, food security,
peace and human rights, ecosystems and education."[4]

CARE, Save the Children, UNICEF, World Vision, and others, integrate WASH projects into their ongoing work with communities or, in some cases, partner with local governments or nonprofits to find the best solution for each community.

Whatever the approach, there is consensus that the health of children, especially, depends on clean water, adequate sanitation, and good hygiene. And girls are disproportionately affected by lack of any or all of those elements. They are considered responsible for water collection, cooking, and caring for younger children and the ill. They must manage their menstrual health. Simply put, easy access to clean water, safe sanitation, and accessible hygiene greatly improves girls' lives.

## WATER

None of us can live without water. As W. H. Auden said, "Thousands have lived without love, not one without water."[5] Sadly, millions are suffering because the water they drink to survive is a conduit for disease.

According to a recent UNICEF study, women and girls worldwide spend 200 million hours each day collecting water for their families.[6] Many walk an hour or more each way with a heavy bucket on their head, a task that is not only time-consuming but also physically difficult, especially for girls. The water source is often a river or lake where animals gather, making it a dangerous undertaking, and the walk itself leaves girls vulnerable to predators, both human and animal.

*Easy access to clean water, safe sanitation, and accessible hygiene greatly improves girls' lives.*

Ironically, much of the water they bring home is unclean and unsafe, full of waterborne diseases and parasites. Contaminated water and poor sanitation are linked to transmission of cholera, diarrhea, dysentery, hepatitis A, typhoid, and polio, according to the World Health Organization. Children often contract parasites from unclean water that cause them to live with chronically poor health.[7]

And because water is scarce, chronic dehydration is common, especially in children. The onset of diarrhea can be fatal in days and, sadly, is often caused by the very water children and babies are given.

Although it sounds like an overwhelming problem, there are several approaches to bringing clean water to people who are living without it. As you'll see, some of these approaches are limited in their effectiveness and fail to address the root issue of the investment of time girls are expected to put in daily to retrieve it.

*According to a recent UNICEF study, women and girls worldwide spend 200 million hours each day collecting water for their families.*

## INNOVATIONS THAT MAKE A DIFFERENCE

### HIPPO ROLLER

For centuries, women and girls have carried jugs to a water source, where they have filled them and then carried the heavy containers back, sometimes for miles, to their homes. The open water containers often become contaminated, and the water is easily spilled.

One of the first innovations in thousands of years is something called the "Hippo Roller." The Hippo Roller was invented in South Africa in 1991 as a way to help transport water in low-income countries. The plastic, barrel-shaped rolling water device has a handle for pushing or pulling and can carry up to 25 gallons of water at a time without a person needing to lift or carry the water. The device can last several years and provides a nonstrenuous method of moving a large quantity of water from the source to a home or village. Many NGOs are now providing these rollers if wells cannot be dug near a village, or if there is no acceptable water source available nearby. To learn more, go to hipporoller.org.

## ADDITIVES

If you've ever gone camping, you may have packed water purification tablets to use when accessing fresh water sources for drinking. These inexpensive tablets use mostly iodine, chlorine, or chlorine dioxide to kill bacteria and parasites. This same method is implemented in some parts of the developing world where chlorine (usually in liquid form) is commonly used to treat drinking water. A capful of chlorine bleach is dropped into a bucket of water, letting it stand for thirty minutes or more.[8] When used properly, the bleach kills most bacteria and viruses. In times of disaster, when drinking water sources may be contaminated, chlorine is still considered one of the easiest ways to provide potable water. In addition, chlorine is often used to clean open water containers which can become contaminated. Chlorine bleach is found in most parts of the world or is easily transportable. NGOs provide it routinely, and it is available at small shops in most regions.

Additives are used when there is no easy way to find a more sustainable solution. They do not address the problem of accessibility to water sources or many of the issues that affect the girls who gather water, but they are an effective way to stop the spread of waterborne diseases.

## SOLAR DISINFECTION

In areas of the world with several hours of intense sunlight each day, a method called solar water disinfection (SODIS) can be used. It may be as basic as filling clean glass bottles with water and exposing them to direct sunlight for at least six hours. Some nonprofit organizations teach this method to communities, which has proven to be highly effective as long as there is sustained sunlight and the water itself is not full of sediment.

To create a larger-scale decontamination method, solar panels may be used to heat the water for a period of time, combining heat and UV rays to disinfect the water.[9] Over the past decade I've seen more and more solar panels popping up in remote areas, harnessing the power of the sun to provide clean water as well as fueling batteries to provide light and power after dark. At a World Vision project in Kenya, huge solar panels powered a pump to disinfect water that was then distributed at a "clean water" facility near a rural school.

Small solar cookers are also used to safely cook food and heat water to boiling. These ingenious stoves are often collapsible, portable devices with reflective surfaces that capture and concentrate the sun's rays to heat food and water to as high as 400 degrees. In addition to providing clean water, these cookers help families prepare food without open fires, not only reducing pollution, but also providing a much safer alternative.[10]

## WHAT YOU CAN DO

### SOLAR COOKERS

Solar Cookers International is a nonprofit organization dedicated to promoting the use of solar cookers around the world. It provides free resources to help people build their own cookers and supports work in various countries. For more information or to support their work, go to solarcookers.org/.

No matter what the method, harnessing the sun to disinfect water is another effective way to make water safer to drink for individual households or entire communities.

## FILTRATION

For communities living near open fresh water, such as lakes, rivers, or streams, water filtration systems are the gold standard for providing drinkable water.

The filtration systems rid contaminated water of many of the bacteria and toxins and often improve the taste of the water as well. Modest homemade systems using sand are surprisingly effective and are being used in many countries. Some organizations even teach communities how to make their own filtration systems using common materials and offer plans for building them.[11]

Commercial water filters are distributed to many communities through development organizations. Sawyer water filters are the most common brand used by non-profit organizations in more than eighty countries. They are often seen in disaster situations where the water is no longer safe and in refugee camps or other places where a portable solution is needed. They are the same filters sold in developed countries to campers and others who need to filter water from natural sources. Family-size filters can provide clean drinking water for an entire year.[12]

*For communities living near open fresh water, such as lakes, rivers, or streams, water filtration systems are the gold standard for providing drinkable water.*

Sawyer is a commercial company with a charitable arm that works with Rotary International and other nonprofits as well as churches and mission teams going overseas to help distribute filters in some of the most remote areas.[13]

Filtration is a relatively elementary method of cleaning water, but it can take time for the water to flow through the system. And

## WHAT YOU CAN DO

**TEACH A COMMUNITY TO BUILD THEIR OWN SAND FILTERS**
A Rocha is an international Christian conservation organization that teaches communities to use sand filters as part of their dedication to "creation care." In Uganda, they provide training to churches and other community groups to not only access clean water, but also avoid cutting down trees and starting open fires. To support the training and building of sand filters, go to shop.arocha.org/product/bio -sand-filter-training-for-a-church-or-community-uganda/.

## WHAT YOU CAN DO

### PROVIDE WATER FILTERS

Water filters provide a simple but effective way to clean water for individuals, a family, or an entire community. The most commonly used filters are made by Sawyer, a company that not only produces filters used by campers and others, but also supports the more than thirty charities that provide filters. To learn more about the charities supported by Sawyer, go to sawyer.com/charities.

Or you can support the Sawyer Foundation directly at donate.sawyerfoundation.org.

like the previous methods, it does not solve the problems associated with collecting the water in the first place. It works best when the natural source of water is nearby.

## CISTERNS

Cisterns are large containers that hold water and, in many cases, collect rainwater for later use. While rainwater may be preferable to drinking water from other sources, cisterns must be closed to prevent contamination from mosquitoes or algae. In some places, roofs and other hard surfaces use gutters and pipes or downspouts to direct the rainwater into tanks.

In the United States, rain barrels are often seen below downspouts to collect rain for watering plants. Similarly, rainwater is captured in developing countries through various catchment systems, although they must be kept clean to prevent pollution. For countries with cyclical rainy and dry seasons, the rainwater has to be collected in large enough containers to last through the dry season, which is often a logistical challenge. But if rainwater can be collected regularly and effectively, it significantly helps women and girls.

## WELLS

In Senegal I rode with World Vision workers into a village where everyone seemed terribly lethargic. Women were carrying buckets of water on their heads as we drove down the dusty road. Men were sitting in the shade and batting away flies. Children napped or played in the dirt without much enthusiasm. It was hot and dry and depressing. The villagers who talked to us explained that their only source of water was nearly an hour's walk away, and much like the pond we'd seen in Mauritania, it would only be replenished when the rains came again. The World Vision representatives explained that they would be able to help the village dig a well, but no one seemed very interested. When we asked if many children were sick, they answered, "Wow," the Wolof word for yes. We said we were sorry about what they were going through and left information with the chief about how he could contact World Vision if the village changed their minds about a well.

The next village we visited couldn't have been a greater contrast. As we approached the village, men were dancing and singing to us, welcoming our visit. Women wore their finest dresses and brought us snacks. Children squealed as they saw us, both excited and scared by our white faces. A group of village leaders greeted us and offered to give us a tour. The first thing they wanted us to see was their well. It stood just a few yards away from the edge of the village, easily accessed by everyone.

One of the men showed us that even *he* could gather the water, which was typically a woman's job but was now so easy even the men could do it! The women all laughed as he demonstrated pumping clean drinking water. I was shocked by the difference between the two villages—located less than an hour apart.

This village had been very much like the first one, with one life-saving difference. They accepted World Vision's offer to help them build a well. World Vision did the front-end work, digging a well deep enough to be safe and sustainable. Then the village took over, committed to maintaining the well. Two years later, the difference in the community was nothing short of miraculous. "Our girls and women don't spend all day collecting water, so now they have time to learn," explained one older man, proud of the progress his village had made.

But that wasn't all. The women in the village decided they needed to do more for their children. World Vision helped them design a functional, clean birthing room so women wouldn't have to give birth on a dirty floor or in a field. The women were extremely proud of their birthing room—no baby had died since its doors opened. Their once-lethargic children were now full of energy and so healthy they wore their parents out! The women then showed us a classroom where the children were using small chalkboards for basic math and writing.

As we started to leave, the women and men thanked us profusely for the well. Seeing their joy and the transformation of their village so soon after seeing the first village was eye-opening for me. Clean, accessible water had changed everything for them.

Wells are an important and sustainable source of water, not dependent on rains and less vulnerable to droughts. Most wells tap into a deep underground aquifer

## WHAT YOU CAN DO

**BUILD A WELL**
One well changes lives in a community. It means women don't spend hours walking, often in dangerous conditions, to collect water. It means girls have time to go to school. It means children are healthier and don't become dangerously dehydrated. Thanks to portable equipment and growing expertise, World Vision can dig a well in most villages for just $15,000. That well can serve the needs of about 250 to 300 people for years to come. While that may seem like a great deal of money, some churches, schools, and other organizations have come together to sponsor a well. If you are interested in sponsoring a well in Africa, go to donate.worldvision.org/give/deep-well.

where water is plentiful and pure. Even in the desert, when wells are dug properly, water is plentiful for drinking, cooking, and washing. For many NGOs, drilling wells has become a major focus because of the enormous impact accessible water can make.[14]

When I asked the World Vision staff why they didn't just build a well for every village, they explained that wells also require maintenance. A village has to spend the time and resources to pump the water once the well is dug. Sadly, many wells have been drilled but not maintained, so NGOs make sure there is commitment up front.

In communities where World Vision operates, local water, sanitation, and hygiene committees are established to manage every new water point. The committee is made up of local residents who collect fees for the well's usage and repairs. World Vision also provides the committees with tool kits and comprehensive training on maintaining and repairing wells. Creating such committees is now standard practice across many government and nongovernmental organizations to ensure that the community takes responsibility for the wells that are dug.[15]

Most wells dug before the nineteenth century were hand dug and are still quite common in many parts of the world. Hand-dug wells are excavations with diameters large enough to accommodate one or more people with shovels digging below the water table. In some cases, larger excavations, called step wells, make it possible for people to walk down to the water source and draw water. These types of wells can be lined with stone or brick. The lining sometimes extends above the ground surface to form a wall to reduce

## DID YOU KNOW?

### JACOB'S WELL STILL PROVIDES CLEAN WATER

On a visit to Israel and the West Bank, our itinerary included a visit to Jacob's Well, the site of the biblical encounter between Jesus and "the woman at the well."[16] I assumed we were simply visiting a historic spot where the well once stood. After entering a monastery and church, we walked down a flight of stairs and—much to my surprise—there was a well with a small winch and bucket. A priest dropped the bucket into the well, and after a surprisingly long time we heard it splash. Then he pulled the bucket up and offered each of us a drink. The water was cold and sweet, drawn from more than a hundred feet down. It was amazing to think that a group of women in the twenty-first century, including myself, were drinking water from the same source that the Samaritan woman drew from for Jesus. For many of us, it was not only a refreshing drink, but a spiritually significant one as well.[17]

contamination and accidental falls. But that means the open surface of the water can still be exposed to contaminants and polluted by the containers that are used to draw water from the well.

Hand-dug wells are inexpensive and low tech, and yet some are as deep as two hundred feet. Because water is generally extracted by hand, they have low operational and maintenance costs. But digging hand wells can be impossible in rocky areas and can be dangerous for people digging them. Besides the physical challenge of digging such wells, if the well isn't dug deep enough, it may tap in to groundwater so close to the surface that it is easily polluted. And in some parts of Africa, tapping into shallow aquifers means they are quickly depleted.[18]

Drilled wells reach water at a much deeper level, but generally the water can only be accessed by a mechanical pump (electric or gas powered). Drilled wells with electric pumps are used throughout the world, typically in rural or sparsely populated areas, though water in many urban areas is supplied partly by municipal wells. Hand pumps can be used in shallower wells. As a child I remember visiting my grandparents who lived on a farm in Indiana and used a hand pump to get water from their well for their livestock and to water their crops. I remember being impressed by how much work it took to pump a bucket full of water. Some parts of the developed world still use well water, although most homes have mechanical systems that pump the well water into the plumbing system.[19]

## SANITATION

Most of us take for granted that a toilet is available whenever we need it. Occasionally we find ourselves in a place where the public bathroom is not very clean or a toilet is out of order, but

## INNOVATIONS THAT MAKE A DIFFERENCE

### HOW A WELL CHANGED ONE GIRL'S LIFE

Twelve-year-old Ajimoh Yaya used to wake up at 4 a.m. each morning, walk more than a mile in the dark to the Abata River, and trudge home with bucketfuls of water for her family's cooking, drinking, and bathing needs. The river was the only water source for Ajimoh's village, Araromi Oke, in Ekiti State, Nigeria. In the dry season when the river was low, it was prone to contamination, causing cholera, diarrhea, and other waterborne illnesses to rage through the community.

The river water didn't just affect the villagers' health; fetching water was difficult and impacted the lives of everyone, especially children. Even though Ajimoh woke up before dawn to take care of her arduous chore, she was often late for school. And because there was so little water for all the household needs, Ajimoh and her siblings weren't able to bathe properly. "I had rashes all over my skin," Ajimoh recalled.

UNICEF collaborated with the Nigerian government to implement a nationwide program for supplying clean water and sanitation to those who need it most. The program aims to create over 11,000 water sources, benefiting more than 5.5 million people.

For Ajimoh, the program has been life changing. UNICEF helped build two wells (boreholes) equipped with hand pumps in her village, one in the middle of the community and the other at her school, St. Luke's Anglican Primary School. "Now that we have the boreholes, nobody in the community goes to fetch water from the Abata River anymore, not even to wash clothes," said Ajimoh. "I now wake up at 6:00 a.m. I bathe twice every day, wash my school uniform every day, help my mother bathe my two brothers, eat breakfast, and still get to school early."[20]

unless we are camping in the wilderness, we expect a toilet will be nearby.

We don't even think about the fact that the toilets we count on are part of an elaborate infrastructure of sewers and wastewater management systems. In many countries this level of infrastructure only exists in major cities, and managing human waste is simply left to communities or individual households. For example, in the community where I live, each household has its own septic system, with a large tank that collects household waste. Periodically, the tank must be pumped out so it doesn't overflow. But our toilets operate just like any others, efficiently flushing away waste.

Sadly, approximately 673 million people in the world have no sewer, septic system, or even an outhouse, so they practice "open defecation"—relieving themselves in fields, ditches, or other open spaces.[21] This generally happens either because toilets are not available or due to cultural practices. Lack of proper sanitation costs the world an estimated $223 billion every year.[22]

> *In many countries, managing human waste is simply left to communities or individual households.*

Open defecation pollutes the nearby water and soil and can easily transmit disease. Children are the most vulnerable since they are often crawling or playing on the ground, and it is one of the factors linked to high child mortality. And when women and girls seek privacy to defecate, away from others and sometimes even after dark, they are exposed to greater risks of assault.

According to UNICEF,

Poor sanitation puts children at risk of childhood diseases and malnutrition that can impact their overall development, learning and, later in life, economic opportunities. While some parts of the world have improved access to sanitation, millions of children in poor and rural areas have been left behind.

Lack of sanitation can be a barrier to individual prosperity and sustainable development. When children, especially girls, cannot access private and decent sanitation facilities in their schools and learning environments, the right to education is threatened.[23]

Helping communities understand the importance of making sure human waste is properly disposed of is an important part of the work done by many international development groups. Simple communal latrines using various filtering or composting techniques are becoming increasingly available. Providing latrines and private places for girls' sanitation needs at schools are also being emphasized so that girls feel safe and comfortable especially during menstruation. According to UNICEF, "In Africa, half of young girls who drop out of school do so because their school doesn't have basic toilets. Lack of toilets puts women and girls at risk of shame and makes them a target for sexual assault."[24]

In 2011, the Gates Foundation launched the "Reinvent the Toilet Challenge."[25] Engineers and scientists have been tasked to design simple, affordable toilets for use in remote areas that don't require electricity, a water supply, or connection to a sewer system. Some of the toilet models provide sanitation for single homes, while others are designed for public or shared toilet facilities.

Even in communities with toilets, waste must be properly contained, filtered, or transported so it doesn't flow into the groundwater or surrounding soil. Communities often start with a communal latrine, either a pit (literally a hole in the ground) or

## INNOVATIONS THAT MAKE A DIFFERENCE

### NOT YOUR TYPICAL TOILET

The Borgen Project, a nonprofit dedicated to fighting extreme poverty, has highlighted five types of toilets that are making a difference in the developing world:

1. **Earthworm Toilets.** These toilets use both aerobic bacteria and earthworms to compost human waste.
2. **The Sulabh Toilet.** The Sulabh toilet is a pan-trap squat toilet that uses a two-pit system minimizing both odor and water waste. Only one pit is ever in use at a time.
3. **The BioFil Digester.** Ghanaian Kweku Anno developed a composting system that uses a primary treatment of both aerobic bacteria and red worms to aerate the solid contents; the BioFil digester then treats what remains through a sand filter into a reed bed.
4. **The X-Runner Toilet (now known as Sanima).** The X-Runner toilet is a waterless urine-diverting portable toilet that was developed by Noa Lerner, an Israeli industrial engineer. The toilet separates urine from feces and minimizes odor due to its enclosed and detachable pan.
5. **The EcoSan Toilet.** This toilet is completely water-free and entirely closed. Developed in the late 1990s by Eco Sanitation Ltd, the toilet relies on dehydration of waste to limit odor and avoid the use of precious water resources. The excrement falls into a conveyer that rotates and mechanically moves the waste every time the toilet lid is opened.[26]

trench. But these provide little privacy, so basic outhouses are usually built around the hole, sometimes with a seat made of wood.

When I visited Thailand, I stayed in a remote village where the community was quite proud of its communal latrine, a small hut which they pointed out to visitors. When I went inside, I was shocked to see a mud floor with a fairly large hole in the middle, smelling like you might expect. I was truly terrified that my footing would give out and I would slide into the hole! I admit that I ate and drank less while I was there, trying to avoid multiple trips to the outhouse.

## DID YOU KNOW?

### CELEBRATE TOILETS

November 19 is World Toilet Day, an official United Nations international observance to inspire action to tackle the global sanitation crisis. It celebrates toilets and raises awareness of the *3.6 billion* people living without access to safe sanitation. "When some people in a community do not have safe toilets, everyone's health is threatened. Poor sanitation contaminates drinking water sources, rivers, beaches, and crops, spreading deadly diseases among the wider population."[27]

## HYGIENE

Most of us wash our hands multiple times a day. During the COVID-19 pandemic, handwashing was strongly recommended as an important method to stop the spread of the virus. But handwashing is not prevalent in many societies where soap and water are difficult to come by or where the small amount of water available is so precious that it is for drinking only. Three billion people do not have a handwashing facility with water and soap at home. Almost half of the schools in the developing world are in the same situation, affecting 818 million school-age children. Roughly 32 percent of health-care facilities in the developing world lack hand hygiene facilities at points where patients are treated.[28]

Diarrhea, the second leading cause of death among children under five, kills more than 525,000 children each year.[29] Some studies show that the incidence of such diseases can be nearly cut in half when handwashing with soap and water is practiced in a community.

> *Almost half of the schools in the developing world lack handwashing facilities, affecting 818 million school-age children.*

Handwashing can stop the spread of typhoid and cholera by removing bacteria, parasites, and viruses from the hands.

Handwashing also helps stop the spread of disease through fecal matter. "Coupled with poor hygiene practices, exposure to fecal matter remains a leading cause of child mortality, morbidity, undernutrition and stunting, and can negatively impact a child's cognitive development."[30]

## MENSTRUAL HYGIENE

For many girls in the developing world, the beginning of their period is the end of their formal education. Going to school while menstruating is difficult for many girls, who either miss so many days each month that it is impossible to keep up or they simply give up and drop out. In some cultures, menstruation also marks the end of a girl's childhood and the beginning of her preparation to be a wife, which also may mean the end of school. In addition, some cultural taboos restrict public discussions about menstruation, and girls who are menstruating are sometimes considered "unclean" and prohibited from taking part in certain activities, including school or religious rituals. For many girls, menstruation is embarrassing and shameful.

In developing countries, access to menstrual pads and the lack of bathrooms or private areas at many schools is problematic.

## INNOVATIONS THAT MAKE A DIFFERENCE

### *SESAME STREET'S* WASH UP! PROGRAM

*Sesame Street*'s global campaign to bring sanitation and hygiene education to kids is called WASH UP! and was created in partnership with World Vision. Since 2015, *Sesame Street* characters have appeared in storybooks, games, videos, and teacher training materials, making healthy habits easy to practice. It is already being implemented in sixteen countries, with more expected to follow.

The recognizable characters have the unique ability to reach children and model behaviors around topics adults may see as taboo, such as toilet use and menstrual hygiene. Raya, an energetic six-year-old character, is guiding conversations all over the world about clean water, handwashing, and proper latrine use. She encourages children to share what they learn with friends and family, making good habits contagious.

WASH UP! programs can be found across sub-Saharan Africa, Latin America, and the Middle East. "In Nigeria, kids who participated in the program were twice as likely to wash their hands after defecation. Children in India who participated were 48 percent more likely to use an improved latrine at home. In just two years, WASH UP! has reached over 52,000 children in Zambia and is now part of the country's primary school curriculum."[31]

In addition, WASH UP! Girl Talk promotes healthy hygiene practices particularly around menstrual health. The overall goal of the program is to empower both girls and boys in school with information and skills to understand puberty and for girls to meet their menstrual health and hygiene needs.[32] To support the program, go to donate.worldvision.org/give /sesame-street-wash-up-kit.

Programs that help girls manage these challenges are often referred to by the initials MHH—menstrual health and hygiene. MHH has become an increasingly important emphasis because girls who can manage their menstrual periods are able to continue school.

According to the World Bank, *at least 367 million children have no sanitation services in their schools.* "This lack of infrastructure and stigma contributes to absenteeism; in one Kenyan study 95 percent of menstruating girls missed one to three school days, 70 percent reported a negative impact on their grades, and over 50 percent started falling behind in school due to menstruation."[33]

*For many girls in the developing world, the beginning of their menstrual period is the end of their formal education.*

The term *period poverty* refers to a lack of access to menstrual products, education, hygiene facilities, waste management, or a combination of these. It affects an estimated 500 million people worldwide.[34] While it mostly affects girls in the developing world, there is increasing awareness that vulnerable women and girls living in poverty in developed countries also have difficulty affording essential products.

The 2019 Academy Award–winning Netflix documentary *Period. End of Sentence.* tells the story of women in a village outside of New Delhi, India, who installed a machine that made menstrual pads, which they sold throughout their district.[35] Not only has the project provided jobs for women, but the availability of absorbent pads, instead of the typical rags,

*According to the World Bank, at least 367 million children have no sanitation services in their schools.*

has allowed girls to stay in school. The pad-making machine and the documentary were partially funded by high school students who raised $55,000 through fundraisers. The movement later expanded into The Pad Project, which works to increase access to menstrual supplies and menstrual hygiene management education.[36]

## WHAT YOU CAN DO

**SUPPORT THE PAD PROJECT**

The Pad Project's programs utilize a social enterprise model. Instead of simply distributing products, these programs employ women to run their own businesses of making and selling menstrual pads. Their programs also involve implementing menstrual hygiene management workshops, all of which are created and run by nonprofit partners to fit the needs of their community members. To learn more or support the work of the organizations, go to thepadproject.org/.

## CLOSING THOUGHTS

Nobel Prize winner Desmond Tutu wisely said, "There comes a point where we need to stop just pulling people out of the river. We need to go upstream and find out why they are falling in."[37]

Perhaps this quote has never been more appropriate than when it applies to girls and water, sanitation, and hygiene. Why are girls dying from preventable diseases? Lack of clean water plays an enormous role. So does lack of good sanitation facilities and simple handwashing. Why are girls being assaulted? They often walk far distances alone to reach water sources. Or they seek a private place to relieve themselves. Why are girls missing school? They spend hours each day collecting and carrying water, so they don't have time to attend school. And when they start menstruating, they lack both menstrual supplies and private facilities.

Clean water, good hygiene, and proper sanitation have an enormous impact on the lives of girls and women. It is an "upstream" solution to many of the problems girls face.

# 4

. . . . . . . . . . . . . . .

# EDUCATING GIRLS

ALL SHE WANTED TO DO was go to school, along with other girls in her community. But her desire for education nearly cost Malala Yousafzai her life. Shot by Taliban extremists after taking an exam at her school in Pakistan, Malala was all the more determined. Her story of perseverance and her articulate voice for girls' education earned her international attention and a Nobel Prize. Today, she is a graduate of Oxford University and continues to advocate for girls through her Malala Fund, which is "working for a world where every girl can learn and lead."[1]

Malala gained international attention even before she was attacked. Fluent in three languages (including English), she wrote a blog for the BBC about life under the Taliban. A documentary was made about her, which may have been one of the reasons she was identified and targeted by the Taliban. If not for her fame, the attack on Malala and her friends would never have been known beyond her region. Instead, a worldwide outpouring of sympathy and outrage followed the assault, and she and her family moved to England to seek medical care and safety. "I tell my story, not because it is unique, but because it is not. It is the story of many girls," she says.[2] Her book *I Am Malala: The Girl Who Stood Up for Education and Was Shot by the Taliban* became a bestseller.[3]

## WHAT YOU CAN DO

### JOIN MALALA

The Malala Fund advocates for twelve years of free, safe, quality education for every girl. The organization advocates at local, national, and international levels for resources and policy changes to give all girls a secondary education. You can support the Malala Fund by purchasing a variety of products (including a mug with the phrase "EDUCATION IS POWER"), helping support advocacy efforts, or donating directly to the cause at malala.org.

The idea that a girl would have to risk her life to go to school is hard for most of us to fathom.

In the developed world, educating children is a given. Unless a child is homeschooled, she must report to a school or her parents will face legal consequences. Schooling is compulsory in every US state and in most developed countries in the world. In the United States, regulations vary from state to state—some require a child to start school at five, while others start at six; some states require a child to remain in school until sixteen, seventeen, or eighteen.[4] In other countries, some require children to start school as early as three years of age and many require schooling until eighteen.

And yet around the world, 129 million girls do not attend school, including 32 million of primary school age, 30 million of lower-secondary school age, and 67.4 million of upper-secondary school age. According to UNICEF, girls are more than twice as likely not to be in school in countries affected by conflict than girls living in non-affected countries.[5]

The challenges to receiving an education vary by country, region, and economic status. Even the recent pandemic has shown how vulnerable schooling is to a public health crisis. While an increasing number of children are able to receive an education online, there are also a growing number whose education has been disrupted by conflict, displacement, and isolation.

*Around the world, 129 million girls do not attend school: 32 million of primary school age, 30 million of lower-secondary school age, and 67.4 million of upper-secondary school age.*

For millions of children, the COVID-19 pandemic meant schools were shut and online learning was not an option. The devastating impact of this interruption, especially for girls, is still being calculated. Sadly, in countries where progress was being made in educating girls, there may be a long-term setback.

The most recent assessment by the Brookings Institute found:

For many girls, COVID-19's associated economic crises exacerbated gender inequalities that are more acute among older adolescents—from increased limitations on their freedom of movement to the need to care for younger siblings and perform household chores to the likelihood of being married off to relieve pressure on sparse household resources. When schools reopened after six months of closure in Uganda, 10 percent of grade 10 girls failed to return compared to 8 percent of grade 10 boys. Worse, 18 percent of grade 12 girls did not come back compared to 2 percent of grade 12 boys. A survey of nearly 4,000 adolescents living in urban settlements and rural counties in Kenya found that 16 percent of vulnerable adolescent girls compared to 8 percent of adolescent boys did not return to school when schools reopened in the country in January 2021.[6]

## BENEFITS OF EDUCATION

I'll never forget visiting the massive garbage dump outside Guatemala City in the 1990s. Long before we saw it, the smell filled the van in which I was riding with other American women visiting the work of World Vision in the Central American country. We covered our noses and mouths with scarves, but the odor seemed to penetrate our pores.

We had been told we were coming to visit a World Vision–sponsored school,[7] and yet all we saw was acres and acres of garbage. One of the largest open-air landfills in the world, the dump outside Guatemala City seems to go on for miles—mountains of spoiled food, raw sewage, chemical waste, biohazard materials, industrial products, rusting cars, and smoking piles of rot. My first thought was *This is a vision of hell.*

Then we saw movement. People were climbing all over the mountains of garbage. Men, women, and children were sorting through the piles. We were shocked to see young children who could barely walk crawling in the toxic stew. It was horrifying.

Our van stopped in front of a little schoolhouse located between two massive garbage peaks. The building was clean and inviting, in sharp contrast to the surrounding area. Inside, a few children sat at clean desks, themselves still dirty but safely inside this haven.

As the local World Vision director began to talk about the school, we were impressed but confused. "Why are there so few children here?" one woman asked.

"The children can see the school from the dump, but they and their family have to choose to come here. For many, life in the garbage dump is all they know, and what little they collect each day helps them and their family survive. They aren't thinking about the future. They are trying to survive each day. As hard as it is to understand, coming to school can be a difficult choice."

The situation in the Guatemala City dump is not so different from other places in the world where expectations for girls are less about their future than their day-to-day contribution to family survival. Choosing to go to school can be particularly difficult for girls, especially if it breaks the norm or goes against family tradition. Yet other than health and safety, there is nothing more important to a girl's future than an education.

"I don't think an education is so much about making a living, it's about making a person," says Tara Westover, author of *Educated*.[8] Westover grew up in a fundamentalist Mormon family in the United States that avoided all government-controlled institutions—including schools. She had to hide her interest in education, even sneaking away from home in order to attend school, and she eventually graduated from high school. The joy of learning and the opportunity to change her life motivated her to attend college at great personal cost. Eventually she earned a PhD from Cambridge University and went on to receive many awards for her writing.

> *The benefits of educating a girl extend beyond her own life to the lives of her children, her community, and even her country.*

The benefits of educating a girl extend beyond her own life to the lives of her children, her community, and even her country. According to the World Bank, "Both individuals and countries benefit from girls' education. Better educated women tend to be more informed about nutrition and healthcare, have fewer children, marry at a later age, and their children are usually healthier, should they choose to become mothers. They are more likely to participate in the formal labor market and earn higher incomes."[9]

Kofi Annan, former UN Secretary-General put it simply: "To educate girls is to reduce poverty."[10]

According to UNICEF, "Investing in girls' education transforms communities, countries and the entire world. Girls who receive an education are less likely to marry young and more likely to lead healthy, productive lives. They earn higher incomes, participate in the decisions that most affect them, and build better futures for themselves and their families."[11]

An African proverb puts it this way: "If you educate a boy, you educate an individual. But if you educate a girl, you educate a nation."

> *Education gives girls the potential to earn better wages, raise healthier and more educated children, and have a voice in her community.*

Education gives girls the potential to earn better wages, raise healthier and more educated children, and have a voice in their communities.

The benefits of education to girls have been measured in many ways. Just look at this list from World Vision International:

- An extra year of primary school education boosts girls' eventual wages by 10 to 20 percent. An extra year of secondary school adds 15 to 25 percent.
- Education is associated with increased contraception use, less underage premarital sex, and lower HIV/AIDS risks.
- When a girl in the developing world receives seven years of education, she marries four years later and has 2.2 fewer children.

- Women invest 90 percent of their income in their households, as opposed to men's 30 to 40 percent, leading to healthier, better-educated children and families.
- Women's labour force participation can lead to reduced poverty, greater political participation, increased agency, and assertion of their rights at the household and community levels.[12]

And according to the World Bank, limited educational opportunities for girls and barriers to completing twelve years of education cost countries between $15 trillion and $30 trillion in lost lifetime productivity and earnings.[13]

UNICEF's statistics show that "only 49 percent of countries have achieved gender parity in primary education. At the secondary level, the gap widens: 42 percent of countries have achieved gender parity in lower secondary education, and 24 percent in upper secondary education."[14]

"Educated boys often leave their villages to work in cities, but the girls often stay in their village and become leaders in their community. An educated girl will pass on her knowledge to her children and work to improve their community by reducing poverty, improve healthcare, and reduce violence against women/girls," according to Tirzah International, an organization that partners with local female leaders to create opportunities for women.[15]

UNICEF adds, "Girls' education strengthens economies and reduces inequality. It contributes to more stable, resilient societies that give all individuals—including boys and men—the opportunity to fulfill their potential."[16]

In June 2021, US Senator Jeanne Shaheen (D-NH) and US Senator Lisa Murkowski (R-AK) introduced a bill to address the unique barriers young girls in developing countries face in accessing a full education. State Representatives Lois Frankel and Mike Waltz introduced companion legislation in the Florida House of Representatives. According to a press release from Senator Jeanne Shaheen,

> The Keeping Girls in School Act would direct the US government to leverage its resources and partnerships with private institutions, NGOs, and federal agencies to create solutions that address the obstacles facing adolescent girls. Supported by UNICEF and many NGOs, the bill would also require the development of a US global strategy to empower adolescent girls. . . .
>
> "When girls are empowered with access to quality education, it sets their societies on the fast track for success and economic development. That's why addressing the global gender education gap must be a critical US policy priority," said Senator Shaheen. . . .
>
> "On the global scale, there are a staggering number of girls who are not in school because their attendance is deterred by unsafe environments, forced marriages, domestic violence, harassment, or poor socioeconomic status. These are all tragic obstacles, but through this legislation we have an opportunity to help," said Senator Murkowski. "Education is a key factor in creating a healthy, successful future, both for individuals and for society at large. I'm proud to reintroduce legislation that will help break down barriers and give millions of girls in primary school and for young women pursuing a secondary education the chance to make attending school a reality."
>
> "When girls are educated their futures are brighter. This means greater prosperity and security for their families,

communities, and the world," said Rep. Frankel. "Eleven million girls are at risk of never returning to school around the world right now, which means there are eleven million reasons that we need to care about this issue. This bill will tackle the barriers keeping girls out of school, and help build a more peaceful, prosperous, and equitable world."

"As a Green Beret who has operated all over the world, I have seen firsthand that in societies where women thrive, extremism doesn't," said Rep. Waltz. "Adolescent girls are disproportionately at risk of dropping out of school than boys. The Keeping Girls in School Act will help ensure girls can safely access the proper education they deserve. Girls' education is essential to our national security and this legislation will help make the United States and the world safer places."[17]

As of January 2023, no action has yet been taken.

## OBSTACLES TO EDUCATION

Barriers to girls' education—like poverty, child marriage, and gender-based violence—differ, depending on the country and the community. Poor families often favor boys when investing in education. In some places, schools do not meet the safety, hygiene, or sanitation needs of girls. In other places, teaching practices are not gender-responsive and result in gender gaps in learning and skills development. Here are some of the most common obstacles.

### PREJUDICE

For girls, especially, schooling is too often viewed by their families or community as a waste of time and money. Girls are valued for their ability to help in the home and become a good wife. Investing in a girl's education takes funds from other necessities. Often families expect their daughters to marry, and therefore it is thought that they don't need schooling beyond the basic level. While many countries guarantee free access to primary grades, all too often girls have few options for secondary school and must travel to another location or board, leaving them unavailable to help in the household.

Kakenya Ntaiya grew up in rural Kenya in a small village called Enoosaen. The first of eight children, she spent her childhood helping her mother around the house.

"Like other Maasai girls, I was engaged from a very young age to be married. But as I reached puberty, I underwent female genital mutilation, known as FGM. . . . FGM was supposed to mark the end of my childhood and, by extension, my education," said Kakenya Ntaiya in a recent TED talk. "But I negotiated with my father in order to stay in school—even after going through FGM.

"Years later I went to university. And in order to get my community's support, I promised to come back one day to repay that support. But years later, when I went back to my village, not much had changed. Girls were still going through FGM, still leaving school, still getting married to men older than their fathers, and still having children when they're teenagers. I did not want to see any more girls go through that. That's when I knew what I needed to do to give back to my community.

*For many girls, getting to school is a long and dangerous journey.*

"I built a school just for girls so that they can be free from FGM and early marriage."

Her goal is simple: "Helping the communities see that each daughter is a treasure, every sister is full of potential, and helping every single girl see that value in herself."[18]

International organizations like World Vision work at every level in a country to help establish the importance of girls' education. "We work with all stakeholders in a girl's life—governments, families, schools, churches, traditional leadership, boys and men and the girls themselves—to create a multi-layered, holistic and sustainable program that targets the barriers to girls' access to education, retention in school and learning outcomes."[19]

> *Extremist groups often object to girls being educated.*

Extremist groups often object to girls being educated. The Taliban has created numerous obstacles to prevent girls from attending school. While allowing boys to return to secondary school, it banned girls from secondary school after it took control of Afghanistan in 2021.[20]

In the local Hausa dialect, the name Boko Haram, the extremist group operating in Nigeria, means "Western Education Is Forbidden." The terrorist organization carried out that decree in 2014. The founder of Boko Haram condemned the reading of any books other than the Koran.[21]

## DISTANCE

In many parts of the world, people live in remote areas—on mountainsides, on vast plains, in small villages, or on farms. Whatever school exists is often miles away, and many of the working poor have no regular means of transportation. There are no yellow school buses in most of the developing world.

For many girls, getting to school requires a long and dangerous journey. In some countries it is not uncommon to hear of a child being bitten by a snake or attacked by an animal en route to school. And even in urban areas, girls may have to walk through slums or dangerous neighborhoods, making them extremely vulnerable to predators.

## INNOVATIONS THAT MAKE A DIFFERENCE

### BICYCLES FOR SCHOOLGIRLS

World Bicycle Relief offers this story:

At 14 years old, orphan Belita would wake up to darkness in the Chuungu village. She rose before 5 a.m. each day in order to make the trek to her school, a full 5 km in the Kalomo district of the southern province of the Republic of Zambia. Belita didn't have time to help her grandmother with morning chores. Instead, she simply would grab a meal and begin to walk.

Even with her early schedule, she struggled to get to school on time. She dreaded the slap on the wrist she received at the front of the classroom each day when she was late. After class, Belita would begin the hike home, arriving at her village with just enough time to help with chores, eat, and, if time allowed, complete her homework.

Fast-forward one year. Belita is now 15 years old and in 7th grade at the Chilal basic school. She has improved her class standing, moving from 10th to 7th in her grade. She no longer has trouble arriving to school on time and can help her grandmother with chores around the house. And Belita now has enough time to complete her schoolwork. She sees herself finishing basic school before enrolling in a nurses' training college. What brought about this improvement in grades, family life and future aspirations? A single Buffalo Bicycle.[22]

For just $165 you can provide a durable bicycle made for rough terrain for girls like Belita to ride to school. Go to worldbicyclerelief.org to donate.

"It's a sad truth, but girls are often assaulted, raped, and even kidnapped on their way to school. So before a girl could learn math or history, she needed to feel safe, she needed to be rested and be well-nourished," says Kakenya Ntaiya, telling about the school for girls she established in her village in Kenya and sharing her experience in a TED talk.[23]

## WHAT YOU CAN DO

### EDUCATE GIRLS IN RURAL AFRICA
Girls in rural Africa face some of the greatest obstacles to receiving an education. CAMFED works in five African countries—Ghana, Malawi, Tanzania, Zambia, and Zimbabwe—to support girls who otherwise couldn't afford to go to school or who are hindered by lack of resources in their communities. Gifts to CAMFED help provide scholarships, school uniforms, supplies, and menstrual pads. To learn more or to donate, go to camfed.org.

Another way of addressing the problem is to create more schools in areas underserved by larger public schools. Although there are private schools (many of them boarding schools) in developing countries that serve the children whose families can afford it, smaller private schools are often started by individuals who teach in their homes or at community centers so children don't have to walk such long distances. Some of these smaller schools have become so successful that they have opened branches. School fees are kept low, and children who can't afford even the low fee are often allowed to attend. Parents often prefer these schools to the public schools because class sizes are small, and the teachers are more dedicated.

In his book *The Beautiful Tree*, educator James Tooley writes

## WHAT YOU CAN DO

### LOANS TO START SCHOOLS

Starting a private school often requires a small loan so the teacher can buy basic equipment and create a classroom, as well as supply materials to the students. Loans are repaid over time as school fees are collected. You can help fund a loan to an "edupreneur" through Edify (edify.org) or Opportunity International (opportunity.org/education-finance).

about his years researching these small private schools. One grateful parent in Nigeria said, "We pass the public school many days and see the children outside all of the time, doing nothing. But in the private schools, we see them every day working hard."[24] Tooley lauds the dedicated individuals who educate children in India and throughout Africa and also make a small income.

Several organizations now offer backing for such schools, as well as lesson plans. Edify is a Christian organization created to help fund small educational start-ups in low-income countries, providing small loans to "edupreneurs" or qualified teachers who set up their own schools and need help procuring resources. It's a win-win situation. For a small fee, children go to schools in their own community and the teacher has means to support her family.[25]

### COST

For families living in poverty, the cost of schooling can be prohibitive, even if it is a nominal school fee or the cost of a required school uniform. According to the World Bank, "over 1.9 billion people, or 26.2 percent of the world's population, were living on less than $3.20 per day in 2015. Close to 46 percent of the world's population was living on less than $5.50 a day."[26] That means a school fee, the cost of school supplies, or a uniform can mean a family goes hungry for days to pay for school.

ONE, a global organization aimed at ending poverty, put it this way in a guest blog post:

> When costs are high and benefits aren't clearly understood, parents are less likely to send their kids to school, and kids are less likely to want to attend. The benefits of education come mostly in the future, but the costs are immediate and top-of-mind.

## WHAT YOU CAN DO

### BACKPACKS FOR SCHOOL CHILDREN

Basic school supplies like pencils, notebooks, and backpacks are too costly for many children living in poverty both in the United States and other countries. To help address the need, World Vision has developed a program to provide backpacks filled with school items to kids who can't afford them.

The packing program can be done by any group—schools, churches, companies, or civic organizations. World Vision supplies the items and individuals fill the backpacks, including a handwritten note of encouragement.

When I visited a refugee school in Jordan, the children (many of whom had fled Syria with nothing) proudly showed me their World Vision backpacks and the note inside from the person who had prepared the gift. They were thrilled to know that someone had personally made each backpack possible.

To host an event to pack supplies for overseas recipients (which include basic hygiene items as well as school supplies), or to supply backpacks for needy children in the United States go to kits.worldvision.org/.

It's true that many families can't always afford large school fees, but data shows that even relatively small costs—such as a six-dollar uniform, a school lunch, books, or basic school supplies—can prevent kids from attending school.

The cost of a school uniform or lunch shouldn't stand between a girl and her future. By eliminating the immediate costs of schooling where we can, we will move toward a world in which every girl gets the opportunities she deserves.[27]

> The cost of a school uniform or lunch shouldn't stand between a girl and her future.

Organizations that offer sponsorship models, such as Compassion International, Food for the Hungry, Save the Children, and World Vision, generally include education fees as part of their support.[28] (In general, these organizations support the entire community in which the sponsored child lives.) Many organizations have special funds to pay for school supplies and uniforms in places where children can't afford them. Pencils of Promise is an organization started by Adam Braun, who gave a boy in India a pencil, the thing the boy said he wanted most in life. With this small beginning, Adam went on to build hundreds of schools in more than 550 countries. The organization also makes sure these schools have adequate sanitation facilities for the children's health and well-being.[29]

When I visited the Evangelical Nazarene Church of Marka in Jordan I saw a great solution to the challenge of affordable uniforms for school. The church (and its nonprofit organization) has developed several small businesses that employ Syrian and Iraqi refugees who have fled violence in nearby countries. One of the businesses sews school uniforms. The refugees are paid for every uniform they sew, and some uniforms are sold to those who can afford to pay, providing an income stream. Other uniforms are provided free of charge to children in need who attend the Good Shepherd Center, which is operated by the church.[30]

## WORK

Before I traveled outside the United States, one of my many misconceptions about people who live in poverty was that they are lazy and could make more money if they worked harder. In fact, once I began to meet people living with scant resources, I was shocked by how hard they had to work just to make it through each day. Collecting water, tending a fire (for warmth and cooking), finding food every day (because there is no refrigeration), caring for children, caring for the home and garden, mending . . . the list goes on. No matter how old they are, everyone in the household is expected to contribute.

From the time they can walk, girls are expected to help with household chores and to care for their younger siblings. They often rise early and cannot leave for school until they have done hours of work. Once they return from school, they have another list of chores, leaving little time for homework.

## WHAT YOU CAN DO

### PENCILS OF PROMISE

Pencils of Promise builds schools, supports teachers, and makes sure children have adequate sanitation in their schools. Using a campaign approach, the organization engages groups from schools and other communities to fundraise together toward a goal. If you'd like to learn more about supporting the work, go to pencilsofpromise.org/take-action/campaign/.

## WHAT YOU CAN DO

### EARLY LEARNING CENTERS

Save the Children focuses on early education for girls. It helps make sure they attend and stay in school. One of its programs helps create early childhood learning centers in villages so girls can begin to learn near their homes. To support Save the Children's education work with girls, go to savethechildren.org/us/what-we-do/education/girls-education.

In Zambia I interviewed a prominent woman who had received an excellent education and risen to a high position in the government. When I asked her about challenges she had faced along the way, she surprised me by saying that the hardest part of her journey to success was leaving the house as a little girl to attend school. She told me,

I was the first girl in my family to attend school. My father encouraged my interest in learning, but my mother needed me to help around the house, so every day I went to school meant she had more work to do. She kept telling me things like, "Girls don't need school. You need to stay home and learn how to be a good wife." I felt terribly conflicted as a young girl because my mother disapproved of me leaving home each day for school. She wasn't being mean or selfish. She just didn't see the point of education. Without my father's encouragement, I never would have finished primary school. If I'd dropped out then, I would never have made it any further than my village.

I'll never forget a trip I took with Opportunity International to Uganda, where we met amazing women who had received small loans and had turned them into modest income-generating businesses. In one small village we listened to a group of women who were only in their second loan cycle (having repaid their first loan, then borrowed again). As they told us about their various income-generating projects, we noticed a group of children sitting quietly to the side along with another woman.

When we asked through our translator about the children, the women smiled proudly. One woman said, "After we repaid our first loan, we all agreed that we should use some of our income to help our community. We hired a teacher so our children can receive an education and have a better life. Now they can stay in our village and help their families as well as go to school. Everyone is happy."

> From the time they can walk, girls are expected to help with household chores and to care for their younger siblings.

We were astounded that these women, who had just begun to create an income stream, immediately chose to give some of their funds back. And the first way they helped their community was by providing education for their children so they could safely learn in their own village.

## ILLNESS

One of the greatest impediments to girls consistently going to school is illness. As noted in chapter 2, many girls are born to mothers who are malnourished and inherit vitamin deficiencies that affect their well-being and daily health. That means they are susceptible to illnesses that sap their liveliness and make regular school attendance difficult.

Without childhood immunizations like the rotavirus vaccine, children can experience regular bouts of diarrhea, which is both embarrassing and energy-depleting. Children with cuts and scratches can become deathly ill if they haven't had a tetanus shot. Even small childhood scrapes can result in life-threatening infections without a topical antibiotic cream or oral medication.

While malaria most often takes the lives of children under the age of five, school-age children who become infected and survive without treatment often suffer debilitating symptoms, such as fever, chills, and body aches for months or even years.

Without pediatric antibiotics, infections such as strep throat and pneumonia often go untreated. Pneumonia claims more children's lives than any other infectious disease, but it can also leave those who beat the odds with complications for years, such as lung infections and difficulty breathing. Untreated strep infections can cause rheumatic fever, resulting in long-term damage to the heart and ongoing exhaustion. Tuberculosis affects as many as one million children a year but often goes untreated, leaving children chronically ill.

One desperate mother who had brought her ten-year-old daughter with respiratory problems to a clinic in rural Guatemala told me, "My daughter has been too sick to stay in school for much of last year. She is falling so far behind that soon it will be impossible for her to return." Another mother told me that her little girl had breathing problems that meant the mile-long walk to school was too difficult for her.

Often I've entered the classroom in a developing country and seen children who look tired and ill, their chins resting on their desks. When a child is too sick to go to school and stays home or comes to school and is too sick to listen, she can easily fall behind in the classwork and lose motivation for returning to school.

## LACK OF SANITATION

For many schools in resource-poor countries, bathrooms are either nonexistent or are simply rudimentary outhouses without running water. This often makes girls feel unsafe or uncomfortable, especially when they begin menstruating. A growing understanding of this challenge has led to an emphasis on providing resources to girls. One advocacy group says, "Gender sensitive sanitation—including clean, safe and separate toilets, with access to water and garbage disposal—is central to ensuring a gender equitable learning environment that addresses the needs of all students, including adolescent girls."[31]

Within the developing world, an increasing number of programs help girls navigate the challenges of menstruation, referred to as MHM (menstrual hygiene management) or MHH (menstrual health and hygiene). For too many years, this issue was ignored until multiple studies showed that girls routinely missed several days of school each month when they had their periods. As they got further and further behind in their studies, the easiest solution was to drop out. A global advocacy group observes,

> *A lack of private bathrooms at school makes girls feel unsafe or uncomfortable, especially when they begin menstruating.*

Lack of attention and access to quality menstrual hygiene management (MHM) in schools can negatively affect adolescent girls' abilities to concentrate, stand up and respond to questions, write on the blackboard, and feel confident and comfortable attending school on days when they are menstruating. Such experiences are often exacerbated by a lack of emotional support; a lack of adequate menstrual materials (pads, cloth, underwear), including emergency menstrual-related supplies in schools; and a lack of private spaces to rest when they are experiencing significant menstrual cramping. And unfortunately, many of these factors lead to disrupted classroom engagement and some absenteeism among girls.[32]

One group working to end the stigma surrounding menstruation (as mentioned in chapter 3) and provide more opportunities for girls is called The Pad Project.[33] Their tagline is "A period should end a sentence, not a girl's education."

## DISPLACEMENT

"Of the 7.1 million refugee children of school age, 3.7 million—more than half—do not go to school," according to UNHCR, the UN refugee agency.[34]

The war in Ukraine is the latest to displace millions of people, mostly women and children. While countries all over Europe are temporarily harboring the latest group of refugees, accommodating their ongoing needs long term is a monumental task. Children who have fled the war are now in countries with different languages, and that makes education a challenge. In countries with overcrowded schools, assimilating a new group of students can be a logistical issue.

For example, Jordan has welcomed millions of refugees from nearby countries, doing its best to provide safe havens and shelter, but the overall impact has been enormous. Some refugees have been in Jordan since the Syrian war began over a decade ago. The country's school system was already struggling before the influx of thousands of additional students. Nonprofit groups, churches, and mosques have all tried to help fill the educational gap for the children.[35]

## INNOVATIONS THAT MAKE A DIFFERENCE

### EMPOWERING REFUGEE CHILDREN

Questscope is a unique organization I encountered in the Za'atari refugee camp in Jordan. There, they used older, well-educated refugees as well as their own staff to help set up schooling for children living in the camps. Their philosophy is unique: "Schools give refugee and low-income youth stability and structure when everything else has been stripped away. Schools also give displaced youth a way to fit into a new community and develop the social skills needed to live in times of peace."[36]

Questscope's approach to education is based on what they call the Reciprocal Learning for Change (RLC) method, specifically developed for youth who have experienced trauma or other severe hardship. I watched the students interacting with their instructors instead of passively listening. They were energized as they helped decide what they wanted to learn and participated in the lesson. Girls were creating a play to dramatize a health lesson for their classmates and younger students. Children who had lost everything were thriving and excited for the opportunity to continue learning. What I witnessed was Questscope's slogan—"Putting the last, first"—in action.

Questscope works primarily in the Middle East and is based on a model developed by their founder, Dr. Curt Rhodes, who has spent more than forty years bringing education to those who are displaced and vulnerable. While their approach is unique, their method is effective. As one instructor explained, "These children have lost control over everything in their lives. We try to give them back some of their power and independence."

To learn more or support Questscope, go to questscope .org/en.

**LACK OF SUPPORT**

Nicole and Vincent Derieux live in Grasse, France, a picturesque city on the French Riviera with a stunning view of the Mediterranean Sea. The children of most families in Grasse receive an excellent education, but the children of the workers (many from Arab-speaking countries in North Africa) who clean hotel rooms, haul garbage, and sweep the streets often drop out of school.

As the Derieux began to learn more about the lives of the mostly Muslim workers, they sensed a great need among the children in particular. "Although they attend French schools, they go home to families who often don't speak French and to conditions that make it very difficult to do homework," says Nicole. "The children often fail in school, because they have no support system." In addition, on school holidays and weekends, the parents work and leave the children unattended.

Nicole, a former French teacher, and Vincent, who grew up in Orange, France, and once served in the French special forces, began to offer their home as a place for kids to do homework. After some success, they began to host camp days when the children could safely play games and enjoy outdoor activities instead of roaming the streets or staying in their tiny apartments. The Parfums de Vie ("fragrance of life") ministry was officially launched in 2008.[37]

Today, the program has grown so much that it is now housed in a former mechanic's garage within walking distance from the local school. After school, children of all ages stream into the garage, sit down at the tables, choose books from the library, and meet with volunteers who help them with their homework.

The effectiveness of tutoring, mentoring, and taking a personal interest in the children has been stunning. Narjes, whose parents are North African immigrants, was failing in grade school because of the difficulty of her living situation. She entered the Parfums de Vie program ten years ago and soon went from failing to being the top student in her class. Her grades were so good that she qualified to enter an elite French boarding school. Now fluent in English as well as French and Arabic, she is in her third year at St. Andrews University in Scotland.

"The children look at Narjes and some of the older students who are excelling and begin to imagine a better future for themselves," says Nicole. "It is wonderful to see a child realize that his or her future can be so much more. And their families are so proud of them."[38] And some of the residents of the town, who often viewed the disaffected children of workers as troublemakers, are now volunteer tutors and mentors with the after-school programs.

## WHAT YOU CAN DO

### PARFUMS DE VIE

The work of Parfums de Vie is supported by direct donations (parfumsdevie.com/) as well as a unique collaboration with the main industry in Grasse—"the perfume capital of the world." Two unique perfumes specially developed to benefit the work with at-risk children are sold in high-end perfumeries as well as directly on the website. To purchase a fragrance, go to villadesparfums.com/fragrances/.

The Derieux also rent out part of a villa on the French Riviera with proceeds supporting the work. For information about booking a reservation, visit stayatvilladesparfums.com/.

## EARLY MARRIAGE

Approximately 40,000 girls under the age of eighteen are married every day—nearly 15 million each year. More than 60 percent of child brides in developing countries have no formal education, according to Theirworld, a global children's charity focused on education.[39]

"When girls are married early, it can have a major impact on their ability to get an education. Many girls who become brides are taken out of school and have very little prospect of completing their education. At the same time, the lack of access to quality education increases the likelihood of early forced marriage."[40]

> *Uneducated girls are up to six times more likely to marry early than those with a secondary education.*

Uneducated girls are up to six times more likely to marry early than those with a secondary education. "In sub-Saharan Africa, 66 percent of women with no education were married before age 18 compared to 13 percent of those who went to school after the age of 12."[41]

## DISRUPTION

COVID-19 was a recent example of massive disruptions to education. According to UNESCO, by the first half of 2020, 194 countries mandated school closures affecting 91 percent of students.[42]

Disruptions to ongoing education can have extreme consequences. Research shows that just three months of missed schooling can result in 1.5 years of learning loss years later. For girls, disruptions like COVID-19 have an even greater impact. The Malala Fund research team estimates that 20 million girls in developing countries may never return to the classroom.[43]

A Save the Children study found that eight out of ten children surveyed in thirty-seven countries reported learning very little or nothing at all during the pandemic. And while children in some developed countries continued online classes, at least one-third of the world's school children could not.[44]

During the Ebola virus outbreak in Liberia in 2014, the Malala

## DID YOU KNOW?

**UN SUSTAINABLE DEVELOPMENT GOAL #4:
ENSURE INCLUSIVE AND EQUITABLE QUALITY
EDUCATION AND PROMOTE LIFELONG LEARNING
OPPORTUNITIES FOR ALL.**
Achieving inclusive and quality education for all reaffirms the
belief that education is one of the most powerful and proven
vehicles for sustainable development. This goal ensures
that all girls and boys complete free primary and secondary
schooling by 2030. It also aims to provide equal access to
affordable vocational training, and to eliminate gender and
wealth disparities with the aim of achieving universal access
to a quality higher education.[45]

Fund discovered that many girls in that country became the sole
breadwinners for their families. Even after the crisis had ended,
girls who reenrolled in school still had to provide for their families,
greatly affecting their school attendance.

Teen pregnancy also plays a factor in girls not returning to
school. COVID-19 school closures meant girls were either confined
to home or had more unstructured time to spend with boys and
men, which "increased risk of sexual violence and exploitation."[46]
A World Vision study projects that up to one million girls in sub-
Saharan Africa may never go back to school because of pregnancy
during COVID-19 closures.[47]

With these factors all playing a role, COVID-19 could
result in severe outcomes and disproportionate effects in girls'
education—20 million girls could potentially be out of school even
when the pandemic is over, and many more will have lost months
of learning.[48]

## WHAT YOU CAN DO

### DONATE A COMPUTER

Giving girls access to computers is one way to help them learn, even when schools are not nearby or when conditions like COVID interfere with their studies. But the digital divide keeps many from having access to computers.

The World Computer Exchange gathers, refurbishes, loads content on, and ships donated computers to partner schools and community organizations in developing countries. So far, these computers have connected nearly 3,600 classrooms for 5 million youth in 53 countries.

To learn more about donating a computer or other digital equipment, go to worldcomputerexchange.org/get-involved /give-computers/.

## CLOSING THOUGHTS

Education changes minds, hearts, and lives, especially for girls. The knowledge girls gain gives them confidence and options for their future. It increases their likelihood of avoiding early marriage, earning a living, and eventually caring for themselves and their children well. It helps girls contribute to their own lives and their communities.

In *I Am a Girl from Africa*, Elizabeth Nyamayaro tells her amazing journey from living in poverty and near-starvation in Zimbabwe as a child to eventually working as a special advisor to the United Nations and founding a nonprofit organization. Throughout the book she documents her determination to get an education. "Education is an

> *At least one-third of the world's school children cannot access remote learning.*

empowering right and one of the most powerful tools by which economically and socially marginalized children and adults can uplift themselves out of poverty."[49]

> *Education changes minds, hearts, and lives, especially for girls.*

The importance of education can't be underestimated. Yet the obstacles to education are often surprisingly minor. Finding ways to overcome these obstacles can unleash the amazing, limitless power of girls and make the world a much better place.

# 5

. . . . . . . . . . . . .

# BREAKING CULTURAL STEREOTYPES

DULCE MARIA IS A BRIGHT TEN-YEAR-OLD with a shy smile. She lives with her grandmother and younger brother on a hillside in rural Guatemala, a two-hour walk to the nearest town. Her home has a tin roof and walls made of mud bricks that do little to keep out the cold or dampness. The home has no electricity, no heat, and no indoor plumbing. But Dulce Maria has big dreams.

Every day she walks to the one-room school where about a dozen children of different ages gather to learn from teacher Edna Galicia. Her teacher can't praise Dulce Maria enough. "She is a smart, hard-working student," she tells me through a translator. "She comes to school every day and is excited to learn. She wants more for her life."

When I ask the children at the school what they want to be when they grow up, Dulce Maria's hand goes up first. "I want to be mayor," she says with confidence. It is an unusual goal in Guatemala, where men dominate government and only seven cities in the entire country have women mayors.

But in San Cristóbal Acasaguastlán, the town nearest Dulce Maria's home, Mayor Jeaneth Ordoñez presides. The mother of three often travels to the rural regions surrounding her city, working to improve the education and health of the citizens. So when she visited the one-room school where Dulce Maria studies, Ordoñez became the girl's role model.

Mayor Jeaneth's story is one of courage, faith, and family support, especially from her husband, Samuel. Samuel grew up in a family where both parents were teachers, and he regularly heard messages about strong, determined women. When Jeaneth had the opportunity to run for mayor, Samuel was the first to encourage her. He ran her campaign and today works for his wife. Without Samuel, she wouldn't be mayor, Jeaneth is quick to say. And without Jeaneth, Dulce Maria wouldn't have a role model or a reason to dream.

## CULTURAL NORMS

Perhaps nothing holds girls back more than cultural norms. Cultural norms can be defined in various ways but they mostly encompass how people in a society live and what they consider "normal." These factors include values and traditions, the language used, the stories told, and the songs sung. Cultural norms determine what is acceptable and what is not, what we can aspire to do and be, and what will bring us the positive attention of our community. As we've seen in previous chapters, the culture in which we live has a profound effect on health standards, education norms, and role expectations. In some parts of the world, women who are overweight are considered beautiful and desirable. In other places, being thin is considered attractive. In many parts of the world, girls are taught from an early age to be subservient, passive, and modest.

> *Nothing holds girls back more than cultural norms: how people in a society live and what they consider "normal."*

"Social norms are informal rules of behavior in a group. They are driven by beliefs we have about how people valuable to us think, behave, and what they expect of us, which in turn guide how we behave in specific situations," report Vincent Petit and Tamar Naomi Zalk in the UNICEF publication *Everybody Wants to Belong: A Practical Guide to Tackling and Leveraging Social Norms in Behavior Change Programming.*[1] "They define what is acceptable or appropriate, what is 'normal.' Harmful behaviors related to childcare or violence against women are often solidified because of shared beliefs that these behaviors are generally accepted and regarded as normal."

In some countries, laws are in place to prevent child marriage, female genital mutilation, gender-based violence, and many forms of discrimination. But despite what the laws say, cultural beliefs often dominate. This is especially true for those living in small communities, in rural areas, or in homogenous populations where expectations for behavior are set and not easily changed. Going against common beliefs can stigmatize or even separate a person from her support system.

> *Going against common beliefs can stigmatize or even separate a person from her support system.*

While it's easy to assume that cultural norms are more dominant in countries where the population is illiterate, or news is not easily accessible, cultural norms often dominate in developed countries as well. I grew up in a church where women were never allowed to preach or even teach Sunday school if men were in the class. Although I loved reading the Bible and playing Sunday school with my younger sister, it never occurred to me that being a pastor was a possible career because my family's religious culture (formed by their theology) told me that only men became pastors. In my small

Midwestern town, women weren't involved in business or government. My role models, like those of many girls of my generation, were teachers, nurses, and homemakers. Television shows often portrayed women who were either scatter-brained, helpless, or overtly sexy. Even in college, when I took an aptitude test to determine what I was best suited for, I was pointed toward a career as a flight attendant.

Cultural messages start early. As a child I remember hearing men tease my father about having two daughters. "Are you going to try again for a son?" was a common question. But to his credit, my father never missed a chance to push back, telling anyone who asked that he couldn't be prouder of his girls. In a time when women mostly worked as secretaries, my father became my role model. He was a businessman who enjoyed talking to me about his work and praised my interest. He brought me along to his office on Saturday mornings, when he'd catch up on the week's work in the relative quiet. I'd do homework; he'd do paperwork. In his own way, he was helping me see that being in business was something I could do. Despite all the messages in my world telling me that business was not an appropriate dream for a girl, my father's encouragement told me that I could do it. When I decided to pursue an MBA after college, my dad was thrilled. Once I started my own business, he loved when I would call him from my office with a question about managing employees or negotiating a contract. Long before Kobe Bryant, my father was a proud "girl dad."

Because of her role model, perhaps one day Dulce Maria will become mayor. Or perhaps she'll teach other girls who want to dream big. Whatever the case, it's easy to imagine Dulce Maria becoming a strong and influential woman because her community supports her dreams.

# CULTURAL PRACTICES
# THAT HURT GIRLS

Both boys and girls are sometimes hurt by cultural practices that make it difficult for them to thrive. But girls are specifically affected by practices that target them because of their gender.

The United Nations Office of the High Commissioner for Human Rights (OHCHR) has identified some specific practices.

Traditional cultural practices reflect values and beliefs held by members of a community for periods often spanning generations. Every social grouping in the world has specific traditional cultural practices and beliefs, some of which are beneficial to all members, while others are harmful to a specific group, such as women. These harmful traditional practices include female genital mutilation (FGM); forced feeding of women; early marriage; the various taboos or practices which prevent women from controlling their own fertility; nutritional taboos and traditional birth practices; son preference and its implications for the status of the girl child; female infanticide; early pregnancy; and dowry price. Despite their harmful nature and their violation of international human rights laws, such practices persist because they are not questioned and take on an aura of morality in the eyes of those practicing them.[2]

According to the Bill and Melinda Gates Foundation,

Adolescence is when girls' and boys' futures really start to diverge. Boys' worlds expand. They rely less on their parents, venture farther and farther from home, and enroll in high school or college or get a job, which puts them in contact with wider society.

At the same time, girls' worlds contract. They transition, sometimes at a very young age, from being subservient to their parents to being subservient to their husbands. Although they enjoyed some measure of freedom while attending primary school, they are expected to return to the confines of the home, to devote themselves to cooking, cleaning, and raising children.[3]

For those of us living in a country where harmful practices seem unimaginable, it's important to understand why they exist and why they are viewed as beneficial. In almost every case, there is a reason why the community views them as a positive practice. Change rarely happens because it is simply imposed, as demonstrated by the number of countries where such practices are illegal but continue, especially in rural areas.

Women and girls tend to be viewed as weak and a burden on the family. Boys are viewed as productive, especially in an agrarian context. Girls cost the family money in places where a dowry is expected, and they can cause a family shame if they become pregnant, even when they are raped (the girl is often blamed) or not seen as pure, leading to such practices as FGM. Education is often seen as unnecessary for girls, who are expected to spend their lives bearing children and caring for the home. In cultures where a bride price is common, the family of the groom must either pay a sum of money or offer property or livestock before a couple can marry. In families living in poverty, this is often a strong incentive to marry off daughters at an early age. Marrying off a daughter can provide much-needed resources to a family living in poverty.

Girls Not Brides is an international organization made up of local groups devoted to ending child marriage, one of the world's most harmful cultural practices. "Child marriage is a global issue. It is fueled by gender inequality, poverty, social norms, and insecurity, and has devastating consequences all over the

*Marrying off a daughter can provide much-needed resources to a family living in poverty.*

world,"[4] according to the nonprofit. The organization estimates that 12 million girls under the age of eighteen are married each year. Girls Not Brides groups all share the same goal: "A world without child marriage where girls and women enjoy equal status with boys and men and are able to achieve their full potential in all aspects of their lives."[5]

The highest rates of child marriages are found in Niger, Central African Republic, Chad, Mali, and Bangladesh. The countries with the highest numbers of child marriages are India, Bangladesh, Nigeria, Brazil, and Ethiopia.[6]

According to UNICEF, factors placing a child at risk of marriage include

poverty, the perception that marriage will provide "protection," family honor, social norms, customary or religious laws that condone the practice, an inadequate legislative framework, and the state of a country's civil registration system. While the practice is more common among girls than boys, it is a violation of rights regardless of sex.

Child marriage often compromises a girl's development by resulting in early pregnancy and social isolation, interrupting her schooling, limiting her opportunities for career and vocational advancement, and placing her at increased risk of domestic violence.[7]

Girls Not Brides reports that especially in times of upheaval, such as refugee situations, girls tend to be married off early as a way to protect them against violence or to provide them with a better future.[8]

## WHAT YOU CAN DO

**SUPPORT GIRLS NOT BRIDES**
Having a wedding? Consider adding Girls Not Brides to your wedding registry as your charity option of choice to bring attention and support to the important work of stopping child marriage. Or you can support one of the local campaigns of the organization that range from leadership training for girls, centers for survivors of FGM, or skills training. Go to girlsnotbrides.org to learn more or to donate.

## HOW CULTURE CHANGES

Margo Day spent her thirty-four-year career in high tech, including a stint at Microsoft as Vice President for US Education. Over the years, she loved bridging her knowledge of technology to describe ways to solve difficult problems, increase productivity, or find new business opportunities. Margo knew that hearing other people's perspectives was crucial to building trust and helping create solutions. And being a woman leader in a traditionally male-dominated field made her realize the importance of being a role model. A woman of deep faith, she wanted to use her expertise to invest in helping others, especially girls.

Taking a leave of absence from Microsoft, she traveled to Kenya with World Vision. There she met thirty-four girls in a rescue center and learned how girls were often married at an early age and also subjected to FGM.[9] Many of the girls she met wanted to continue their education instead of marrying.

Margo's heart was broken by the girls she met who simply wanted to live their lives and pursue their education. And that's where her years of training helped her. "One of the most important lessons I learned from my time at Microsoft is to listen with empathy," says Margo. "People have reasons for what they do, what they believe, and what they think the future may hold. You have to start there. You can't just come in and tell people you are going to solve a problem if they don't even think they have one."[10]

On her first trips to Kenya, Margo spent hours sitting on the ground and listening to the girls affected. What she heard helped her form a plan. "You have to get to the root causes . . . you can't just tell people to stop doing something without providing a better option."

If a family chose to marry their daughter at an early age, there was really no alternative for her. If the daughter refused FGM and marriage she brought shame to herself and was either beaten into compliance or had to run away without support, making it nearly impossible to survive. Margo worked with World Vision to build a secondary school for girls in Kenya where they could live, learn, and thrive. Several of the girls enrolled in the school today escaped from being forced into an early marriage.

"I had the courage to leave because I had heard about this school," one girl told Margo. "Now my family sees that marriage was not the only alternative. They now want my younger sisters to go to school."

"Once the school was built, the question became how to help the community understand the severity of harm of FGM, yet still hold the beautiful norm of transitioning from a girl to a woman and having a place in the community," said Margo.

Margo also worked with World Vision to establish an alternative rite of passage. "The practice of FGM was partially a celebration of a girl becoming a woman. There was good intent behind the practice; we just needed to find a way to redirect that toward a more positive outcome."

World Vision worked with religious and tribal leaders first, in order to gain their support and to help them understand why FGM was harmful. Working together, they created the alternative rite of passage training and ceremony, where girls' transition into womanhood is celebrated in a positive way. Because it was a widely held belief that girls were not marriageable if they had not been cut, the tribal and religious leaders began to speak publicly against the practice and supported families who chose not to follow tradition.

The alternative rite of passage training was so popular that boys asked for a parallel event. World Vision created a boys' track that educates young men on the physical and psychological toll of FGM. It also teaches boys to tell their parents and tribal leaders that they refuse to engage in child marriage or force a young woman to whom they are betrothed to undergo the cut.

Margo has now taken early retirement from Microsoft in order to spend full time on the Mekuno Project, which identifies itself as "a coalition and fund dedicated to eliminating the root causes of FGM and child marriage in Kenya and creating the conditions for girls to flourish in futures they design." Partnering with World Vision and the Global Give Back Circle, the Mekuno Project provides alternatives for girls so they can be educated instead of marrying young. The program also helps educate leaders, practitioners, and families about FGM and helps them envision a better future for their daughters.[11]

"Culture changes in Kenya the same way it changes in the US," Margo explains. "You have to respect the decision makers and their experience. You have to listen to how they identify problems and solutions and understand their challenges. Then you have to help them solve their problems in a way that creates a positive outcome. Ironically, the same methods work with tribal leaders that I used with corporate executives.

"At one point in my life I was focused on helping people adapt to new software. Now I'm focused on helping girls live full lives. I'm so grateful that my training at Microsoft prepared me for this."

## WHAT YOU CAN DO

### EMPOWERING GIRLS IN KENYA

The Kenya Big Dream is the World Vision project that Margo Day partners with to change harmful social norms, reduce financial incentives for child marriage, and promote education and life skills training for girls. Learn more at worldvisionphilanthropy.org/kenyabigdream.

In Kenya, changing beliefs about coming of age, female cutting, and early marriage has taken patience and a process of involving elders, religious leaders, and families. Change has taken years to accomplish. In the case of the #LikeAGirl campaign (discussed in chapter 1), the power of social media swept across the internet, going viral soon after it first aired.

The increased use and availability of the internet offers positive and negative opportunities for cultural change. In some cases, it connects people in more isolated communities with those who have access to the best resources in the world. In other cases, it magnifies and amplifies misinformation and behavior that can be dangerous to girls. It provides a frighteningly efficient vehicle for sex trafficking. And it creates opportunities for bullying that can ruin the life of a girl with one post.

For girls like Malala Yousafzai, it means a local campaign against

> *The increased use and availability of the internet offers positive and negative opportunities for cultural change.*

the Taliban to allow girls to go to school can become a worldwide movement that wins her a Nobel Prize. It shows everyone that the convictions of one girl can truly make a difference.

## GIRLS LEADING CHANGE

Teenage filmmakers Galle Mambo and Shneider Remi Adams knew that some of the cultural norms in their native Cameroon were obviously hurting girls. But in order to change the customs, they felt they needed to first understand why people would choose to practice them. So the two set out to interview a variety of leaders about how to implement changes in their culture.

Working with Advice Project Media, a nonprofit that trains students in journalism and advocacy, Galle and Shneider created the documentary *Hidden Truths: Exposing Cultural Practices That Hurt Teen Girls in Cameroon.*[12]

In the film, they ask community leaders and citizens about the issues of child abuse, rape, and the practice of breast ironing in which a girl's breasts are pressed with hot objects like rocks and cooking spoons in order to flatten them. The very painful practice is often inflicted by a girl's own mother in a misguided attempt to keep the girl's breasts from developing and thereby making her look younger, and supposedly guarding her from sexual harassment and rape. The practice is dangerous, resulting in burns, cysts, infections, and permanent scarring. It also can make it difficult when she is a mother to breastfeed a baby.

The documentary shines a light on a movement to eliminate breast ironing. But it also exposes the fact that rape is an all-too-common event in the lives of girls in Cameroon, who are often blamed for inviting that outcome by dressing provocatively or walking alone. One person interviewed guessed that 80 percent of rapes go unreported because the victim does not want to live with the shame or bring shame to her family.[13]

## WHAT YOU CAN DO

### HELP STORIES BE TOLD
Advice Project Media is a nonprofit that supports citizen journalists. In addition to offering local classes, the organization hosts global leadership and empowerment summits for teen girls and women and intensive writing programs for adults and youth. To learn more, go to adviceprojectmedia.com.

Another cultural practice inflicted on girls is called *leblouh* or force-feeding. It is practiced in countries where an obese girl is considered desirable and a sign of wealth. A girl is force-fed either to make her more attractive to a potential husband or in preparation for marriage. It is customary in some parts of Mauritania, Niger, Uganda, Sudan, Tunisian, Nigeria, Kenya, and South Africa.

Girls as young as six are force-fed enormous quantities of fatty food and liquid. If they don't eat, they are often punished by their mothers, who view it as the best way to secure a good future for their daughters. "This tradition is one that's highly disturbing as the children are usually forced to consume about 16,000 calories daily. This leaves them constantly bloated and eventually obese—looking way older than their actual age and leaving them vulnerable to various health challenges," said Belinda Mallasasime in "The Culture Where Girls Are Force-Fed into Obesity (to Be Sexy)."[14]

Sexual "cleansing" is a ceremony where a girl has sex as a cleansing ritual following her first menstruation. It is considered a rite of passage and a form of initiation of young girls into womanhood. It is known as *kusasa fumbi*, which literally means "brushing off the dust," interpreted as shaking off inexperience in sex by actually having intimate relations. It is encouraged in parts of Zambia, Malawi, Uganda, Tanzania, Mozambique, Angola, Ivory Coast, and Congo.[15]

Another form of sexual cleansing is imposed when a newly bereaved widow is made to have sex with a sex worker or the deceased's relative. Widows who are not cleansed are ostracized and discriminated against. Sexual cleansing was one of the factors in spreading HIV/AIDs during the early days of the pandemic. A man who died was often infected, and his then-infected widow would pass the infection on to the relative. Widow cleansing was outlawed in Kenya in 2015 but is still widespread.[16]

An article in *The Atlantic* sheds light on a practice in some parts of Malawi, where girls as young as eight undergo something called "initiation." The girls, accompanied by older women, are told they will become women, learning to cook, clean, and have sex.

Initiation is a centuries-old practice in the region, according to Harriet Chanza of the World Health Organization. In many agrarian communities, she notes, "There's nothing like adolescence. You are either a child or an adult." Initiation is meant to establish the gender norms that boys and girls are expected to follow as men and women. The emphasis on having sex may also have a darker purpose in a country where nearly three-fourths of the population lives below the poverty line. Chanza, who is based in Malawi, says that some parents may actually want their daughters to get pregnant at a young age. A girl is often married soon after she is found to be pregnant, deferring the cost of caring for her and her baby from her parents to her husband.[17]

Once a girl has gone through the initiation, she is encouraged to have sex with an older man. Some men, called "hyenas," are employed just to have sex with the girls, making sure they have learned enough. This has been a factor in spreading HIV and other sexually transmitted diseases as well as early pregnancy.[18]

## GENDER-BASED VIOLENCE

Gender-based violence (GBV) is most common within households and is often based on cultural views within a community. When I attended a training session in Zambia with women who discussed GBV, one woman said, "He hits me because he loves me." I was shocked to see other women nodding in agreement. Later the facilitator told me that the cultural norm in Zambian culture was sometimes so skewed that a man felt he wasn't being "manly" if he didn't hit his wife, and a woman thought the man didn't love her if he didn't hit her, showing his possessiveness.

> *Gender-based violence is most common within households and is often based on cultural views within a community.*

CARE has published the *Gender, Power, and Justice Primer*, which examines cultural issues affecting women and girls. In the section on GBV, it notes the following false beliefs that are used to justify violence:

- A man has a right to physically discipline a woman over "incorrect" behavior.
- Intimate partner violence is a "taboo" subject to discuss publicly.
- Sex is a man's right in marriage.
- Sexual activity (including rape) is a marker of masculinity.
- Girls are responsible for controlling men's sexual urges.
- For child marriage, norms perpetuating the practice include parental pressure to control girls' sexuality.
- Value on girls' virginity at marriage as a reflection of family honor, and fears of pregnancy before marriage.[19]

## WHAT YOU CAN DO

### SUPPORT GROUPS FIGHTING GENDER-BASED VIOLENCE

For more than two decades, CARE has been addressing the root causes driving gender-based violence (GBV) and supporting survivors. In 2020, CARE directly reached over 2.4 million people with information and services and implemented ninety-two GBV projects in thirty-four countries. To learn more or to support the work, go to care.org/our-work/health/fighting-gender-based-violence/.

World Vision believes that gender-based violence and discrimination costs everyone. The organization addresses gender inequality around the world by working with entire communities—women, girls, men, and boys—to transform discriminatory practices together. World Vision also works with faith leaders to acknowledge and act upon gender injustices within their communities. To learn more or to donate, see worldvision.org/our-work/gender-equality.

# RELIGIOUS BELIEFS

Because religion is an important aspect of culture, working with faith leaders is an important part of changing harmful practices against woman. Sometimes respected faith leaders must be the ones to deliver messages about existing laws to the men in a community. Through the program Channels of Hope for Gender developed by World Vision, faith leaders come together to discuss gender beliefs, myths, and harmful practices. When I attended a session in Kenya in 2015, leaders from different faith backgrounds discussed the practices in their communities that hurt women and girls and examined the original texts that have often been used to support them. For some Christian leaders, the idea of male leadership is deeply ingrained in their beliefs.

The Channels of Hope for Gender website explains it in detail:

Faith leaders are often incredibly influential in the community; their interpretation and the resulting application of religious texts shapes male and female relationships. In some instances, religious text has been used to validate cultural practices that keep women on the fringes of processes that are critical to their own development and to that of their families and communities. Other prejudices extend more power and privilege to males at the expense of females. This can result in a lack of equitable access and control of family and community resources, as well as gender-based violence. This power imbalance negatively impacts on the well-being of women and girls and the development potential of entire communities.[20]

I witnessed faith leaders struggling to examine their beliefs and how they affected their congregations and communities. Some seemed very set in their ways. Others were open to change as they walked through a series of exercises. It was evident that all of them appreciated coming together with other clergy in their region and seemed genuinely committed to improving the lives of women and girls.

## WHAT YOU CAN DO

### HELP EDUCATE RELIGIOUS LEADERS

Religious leaders in most communities have a tremendous influence. Opening their minds and hearts to the importance of supporting girls and women is critical to bringing about change. Channels of Hope for Gender challenges faith leaders to see men and women created by God as equals and to treat each other accordingly. This understanding empowers both women and men to celebrate who they are, moves people toward healthier relationships, and contributes to reducing gender-based violence. To learn more, go to wvi.org/church-and-interfaith-engagement/channels-hope-gender.

In their book *Half the Sky*, Nicholas Kristof and Sheryl WuDunn look at various ways women are oppressed in the world and ask the question, "Is Islam misogynistic?" They note that women in some majority-Muslim countries can't be seen by a male doctor, even if they are terribly sick. They note that eight of the ten countries that are rated worst for women by the World Economic Forum are majority Muslim. Yet they point out that the Koran shows Muhammad as respectful of women and his wife, Aisha, as the first Muslim feminist. "Muslims sometimes note that such conservative attitudes have little to do with the Koran and arise from culture more than religion."[21]

"In short, often we blame a region's religion when the oppression instead may be rooted in its culture," the authors conclude.[22]

The Taliban's takeover in Afghanistan in 2021 has resulted in huge setbacks for women and girls. The Taliban have banned women and girls from secondary and higher education and altered curricula to focus more on religious studies. They dictate what women must wear, how they should travel, workplace segregation by sex, and even what kind of cell phones women should have. They enforce these rules through intimidation and inspections. Human Rights Watch reports, "'The future looks dark,' said one woman who had worked in the government. 'I had many dreams, wanted to continue studying and working. I was thinking of doing my master's. At the moment, they [the Taliban] don't even allow girls to finish high school.'"[23]

*Some evidence indicates that being confined in homes has increased gender-based violence and early marriage of girls who are not in school.*

The COVID-19 pandemic has also created more challenges. Some evidence indicates that being confined in homes has increased GBV and early marriage of girls who are not in school. Girls Not Brides estimates 10 million more girls will be married as children over the next decade due to the COVID-19 pandemic.[24]

## CLOSING THOUGHTS

Cultural norms often work against girls, creating low expectations for their future and giving them messages that limit who they believe they can be. Changing culture isn't easy. But offering role models, changing the minds of thought leaders, showing alternative paths, and equipping girls to become leaders are all ways to help change negative cultural messages and norms.

# 6

. . . . . . . . . . . . . . . .

# PROTECTING
# VULNERABLE GIRLS

HER CLOTHES WERE MISMATCHED AND WORN; a tattered red sweater too large and pink pants too short. I guessed she was about ten years old as she kicked a dirty rubber ball with other children in a small clearing. But despite her clothing, the little girl playing with the other children in a small village in Bosnia stood out from the others. She was the only child with blonde hair and blue eyes, and to my American eyes she was particularly pretty. I was watching the group with a local humanitarian worker who was trying to help resettle the women and children displaced by the war.

I pointed out the little girl to my companion and remarked about her beauty.

"Yes, it's too bad," she replied, startling me with her response. I thought perhaps she hadn't understood me, although her English was very good. Sensing my confusion, she continued, "It's especially hard to protect the pretty ones."

I was shocked. It had never occurred to me that being attractive was one more vulnerability for a refugee. As an American I was drawn to what I considered attractive. It was another moment when I was struck by how little I understood about the needs of

*Being attractive is one more vulnerability when you are a refugee.*

the world and how my view of the situation was limited by my own experience. Being pretty was an advantage in my world. Here, it was cause for concern.

I was visiting Bosnia during the aftermath of the Balkan war along with a group of women from the States. As part of a group called Women of Vision, we were looking for ways to help the thousands of women and children displaced by the war. While the men had either gone off to fight or been killed, the women and children were left to fend for themselves. Most had fled their homes and seen their villages destroyed. These refugees were being housed in a community building in a village more than a hundred miles from their home. They were crowded into one large room with not enough beds for everyone, so they had to take turns sleeping. It was a heartbreaking situation.

Since that day I've encountered refugees in many other situations. But I've never forgotten that little girl in Bosnia. And one of my prayers has been for God to protect little refugee girls, especially the pretty ones.

Girls who are displaced from their homes because of conflict or natural disaster are just one example of those who are vulnerable. In every large city there are numbers of street children—runaways or throwaways (a heartbreaking term for abandoned children)—living on their own or in groups. Other girls, especially those living in

*Girls fall through the cracks of society into an abyss that is truly full of evil.*

poverty, are lured from their homes with promises of jobs that will provide enough money to support their families. Sadly, the majority of those girls end up being trafficked for either labor or sex.

This is probably the most difficult chapter for me to write. Girls fall through the cracks of society into an abyss that is truly full of evil. They get separated from loving families through conflict, trauma, or accident. Or they are abandoned by parents who are unwilling or unable to care for them.

## REFUGEES AND IDPS

For most of us, the thought of becoming a refugee is an unimaginable horror. To suddenly be uprooted from your home—leaving behind everything you own, your community, and everything familiar to you—and run for your life is a terrifying scenario lived out by approximately 89.3 million people in the world.[1] Those who cross a border into another country are called refugees. Those who are displaced but remain within the boundaries of their own country are called internally displaced people (IDPs). Although displaced people long to return home, many will never be able to for fear of violence or persecution.

CARE tells the sobering truth.

Refugees are uniquely vulnerable. But refugee girls doubly so. When extreme violence, hunger or climate drives them from their homes, they are the first to be trafficked for sex or child labor; the first to be exploited as tools of war; and the first to lose their childhoods. Meanwhile, they are the last to be fed, the last to be enrolled in school and, too often, the last to be valued.[2]

*Refugees are uniquely vulnerable. But refugee girls doubly so.*

One of the most recent crises to create a flood of refugees is the war in Ukraine. In 2022

## WHAT YOU CAN DO

### SUPPORT REFUGEE RELIEF ORGANIZATIONS

War, famine, floods, earthquakes, and other natural and man-made disasters often result in families being displaced. Sometimes the loss of home and community means they must start over again in another place without any of their belongings or familiar support systems.

Helping displaced people (both refugees and internally displaced people) is a specialty of several international organizations. While many other groups may respond to particular disasters, the following groups have ongoing work and are prepared to respond to the next crisis. They are all highly ranked by Charity Navigator and have specific specialties in refugee services. Here is a list for you to learn more about each of them or to donate:

CARE, care.org
Church World Services, cwsglobal.org
International Rescue Committee, rescue.org
Oxfam, oxfam.org
Save the Children, savethechildren.org
UNICEF, unicef.org
World Relief, worldrelief.org
World Vision, worldvision.org

as the first refugees, mostly women and children, arrived in foreign countries seeking safety and shelter, humanitarian workers and police feared they would be vulnerable to human traffickers pretending to be Good Samaritans. "The war in Ukraine is leading to massive displacement and refugee flows—conditions that could lead to a significant spike in human trafficking and an acute child protection crisis," according to Afshan Khan, UNICEF's regional director for Europe and Central Asia, in an interview with NPR. "Displaced children are extremely vulnerable to being separated from their families, exploited, and trafficked. They need governments in the region to step up and put measures in place to keep them safe."[3]

Women and children made up the majority of Ukrainian refugees crossing into other countries because men were required to stay behind to fight. A similar situation occurred during the war in Syria, where men stayed behind to fight or protect property, sending their wives and children away from danger. Women and children traveling alone are especially vulnerable.

## DID YOU KNOW?

**DEFINITIONS OF DISPLACED PEOPLE**

**Refugee:** A person who has been forced to leave their home and cross a national border. Generally, a refugee cannot return home because of war, persecution, or natural disaster.

**IDP:** An internally displaced person has been forced to leave their home but remains within the boundaries of the same country even though the person cannot return home.

**Migrant:** A person who willingly leaves home in order to find a better place to work or live.

**Asylum seeker:** A person who has left their country as a refugee and can't return because of political, ethnic, religious, or other persecution, and is seeking a safe haven in another country.

**Immigrant:** A person who has come to live permanently in another country.

**Guest worker:** A person with temporary permission to work in another country.

The Syrian war, which began in 2011, has resulted in more than half the population being internally displaced and nearly 6.6 million people fleeing to neighboring countries.[4]

Sometimes entire families flee conflict, but more often women and children must survive on their own. I met a woman who went by the name Laila[5] at a makeshift medical clinic in Jordan near the Syrian border. She and her daughter had bad colds, and the baby had a terrible diaper rash because Laila couldn't afford to buy diapers to change her. Laila spoke a little English and told me her story with the help of a translator.

*Sometimes entire families flee conflict, but more often women and children must survive on their own.*

She and her husband had both been teachers in Damascus. They were happy and had a good life. They had just found out she was expecting their second child when the civil war began. Her husband decided that Laila and their daughter should go to Jordan for safety, just until the unrest died down. They thought it would be a matter of weeks before he would either join her or she would be able to return home. But weeks turned into months. She gave birth in Jordan and now was trying to survive on her own with two children. She had stopped hearing from her husband nearly a year before and feared he had been killed. There was no room in the refugee camps for her, so she had been renting a small room until her money ran out. A family took pity on her and had let her stay in their unheated outbuilding where she and her young children were living.

Laila, like many women, was simply focused on fleeing violence and finding safety for her children. But after avoiding the immediate danger of war, the women then begin to deal with the long-term problems of protecting their children and themselves.

According to a UNHCR report about women and girls in conflict zones,

> No one is spared the violence, but women and girls are particularly affected because of their status in society and their sex. Sexual and gender-based violence (SGBV)—including rape, forced impregnation, forced abortion, trafficking, sexual slavery, and the intentional spread of sexually transmitted infections, including HIV/AIDS—is one of the defining characteristics of contemporary armed conflict. Its primary targets are women and girls.
>
> Women and girls, like men and boys, also risk abduction and forced recruitment by armed groups, whether as fighters, for sexual exploitation or other tasks. The number of single- and/or child-headed households increases during conflict, and female adolescent heads of household are particularly at risk of rights violations and marginalization.[6]

I met a woman in Guatemala City who told me that her husband had been killed by a gang and she had no choice but to flee her village with her daughter and young son. She had no idea where she would go, but staying in the same place would certainly lead to her death and the abduction of her children. So they joined the millions of people on the run. She hoped to join the throng of people heading toward the United States, even though she knew the trip itself would be perilous and potentially futile. "If we stay, we die," she told me matter-of-factly, shrugging her shoulders.

In 2020, children made up less than one-third of the global population, but almost half among the world's refugees. Worldwide, 36.5 million children under eighteen were forcibly displaced. Some

## WHAT YOU CAN DO

### TEACH ENGLISH TO IMMIGRANTS

For refugees who are resettled in America or immigrants who migrate to the United States, learning English is an important step toward integrating into American culture and having full access to education and employment.

Teaching English as a foreign (or second) language is a valuable skill to have and an invaluable ability to pass on. Teaching English to non-native speakers is a specialty that can be learned through in-person classes or online at tefl.org.

Offering basic skills and language classes at your church, school, or community center can provide immigrants a safe place to seek advice, translations, and help in navigating education and employment questions.

live in refugee camps, some are internally displaced within their own country (IDPs), some are simply on the move.[7]

Nearly three million Syrian children, particularly girls, are missing out on their education.[8] Syrian girls often are married off early as parents seek to protect them, but child marriage often makes it impossible for girls to attend classes. Schools lie in rubble across Syria. Syrian children in neighboring countries, including Lebanon and Jordan, are often unable to enter the already strained public school system and must rely on humanitarian groups that have set up private schooling for them. Displaced families often pull their daughters out of school to earn money for food and rent. Girls are two-and-a-half times more likely to be unable to go to school in conflict-affected countries than their counterparts in conflict-free countries, according to UNICEF.[9]

And because of the sheer numbers of displaced people and the limited capacity of refugee camps, women like Laila end up fending for themselves and their children in a foreign country.

Refugee camps are created as temporary facilities to provide immediate assistance and protection to people. Refugee camps were designed as a short-term solution to keep people safe during emergencies, but some people live in camps for years or even decades. In Jordan, two enormous camps, Za'atari and Azraq, house most of the 130,000-plus refugees from Syria.[10]

I first visited Za'atari in 2014, two years after it had opened. People were living in tents and makeshift shelters, and most believed their situation was temporary. When the war ended, they wanted to go home. But some of the 80,000 inhabitants have lived there for a decade, many of whom have never known another home. The main street in the camp has been nicknamed Champs-Élysées because it is filled with stores and even restaurants established by Syrian entrepreneurs. But the camp has not been a safe place for girls. The child marriage rate is as high as 25 percent, according to UNICEF. The number of babies born to girls younger than eighteen has soared.

> *In 2020, children made up less than one third of the global population, but almost half among the world's refugees.*

Save the Children says that many refugee families marry off their daughters to provide them with financial security or protect them from sexual violence perpetrated by other men in refugee camps.[11]

## STREET CHILDREN

In almost any large city in the world you will find them. In some cities they are hidden from view in the wealthier parts of town, but they are still there. They are street children—poor or homeless young people who are either forced to or have chosen to live on the

## INNOVATIONS THAT MAKE A DIFFERENCE

### SAFE HAVENS FOR DISPLACED CHILDREN

Established by UNICEF and UNHCR, along with local authorities and partners, "Blue Dots" are safe spaces along border crossings that provide children and families with information and services. They also identify and register children traveling on their own and connect them to protection services.

For children, "Blue Dot hubs provide a safe, welcoming space to rest, play, and simply be a child at a time when their world has been abruptly turned upside down in fear and panic, and they are facing the trauma of leaving family, friends, and all that is familiar."[12]

Child Friendly Spaces (CFS) are areas set up in emergency settings such as refugee camps to provide safe and supportive programs for children. The objective is to give children the opportunity to play and learn and offer support to both them and their families during times of displacement and trauma. Typically operated by NGOs, they often are staffed by local community members or people from the same country or culture as the children. They are called by various names, including Child Centered Spaces (CCS), Safe Spaces, Safe Play Areas, and Child Friendly Spaces/Environments (CFS/E).[13]

The spaces I observed in Jordan were operated by Mercy Corps, World Vision, and Save the Children and resembled day care centers or community youth programs, offering younger children the chance to play and older children the opportunity to participate in sports. Some operated within refugee camps, and others were in communities where many refugees lived. While the children were involved in activities, the parents had time to do other tasks.

streets. *Streetism* is a term that means "living on the streets or being of the streets" and is used especially in some parts of Africa. The total number of children living on the streets throughout the world is estimated to be at least 100 million. In India alone, there are an estimated 11 million children living on the streets.[14]

> *The total number of children living on the streets throughout the world is estimated to be at least 100 million.*

Sometimes these are children with some disability or other condition that makes it difficult for their family to provide adequate care. In other cases, families are simply too poor to care for all of their children, or sometimes girls attract the attention of a male in the household and are sent away by a jealous wife. Sometimes girls who are being abused in their home run away from the situation and find themselves on the street. Estimates of how many children go missing worldwide each year are as high as 8 million,[15] but the International Center for Missing and Exploited Children says there is no reliable statistic because so many children never get reported or counted. This is almost always the case when children are thrown out of their homes or are in such dysfunctional homes that the street becomes their preferred alternative.

In the Academy Award–nominated movie *Lion* we glimpse the brutality of life on the street through the eyes of Saroo, a five-year-old who falls asleep on a train and ends up thousands of miles away from the safety of his village and family in Kolkata (Calcutta). Based on a true story chronicled in the book *A Long Way Home*, Saroo is fortunate to end up in an orphanage and to be adopted by an Australian couple. But during his time on the street, he sees how children are manipulated and abused by adults and even other children.[16]

Children often end up on the street after experiencing trauma.

They are understandably suspicious of adults and fear authorities who will either return them to their unsafe home or place them in orphanages or foster homes. Gangs exploit children, and merchants often call on the police to get rid of them because they frighten customers away by begging.

When I visited Casa de Luz in the Dominican Republic, a home for children with disabilities, I learned that almost all the children living there had been rescued from the streets. In some cases, their families simply couldn't care for their special needs and abandoned them. But in others, their only relative had died and there was no social safety net to catch them. Sadly, this home can care for only a small number of the children who need help.

Given the high number of children who end up alone and outside their home, the UN established guidelines in 2009 to guide governments and organizations in helping effectively. Called "United Nations Guidelines for Alternative Care of Children," this document establishes principles for adoption, foster care, and orphanages.[17]

The AIDS crisis left more than 16.5 million children orphaned worldwide, according to SOS Children's Villages, an NGO that offers care through a unique foster village program.[18]

In *Walking the Bowl*, a book about the lives of street children in Lusaka, Zambia, authors Chris Lockhart and Daniel Mulilo Chama

## WHAT YOU CAN DO

### SUPPORT SOS CHILDREN'S VILLAGES

SOS Children's Villages are dedicated to the care of orphaned and abandoned children. Operating in 137 countries, the organization's goal is "to make sure no child grows up alone and unsupported." To learn more or donate, go to sos-usa.org.

tell true stories of boys and girls who either fell through the cracks after family members died or who were sent out of their homes by jealous new wives or husbands who didn't want to care for children from a previous relationship.

"Girls were in high demand, a prized commodity, especially since so few spent any time on the streets, at least in the conspicuous ways that the boys did. Street girls . . . did not stand on street corners, did not tug at shirtsleeves, did not ask to wash your car or shine your shoes," says Timo, one of the narrators in the book. In fact, Kapula, the girl he was describing, had been sent to the streets by her aunt, who relied on her to bring back money from soliciting sex. Kapula was barely sixteen.[19]

We learn from Kapula what life on the street is like for any unattached girl:

> Every boy who discovered her sleeping spot rolled her.
> They called it rolling because the boy literally rolled the
> girl over in order to do his business. They knew it was
> open season when it came to unattached girls who slept on
> the streets. The girls couldn't do anything about it. If they
> resisted, they were beaten as well. So they just rolled over
> and endured it or pretended like nothing was happening.
> On any given night, a girl could easily be rolled by as
> many as ten different boys.[20]

It's easy to look at cities like Kolkata or Santo Domingo or Lusaka and imagine the problem is far away. But it also exists in first-world countries. The drug crisis in the United States is just one underlying factor in the increasing number of children who have fallen through the cracks when their parents died or became so addicted that they essentially abandoned their children. Children end up with relatives who don't want them, grandparents who are too old to care for them, or the foster system that includes many wonderful people, but also too many foster parents who rely on it to make money and don't properly care for the children.

"It's a cold, hard, cruel fact that my mother loved heroin more than she loved me," says Holly, the main character in the young adult novel *Runaway* by Wendelin Van Draanen. The book follows Holly through abusive foster homes until she finally escapes and has to face the reality of making it on her own. The novel is based on interviews with many young women who experienced the same scenario.[21]

Many homeless shelters don't accept unaccompanied minors, so children are left to find shelter and safety on their own. That means they end up in parks, abandoned buildings, or homeless enclaves doing their best to survive. Social workers or authorities who encounter these children are often required by law to report them, so the children hide from the very people who might be able to offer help in an emergency.

## WHAT YOU CAN DO

### LEARN MORE ABOUT STREET CHILDREN

Consortium for Street Children is a global alliance that exists to be a voice for street children and ensure their rights to services, resources, care, and opportunities are met. Learn more at streetchildren.org.

The mission of the National Runaway Safeline (NRS) is to keep America's runaway, homeless, and at-risk youth safe and off the streets. Their website offers resources for children at risk, including concerned adults and organizations wanting to help. Learn more at 1800runaway.org.

Life on the street is especially dangerous for girls, who often work hard to make themselves look unattractive or even to pass as boys so they have less chance of being sexually assaulted or sold into prostitution. But as many as 20 percent of girls who are homeless end up pregnant.[22]

> *Life on the street is especially dangerous for girls, who often work hard to make themselves look unattractive or even to pass as boys.*

The most prevalent type of reported missing children in the United States are runaway/thrown away children. According to the National Runaway Safeline (formerly the National Runaway Switchboard), between 1.6 and 2.8 million youth run away each year in the United States. Children can begin running as young as ages ten to fourteen. The youngest are the most at-risk for the dangers of street life.[23]

Sometimes children come together to form their own "family," with the older ones caring for the younger. Children who are homeless also miss school and have little or no access to medical care. If they seek care, doctors are required to report them to social services that often put them in the foster care system. Even under the best circumstances, children in the United States generally age out of the foster care system when they turn eighteen or twenty-one, depending on the state, leaving them without resources and often with poor or little education.

An initiative of the University of Chicago's Chapin Hall called Voices of Youth Count found that one in thirty adolescent minors (ages thirteen to seventeen) endured some form of homelessness in a year.[24]

SchoolHouse Connection, a national nonprofit organization working to overcome homelessness through education, explains,

Unaccompanied youth are at a much higher risk for labor and sex trafficking, assault and other forms of victimization than their housed peers. Most unaccompanied youth are unable to access safe housing or shelter, for a combination of reasons, including: being too young to consent for services without a parent; fear of child welfare involvement; and the lack of services overall: more than half of those who seek shelter cannot access it because shelters are full. The risks for unaccompanied youth also extend to many infants and toddlers, as research indicates as many as 20 percent of homeless youth become pregnant. In fact, unmarried parenting youth have a 200 percent higher risk of homelessness than youth without children. Providing appropriate services to keep unaccompanied youth safe and secure permanent housing for them requires inter-agency collaboration and strategies that recognize the unique developmental needs and strengths of young people.[25]

## FOSTER CARE

Foster care is a program for placing a child (in the United States, generally under the age of eighteen) into a group home or private home of a caregiver, referred to as a foster parent. Arranged through the government or a social service agency, the placement is intended to be temporary until the child can safely return to her home, be reunited with relatives, or be permanently placed in an adoptive home. The group home or foster parent is compensated for expenses.

Depending on the country, a child can "age out" of foster care at eighteen and lose access to support. In the United States, an estimated 20 percent of those children immediately become homeless.

An estimated 60 percent of child trafficking victims are current or former foster youth, according to the National Foster Youth Institute. The Institute aims to "transform the child welfare system by building a national grassroots movement led by foster youth and their families."[26]

## WHAT YOU CAN DO

### BECOME A FOSTER PARENT

A good foster home is a life-changing gift to a child who has lost her family or been removed from a difficult or unsafe home. Becoming a foster parent can change a child's life and offer stability after turmoil. Foster placements are needed for both short- and long-term care. Emergency placements may be for a day or two until family members can be located, while longer-term placements may last for years. Each country has different requirements, and in the United States, individual states may differ. To learn more, go to your state's website and search for foster care.

# TRAFFICKING

Child trafficking is the buying and selling of children for the purpose of exploitation. Although it may be for labor, in the case of girls it is more often to work in the sex trade. Trafficking is a multibillion-dollar business, and recruiters of young girls make a great deal of money supplying the never-ending demand for virgins and innocent-looking girls. Nearly all children sold into labor work extremely long hours under difficult circumstances and are housed in inhumane conditions.

Recruiters often come to rural and remote villages, promoting opportunities for children to receive an education while working

## DID YOU KNOW?

**DEFINITIONS OF MISSING CHILDREN**

According to the International Center for Missing and Exploited Children, there are various definitions used to describe a missing child:

**Endangered runaway:** A child who is away from home without the permission of parent(s) or legal guardian(s). The child may have voluntarily left home for a variety of reasons.

**Family abduction:** The taking, retention, or concealment of a child or children by a parent, other family member, custodian, or his or her agent, in derogation of the custody rights, including visitation rights, of another parent or family member.

**Non-family abduction:** The coerced and unauthorized taking of a child by someone other than a family member.

**Lost, injured, or otherwise missing:** A child who has disappeared under unknown circumstances. Facts are insufficient to determine the cause of a child's disappearance.

**Abandoned or unaccompanied minor:** A child who is not accompanied by an adult legally responsible for him or her, including those traveling alone without custodial permission, those separated by an emergency, those in a refugee situation, and those who have been abandoned or otherwise left without any adult care.[27]

in a restaurant, providing childcare, or doing domestic work. Some families and girls themselves see this as an opportunity to find a better life in a large city. Heartbreakingly, some families living in poverty even sell their children—especially daughters—to support the rest of the family and lessen the burden of one more mouth to feed. In some Asian countries, daughters accept the fact that they must help support the family in this way. In Eastern Europe, the high rate of unemployment often makes girls susceptible to job offers in Europe and the United States that too often end up being in the sex trade. Sometimes girls are even trafficked by their boyfriends.

But any girl who falls through the cracks, whether displaced by conflict or on the street because of a bad family situation, can easily fall prey to traffickers. Gangs and organized criminals are constantly on the search for unaccompanied girls they can sell into trafficking. The scope of the problem is almost impossible to fathom.

> *Any girl, whether displaced by conflict or on the street because of a bad family situation, can easily fall prey to traffickers.*

While horrifying to consider, the industry continues to grow in nearly every country of the world, including the United States. In order to combat this, Congress established the Office to Monitor and Combat Trafficking in Persons (TIP Office) as part of the US State Department's efforts to stop this heinous practice. Here is their stated mission:

> The TIP Office leads the Department's global efforts to combat human trafficking through the prosecution of traffickers, the protection of victims, and the prevention of human trafficking by: objectively analyzing government efforts and identifying global trends, engaging in and supporting strategic bilateral and multilateral diplomacy, targeting foreign assistance to build sustainable capacity of governments and civil society, advancing the coordination of federal anti-trafficking policies across agencies, managing and leveraging operational resources to achieve strategic

priorities, and engaging and partnering with civil society, the private sector, and the public to advance the fight against human trafficking.[28]

Every year the office releases the Trafficking in Persons (TIP) Report, ranking countries by their efforts to recognize and combat trafficking. Its website also offers helpful resources about how individuals, faith groups, and others can combat trafficking.

> *Girls who have been trafficked are both traumatized and stigmatized.*

In his book *Not for Sale*, author David Batstone writes about this difficult subject in an educational and hopeful way by telling stories not only of those who have survived trafficking, but also of groups like World Vision, Save the Children, and International Justice Mission that are working around the world to help survivors. He also highlights individuals he calls "abolitionists," who are working on the front lines to stop the traffickers and rescue those trafficked. The work is not for the faint of heart. Individuals who try to come up against this enormous evil force find themselves targeted by organized crime, international syndicates, and even corrupt police and officials who in some countries help facilitate the flow of persons across borders or look the other way in exchange for a bribe.[29]

And while rescuing girls is especially worthy work, the challenge in many cases is what to do next. While traveling with World Relief in Cambodia, I heard the distressing stories of girls who had been trafficked into the country from Vietnam. Although they had been freed from a brothel, they couldn't find other work. They couldn't return to their families because they were considered dishonored, and in Cambodia they had no status as foreigners. Fortunately, World Relief had partnered with a local group helping the girls find jobs and survive. Sadly, I learned that some of them had returned to the brothel because it was either work there or starve.

Girls who have been trafficked are both traumatized and stigmatized. Even if they escape or are rescued, they face a difficult path. They may become pregnant and have to care for a child when they are still children themselves. If they return home, they often find that they are no longer welcome and are not considered marriageable, making them both a burden and an embarrassment to their family. In some countries, girls who have been trafficked and end up in brothels are then subject to criminal charges of prostitution if they escape, or if they have been trafficked across borders, the girls are deported or charged with immigration violations. There are too many stories of girls who escape and go to the police who are receiving payments from brothel owners or traffickers and return the girls back to their captors.

Organizations like World Vision, International Justice Mission, Save the Children, The Exodus Road, and others provide aftercare services to children who escape or are rescued from sex trafficking. These services include both medical and psychological care,

## WHAT YOU CAN DO

### MOBILIZE YOUR CHURCH TO COMBAT TRAFFICKING

*Ending Human Trafficking: A Handbook of Strategies for the Church Today* is a practical guide to understanding trafficking and helping your house of worship become a positive force to combat human trafficking. Providing a theological, educational, and practical framework to address the issue, it helps congregations and others respond effectively. You can order it on Amazon.

ongoing counseling, education, and job training so they can eventually support themselves.

Many organizations also work to prevent trafficking and shine a light on systems that enable traffickers. The Polaris Project is one such organization. This initiative operates the US National Human Trafficking Hotline and works to disrupt trafficking at every level.

The Global Alliance Against Traffic in Women (GAATW) is a network of nongovernmental organizations from all regions of the world who share a deep concern for the women, children, and men whose human rights have been violated by the criminal practice of human trafficking.

> *Many organizations also work to prevent trafficking and shine a light on systems that enable traffickers.*

GAATW works for changes in the political, economic, social, and legal systems and structures that contribute to trafficking in persons and other human rights violations. GAATW also promotes and defends the rights and safety of migrants and their families against the threats of a globalized and informal labor market.[30]

Though both boys and girls are affected by child trafficking, gender overwhelmingly plays a role in certain types of forced work—especially when it comes to sexual exploitation and forced marriage. In these forms of modern slavery, women and girls represent 99 and 84 percent of total victims respectively. Because of this, ending trafficking requires addressing harmful social norms.[31]

Because the internet has become an effective method of recruitment, technology companies have come together in the Tech Coalition, a global alliance of technology companies that "work together to drive critical advances in technology and adoption of best practices for keeping children safe online"[32] and "help our members better prevent, detect, report, and remove online child sexual abuse content."[33]

## CHILD SOLDIERS

A horrifying and growing trend is using children in military campaigns. Perhaps the most visible example has happened in Uganda and South Sudan with the Lord's Resistance Army, a militant and supposedly Christian group organized by cultlike leader Joseph Kony.

According to the Enough Project, the Lord's Resistance Army (LRA) has been one of central Africa's cruelest and most enduring armed groups over the past thirty years. The LRA has abducted more than 67,000 youth, including 30,000 children, for use as child soldiers, sex slaves, and porters, and has brutalized communities since its inception in 1987. It was designated as a terrorist group by the United States in 2001 and prompted the first-ever arrest warrants in 2005 by the International Criminal Court against LRA's leader, Joseph Kony, and other top commanders. Unfortunately, Kony has managed to evade authorities to this day.[34]

The Human Rights Watch, founded in 1978 as the Helsinki Watch, has worked alongside other organizations that focus on international human rights violations, including forcing children to be soldiers.

> Thousands of children are serving as soldiers in armed conflicts around the world. These boys and girls, some as young as 8 years old, serve in government forces and armed opposition groups. They may fight on the front lines, participate in suicide missions, and act as spies, messengers, or lookouts. Girls may be forced into sexual slavery. Many

are abducted or recruited by force, while others join out of desperation, believing that armed groups offer their best chance for survival. We are working to prevent the use of child soldiers and to hold accountable the people who send children to fight.[35]

One internally displaced girl from Sierra Leone called Marion tells her horrifying experience when she was seventeen:

My family and I were hiding in a room during an attack when a rebel broke in. My mother was asked to give one of her children up or else the entire family would be killed. My mother gave me up. The rebels took me with them, and on our way to their camp I was raped by seven of them. I was bleeding heavily and unable to walk any further. They threatened to kill me if I did not go with them. I was held by them for one year. I became pregnant and decided to escape. Upon my arrival in Freetown, I was rejected by my family and my community. I asked myself, "Who will help me now?"[36]

The *Guardian* reports that since 2012, more than 2,000 women and girls have been abducted in Nigeria by the militant Islamist group Boko Haram, including the 276 girls taken from their secondary school in Chibok in 2014. The kidnappings spawned the #BringBackOurGirls campaign, which attracted global attention.[37]

The women and girls who were eventually released from captivity said they endured physical and sexual violence and were forced to marry militants. Some were trained to fight and or forced to become suicide bombers. Boko Haram is known to use girls as young as seven as suicide bombers because they do not attract suspicion. As a result, the girls who were eventually released from the group were considered untrustworthy and even were rejected by their families who feared the girls had been brainwashed and would eventually turn on their own communities.[38]

## CLOSING THOUGHTS

The heartbreaking stories show how broken systems let children fall through the cracks, into the hands of predators or into other unimaginable circumstances. We often call these children victims, not because of their inherent weakness, but because they have been exploited and not protected by the very structures meant to care for them, including their own families.

Circumstances including poverty and displacement create more potential for vulnerability. But even in relatively wealthy countries, including the United States, children end up on the streets or in less-than-ideal homes. The wounds from these types of childhood traumas produce lasting scars. It is especially dangerous and can even be deadly for unprotected girls. And yet girls who escape share amazing stories of resilience.

A girl named Kashi was first trafficked when she was five years old, then later sold to a brothel owner. With the help of International Justice Mission, she not only escaped, but boldly testified in court against her abusers. You can read her story and other stories of survival at ijm.org/stories.

# 7

## OFFERING GIRLS ECONOMIC FREEDOM

LINDA WILKINSON DIDN'T KNOW WHY she was in Zambia. She knew how she had arrived there—her husband had accepted a job to run RAPIDS, a consortium of nonprofits working to combat AIDS. But Linda, a woman of deep faith, also believed God had a purpose for her, and she arrived in Zambia with a dream of making a difference in the lives of Zambians.

Linda was praying that God would show her what to do. It wasn't hard to find needs in Lusaka, the capital of the poor AIDS-ravaged country. Funeral processions caused daily traffic jams near the cemetery, and children begged on every street corner.

Katherine was one of the first Zambians Linda met. She was a friend's maid who was helping Linda unpack. Katherine told Linda about a widow she had met the night before who had come begging at her door, asking for food to feed her five children. She added that there were thousands of people with the same story living just outside Linda's front gate.

The story of the widow and her needs prompted Linda to leave her comfortable neighborhood and go with Katherine to Ng'ombe, one of the worst slums in Lusaka. There she met Rhoida, a widow in her early forties who, says Linda, was "beaten down." Linda was compelled to help her but soon she discovered that Rhoida was just one of many desperate widows. There were also countless grandmothers who were trying to survive and provide for their grandchildren.

As Linda began to help the widows, she realized they needed a place to meet and to help teach the children who were not in school. She found an old bar and brothel in the middle of Ng'ombe and, with the donations of friends, purchased it and cleaned it out. Linda named the center Chikumbuso, which means "remembrance." A sign in the community reads: "Remember those who have died, remember where we came from, and remember to do for others."[1]

Linda wanted to find a way for the women to generate income and form a community, so she searched for simple microenterprise projects. "I was having a hard time coming up with a microenterprise that worked and one that united us as a group of women," said Linda. "A Dutch friend, Nelique Brons, heard about Chikumbuso and asked if she could help. The bags were her idea."[2]

The "bags" are handbags and totes made from strips of plastic bags that once littered the streets of Lusaka.[3] The bags are cleaned and then cut into strips and crocheted into bags sold on the Chikumbuso website, in local markets, and by visitors who take them home and sell them to friends.

The first bags were simple. Today, they are multicolored works of art that sell for as much as ninety dollars. The community also produces other products like aprons, computer sleeves, and placemats, all sold on the website. Linda's prayer that God would show her what to do has significantly changed lives. "Over 80 widows and 300 single moms have built better financial futures by making beautiful, handcrafted items. Thanks to these products, thirty women have bought and built their own homes, more than

150 single mothers have started their own businesses or found formal employment, and mothers have paid school and university fees for over 300 of their children."[4] Chikumbuso also runs a school for kindergarten through seventh grade, provides scholarships for children to attend secondary schools, and even helps graduates attend college.

## WHAT YOU CAN DO

### BUY A CHIKUMBUSO BAG
The Chikumbuso website tells the story of Chikumbuso and also showcases the beautiful bags and other goods made by the women. Buy a bag or two, knowing you are supporting women and girls who are in turn helping others. Go to chikumbuso.com/shop.

Chikumbuso also started a separate skills training program. The center bought several sewing machines, hired a seamstress, and began a free tailoring class for single moms. Each year the program offers a class for twenty to thirty new students—now including young men—training them in a lifelong skill. To date, this project has helped more than three hundred youth learn a skill and start their own business.

Over the last fifteen years, I've visited Chikumbuso several times and have seen it grow from a small community to an impressive enterprise. The women who weave the bags are truly artists who take pride not only in their ability to support themselves and their families, but also in the unique and colorful designs they create.

Linda, who lives both in the United States and in Zambia, knows Chikumbuso has succeeded because the group of women continues to thrive and make decisions that benefit the entire community.

## DID YOU KNOW?

**MICRO TERMS**

**Microenterprise:** A business operated on a small scale, often within a community, operated by a sole proprietor and fewer than ten employees. It is typically started with a small loan.

**Microloans:** Small business loans extended to micro-entrepreneurs who usually have little or no credit history or collateral. The loans typically have short repayment periods and high interest.

**Microcredit:** Extending credit in small amounts to entrepreneurs in the developing world.

**Microsavings:** Accounts with no minimums and typically no fees that allow people with very small amounts to safely save their money.

**Microfinance institution (MFI):** An organization that provides credit to microentrepreneurs in need of a small loan to start or expand their business. Types of institutions included NGOs, credit unions, and even commercial banks.

**Microinsurance:** The protection of low-income people against specific perils in exchange for regular premium payments appropriate to the likelihood and cost of the risk involved.[5]

From the beginning, the women placed a portion of the income from each product sold into a communal pot for people in desperate straits. Even as they continued to work themselves out of poverty, they offered a hand to others who needed help.

The women of Chikumbuso are both artists and entrepreneurs who continue to expand their product line. Some have even started their own businesses and now employ others. The women of Chikumbuso demonstrate what I have seen over and over around the world: Women living in resource-poor countries are some of the most resourceful people in the world. Even without a formal education or business training, they find ways to take a simple idea and build businesses to support their families. And when they do generate income, it goes to keeping their children safer, healthier, and more educated. Study after study shows

> *Women living in resource-poor countries are some of the most resourceful people in the world.*

that women want a better future for their daughters. One of the best ways to strengthen girls is to provide economic opportunities for them and their families.

## MICROFINANCE

BeadforLife is a nonprofit started in 2004 in Kampala, Uganda, that, like Chikumbuso, began by using free materials—in this case, discarded paper that was then ingeniously rolled into beads and strung together. The often brightly colored jewelry has been sold in many shops and boutiques in the United States and supports hundreds of women living in poverty.

An article in *Forbes* highlighted the work:

"Instead of just doling out money, we want to identify women who can use the bead-making skills we teach as a stepping stone to do something more," says Torkin Wakefield, co-executive director of BeadforLife.

Most of the women BeadforLife works with never completed grammar school, held a steady job, or had a bank account. Some have AIDS, malaria, or other debilitating diseases, and many have several young children who depend on their care. "We are working with the poorest of the poor," says Rashmi Nakhooda, coordinator of the entrepreneurial program.

But their chances of success depend on the same traits as entrepreneurs in Silicon Valley or Shanghai, Nakhooda adds, namely "having a dream, a focus, and being extremely hard-working."[6]

Like the women of BeadforLife, many other women build their businesses with the help of microloans, small amounts of money provided by a microfinance institution. Microfinance began in the 1970s in Bangladesh when Muhammad Yunus founded Grameen Bank with the then-unique idea of giving small loans to under-privileged men and women who were not qualified to receive typical bank loans. Yunus believed that people living in poverty did not want handouts, but too often lacked the means to move out of their situation.[7]

> *Many women build their businesses with the help of microloans, small amounts of money provided by a microfinance institution.*

People without a credit history, property, or other forms of collateral didn't qualify for loans, and loan sharks offered money with crippling high interest. Microloans were an alternative, offered in small amounts for brief periods of time. The original model of microloans used a small group or cooperative model. In this model, individuals formed a group and received financial training in order to receive a loan from Grameen.[8]

Today, of the more than 140 million microfinance institution borrowers worldwide, 80 percent are women. Studies confirm that female borrowers of regulated MFIs have lower write-offs and portfolio risk, and fewer provisions than men, making them ideal clients. Additionally, women spend 90 percent of their income on family needs compared to only 35 percent of men.[9]

The growing popularity of MFIs has meant that there are now more than 10,000 microfinance institutions around the world with more than $120 billion in loans, according to the Microfinance Barometer.[10]

While serving on the board of Opportunity International, I saw the transformative power of microloans in the lives of women. I met a woman in Uganda whose first loan allowed her to buy a calf—and a few years later she

> *There are now more than 10,000 microfinance institutions around the world with more than $120 billion in loans.*

owned an entire herd of cattle. Another Ugandan woman bought a sewing machine with her first loan. Five years later, she employed a dozen women and produced everything from aprons to bridal gowns. Her children and all the children of her women employees were in school. The ripple effect of small loans was amazing.

When I took a group of American women business owners to the Dominican Republic, we visited women who had started small businesses with loans from Opportunity International. One woman had used her first loan to buy bulk quantities of liquid soap, which she repackaged in smaller bottles, adding fragrance and a pretty label. She proudly told us that she was making nearly fifty cents on each bottle after the cost of her supplies.

Another woman invited us to the home she had built with her earnings. She pointed proudly to the roof that didn't leak and the floors that were concrete, not dirt as in many rural homes. Her first loan gave her funds to buy sugar, milk, and other ingredients to make the popular caramel fudge (*dulce de leche*) sold in small stores

## WHAT YOU CAN DO

### SHOP THE TIRZAH BAZAAR

Tirzah International supports local microenterprise and leadership development programs for women and girls. They offer a "sister to sister" program that allows women donors to support women-run enterprises. Learn more at tirzah.org. The work is also supported by handcrafted works with all profits supporting the organization. Products can be purchased at thetirzahbazaar.com/.

throughout the Dominican Republic. When her girls weren't in school, they helped with the family business. She and her daughters made the fudge, wrapped it in small pieces, and sold it to local stores. Soon, she bragged, she was known for making the best *dulce de leche* in the area, and her candy was in great demand. Within two years, she had made enough money to build her sturdy house.

As one of the American visitors said, "We thought we might come here and help give these women entrepreneurs some tips for running their businesses. Instead, we've been amazed by how much we've learned from *them*."

Of course, not everyone who receives a loan has the drive or skills needed to grow a business. Many use their loans to buy produce and resell it each day for a small markup. Others buy items like candy or soda in bulk that they then offer in small shops or from carts. In these instances, the borrowers are still able to make a living, but growing the business can be limited.

Microloans can be made to individuals or to a group, which often shares the responsibility as well as the profit from individual enterprises. Opportunity International and others describe it as a "Trust Group"—a group of between ten and thirty entrepreneurs who share personal and business advice, receive financial training, and vote on loan-related topics. Members of the group ensure one another's loans, which builds a safety net through peer guarantees and creates a community based on collective success. As a result, Trust Group members encourage and support one another as they build their businesses and support their families.[11]

Whatever it is called, a group (usually of women) helps provide support to one another in many ways. If one member is ill, the others can choose to cover her loan payment for the period. Often the women discover many ways that working together has benefits. For example, one woman might open a storefront and purchase products from other women in the group who grow produce.

One of the most unique microfinance approaches is through Kiva, an organization that crowdfunds loans. With an investment of as little as twenty-five dollars, individuals can go online and invest in entrepreneurs from countries around the world who are seeking loans for everything from a produce stand to a dress design business.[12]

The Acumen Fund, started by Jacqueline Novogratz, takes a different approach. When she left her job on Wall Street and moved

## WHAT YOU CAN DO

### MAKE A LOAN

Kiva's motto is "Make a Loan, Change a Life," and unlike other microfinance organizations, Kiva, a crowdsourcing platform, allows the person making the loan to actually choose the recipient and her business. The person making the loan can ask for repayment or reinvest the money to support other entrepreneurs. To learn more or to make a loan, go to kiva.org.

to Rwanda, Jacqueline wanted to create "a venture capital fund for the poor" made possible by a microfinance group that helped women.[13] The Acumen Fund invests in entrepreneurs who are delivering services such as clean water, affordable housing, alternative energy sources, and reliable transportation to people living in low-income communities. They measure results on both the capital flowing back to the fund and also on the social impact of the investments. "My passion was using business models to create effective, sustainable systems where government or charity alone had failed poor people," said Novogratz.[14]

The Acumen Fund also runs an online academy where budding entrepreneurs can find master classes in everything from basics of finance to public speaking. The free courses are meant to help individuals develop skills so they can grow socially responsible businesses.[15]

## INNOVATIONS THAT MAKE A DIFFERENCE

### BECOME A SOCIAL ENTREPRENEUR

Do you want to change the world? Do you see a social issue you'd like to tackle? Wonder where to start? The Acumen Academy offers courses on social entrepreneurship, basic finance, how to apply for grants, and other topics. Most courses are free or offered for a small fee and are taught by experts in the field or experienced social entrepreneurs. Learn more at acumenacademy.org/coursecatalog/.

## MOBILE MONEY

Mobile money allows people to deposit, withdraw, and transfer money directly from their phones. This flexibility allows people without bank accounts to easily and securely manage their money.

Mobile money is also helpful for sending money to relatives in rural areas and in emergencies when people need quick money transfers.[16]

Mobile money is different from mobile banking. According to the International Monetary Fund, mobile money is a financial service offered to its clients by a mobile network operator independent of the traditional banking network. A bank account is not required to use mobile money services—the only prerequisite is a basic mobile phone. Mobile banking uses an app on a mobile device to access and execute banking services, such as check deposits, balance inquiry, and payment transfers.[17]

For women and girls especially, mobile money gives them a safe way to access money without fear of being robbed. It also gives them a way to save money that is not obvious, providing personal insurance and protection in emergencies. In general, unlike traditional bank accounts, there are no age restrictions to open a mobile money account, making this a good option for adolescent and teenage girls.

> For women and girls especially, mobile money gives them a safe way to access money without fear of being robbed.

Mobile phones can be used for financial services in three different ways: for micropayments through mobile commerce (m-commerce), as electronic money (e-money), and as a banking channel. CGAP, a think tank dedicated to empowering people living in poverty, says,

> In the Philippines, Globe Telecom lets customers load cash (or G-cash) onto their mobile phones at partner merchants or Globe outlets. For one million customers, G-cash is real value that can be stored and withdrawn as hard cash, transferred to a friend across town or across the world,

or used to pay for products at restaurants and stores. In addition, customers of Globe, and of Safaricom in Kenya (which has a similar product called M-Pesa), can use their virtual money to repay loans to, or make deposits in, microfinance institutions.[18]

## REMITTANCES

Money transfers sent by immigrants back to their country of origin are known as remittances. They are often sent to families to cover living costs, education, or health needs, and represent a significant amount of income to many resource-poor countries. In 2021 alone, $589 billion was sent overseas, more than the amount spent on international development. In that same year, the top five remittance recipients in current US dollar terms were India, China, Mexico, the Philippines, and Egypt.[19]

Migrant women who take overseas jobs tend to make lower salaries than men, but research has found that "while women typically earn less than men and pay more in transfer fees, the average remittance amounts they send are the same as or even greater than those of men," implying that they tend to remit a larger portion of their earnings than do men.[20]

Remittances used for education supports not just the giver's own children, but often is shared with relatives, friends, and even other people in the community.[21]

## SKILLS AND VOCATIONAL TRAINING

Not every girl has the opportunity to go to college or even receive a secondary education. Primary schools may be located within a community, but secondary schools are often farther away or may require boarding. School fees and uniform costs often make families hesitant to support a girl's continuing education. And sometimes family circumstances simply prevent a girl from continuing in school.

Choity, who lives in Bangladesh, was forced to quit school at thirteen when her father left the family. Getting two jobs, one as a maid and the other as a laborer, she worked hard but was abused and made just ten dollars a month. She cried about leaving school.

She thought, *If I don't go to school, I can't be anything. I can't get a job. I can't prosper.*

Then World Vision opened a Child-Friendly Learning and Recreation Center as part of their child protection work in Bangladesh. The staff worked with Choity and other girls, teaching curriculum that prepared them to return to school or offering them vocational training.

By the time she entered the program, Choity felt she had been out of school too long to return, so she chose vocational training and learned to sew. World Vision staff also taught her life skills like

> *Too often, dropping out of school results in early marriage or being sent to work for a relative.*

negotiation, bartering, decision-making, stress management, and good communication through role-playing games. And perhaps most importantly, they taught Choity and the other girls to dream about their future.

As part of the program, Choity received a sewing machine. She now has her own sewing business. And the World Vision staff also helped her create a vision board.

"Now all the dreams are in front of me, and it will remind me to go on," Choity said.[22]

Too often, dropping out of school results in early marriage or being sent to work for a relative, a situation that may result in a girl essentially becoming a servant or even a young sexual partner to the older relative. But if a girl can acquire a skill that produces income for her and her family, she can be protected from marriage or other dependency. World Vision, Girls Not Brides, and other groups advocate for what they call "safe space programs," which help girls learn life skills and health and financial literacy, and offer the opportunity to meet friends and mentors in an informal setting to learn about the services they can access in their community.[23] These programs may include a microfinance element or, in an agricultural setting, might provide an animal that the girls can raise.

## WHAT YOU CAN DO

### SUPPORT AN INCOME GENERATION PROGRAM

Small organizations in dozens of countries are working to offer job training and other skills to girls. Donors can select the country and program they would like to support, such as basket-weaving courses in Congo or computer skills in the Dominican Republic. To choose a program to support, go to girlsnotbrides.org/take-action/donate-our-members/.

A growing trend in the developing world is to offer technical and vocational education and training (TVET) as a supplement or alternative to traditional post-secondary education. Through TVET, girls obtain useful skills that help them make a living, offering an alternative to early marriage. The benefits of TVET can be observed in several developing countries:

In Delhi [India], a six-month project to train young women on stitching and tailoring resulted in a 6 percent increased likelihood of employment. They also had higher earnings and a better chance of owning a sewing machine if they completed the program.

*In Delhi, India, a six-month project to train young women on stitching and tailoring resulted in a 6 percent increased likelihood of employment.*

A study performed in Nepal found that graduates of TVET programs overall had better standards of living and higher literacy rates. They also contributed greatly to socio-economic development by improving infrastructure in the regions where they worked. . . .

When TVET programs were implemented in Sri Lanka, 58 percent of course graduates were able to get jobs after just a six-month program. That's over twice the amount generally returned by a year of formal education. Overall, prioritizing TVET in developing countries has been shown to have tremendous benefits.[24]

Some NGOs create these programs in communities by offering courses to girls in weaving, sewing, cooking, and agricultural skills that usually take less than a year to complete and require little or no investment by the girl or her family. Opportunity International, in addition to helping support microfinance, supports skills building and apprentice work. Their website reports,

In Ghana, the Youth Apprenticeship Program (YAP) pairs young people with successful business owners and artisans who mentor the apprentices and provide training in a marketable craft or skill. In addition, program participants receive ongoing business management training, and upon graduation, they can apply for an Opportunity loan to start their own business.

For Joyce, a hairdresser in Kumasi, Ghana, YAP was so valuable that she took on her own apprentices after finishing the program and establishing a successful shop. She is a young business owner who is now mentoring other girls in her community to support themselves, too.[25]

Globally, youth experience the highest rate of unemployment of any age group. Unemployment rates are even greater for young women than young men. And in many countries, women are disproportionately burdened with household responsibilities, including caring for children or elderly family members.[26]

> *Globally, youth experience the highest rate of unemployment of any age group. Unemployment rates are even greater for young women than young men.*

UNICEF has proposed specific skills training for girls. In 2020, the organization reported,

The world today is home to an estimated 600 million adolescent girls. These girls are our future leaders and change agents; however, globally, and particularly in developing countries, they are persistently and disproportionately excluded from critical education and skills-building opportunities. This exclusion limits girls' opportunities, threatens their successful transition to adulthood, adversely impacts their long-term health and well-being, and robs the world of their potential contributions. Investment in skills-building initiatives is one critical pathway to building girls' and young women's self-confidence and resilience, increasing their access to opportunities, ensuring their equal participation in the labor force, and promoting their empowerment. Ensuring that programs are tailored to meet girls' unique needs and that girls themselves fully participate in the design and implementation of such initiatives (an approach often referred to as girl-centered programming) are central principles to the efficacy and impact of these programs.[27]

## DID YOU KNOW?

**TYPES OF SKILLS GIRLS NEED**

UNICEF has suggested four specific categories in which girls require skills training:

**Foundational skills:** Basic math and literacy.

**Transferable skills:** Also called "life skills" or "soft skills," they include problem-solving, negotiation, managing emotions, empathy, and communication.

**Job-specific skills:** Known as technical and vocational skills, they are associated with occupations such as sewing or carpentry and support the transition of older adolescents into the workforce.

**Digital skills:** Digital skills and knowledge enable children to "use and understand technology, search for and manage information, create and share content, collaborate, communicate, build knowledge, and solve problems safely, critically, and ethically."[28]

A recent World Bank study focuses on digital jobs as "new employment opportunities for young women in developing countries" and the study "lays out how jobs in the digital economy can increase young women's productivity, earnings, and financial independence. . . . Working in the digital economy also offers young women the flexibility to overcome mobility constraints and combat restrictive gender norms."[29]

One unique program started in Hanoi when Jimmy Pham, a Vietnamese man living in Australia, returned to Hanoi and saw many young people living on the street. When he asked them what they wanted, they told him they needed skills to get a job. So Pham, who had been trained in the hospitality business, started a nonprofit to help them. KOTO stands for Know One, Teach One—learning should be passed on; knowledge is meant to be shared. KOTO is a hospitality training center in Hanoi, giving at-risk and disadvantaged youth the opportunity to break the poverty cycle by forging a better future for themselves, their families, and their communities. The organization reports,

> Twenty-two years later, our over 1,200 KOTO graduates now include executive and sous chefs, hotel and resort general managers, business owners as well as university graduates. All are contributing to their families and society.
>
> KOTO continues to be acknowledged as a leading unique not-for-profit social enterprise, not only in Vietnam but also internationally. Today, KOTO provides more than a hundred at-risk and disadvantaged Vietnamese youth each year an opportunity to undertake a twenty-four-month holistic hospitality training program to end the cycle of poverty and empower trainees to realize their dreams.[30]

## CLOSING THOUGHTS

Although education is important, not every girl has the opportunity to complete secondary school or go on to college. But teaching girls basic life skills and empowering them to make decisions about their future offers them a chance to make strong, independent choices.

By finding a path to financial freedom, girls can avoid the pitfalls of early marriage or other compromising situations that leave them vulnerable to gender-based violence or other perils. Not every girl will become an entrepreneur. But it is important to offer girls paths to a better life in whatever way they choose to move forward. Skills training may give them options for a future that is free from many of the hardships they would otherwise endure. And when girls and women prosper, their communities do too. They tend to invest in their families and lift everyone around them out of poverty. One of the best weapons for fighting global poverty is to invest in the women and girls of the world.

> *Teaching girls basic life skills and empowering them to make decisions about their future offers them a chance to make strong, independent choices.*

# 8

## CARING FOR DISABLED GIRLS

SOME OF US WERE ADMITTEDLY NERVOUS as the van pulled up to a cement block building outside Santo Domingo in the Dominican Republic. We were on a mission trip with a group from our Washington, DC, church, visiting both a partner church and some of the nonprofit organizations our members supported. On this day, we would be spending time at a home for disabled children called Casa de Luz (House of Light).[1]

We were scheduled to spend two hours at the orphanage. Only a few of us had experience with disabled children. The rest of us wondered how we would be able to help, how we would react, whether this would be a depressing visit on an otherwise upbeat trip. The one person who had previously visited Casa de Luz tried to reassure us that once we saw this place, we would understand.

She was right. As we walked in the front door, we saw light streaming through large windows and colorful murals brightening the hallways. A girl in a wheelchair greeted us with a lopsided grin. Another boy, much too short for his age and with a twisted spine, said, "Hello!" and gestured for us to follow him. We immediately relaxed.

The House of Light was well named. Everything about the facility was full of light. Even the children who were nonverbal or confined to their beds were being cared for by individuals who treated them as if they were their own children. Some sang to them as they cared for their needs. Others sat and stroked their hands. There was nothing depressing about this facility.

Started by Pastor Lucas Carvajal and his wife, Tempora, the House of Light was created to be a loving home for children with disabilities. While raising a disabled child of their own, the Carvajals realized how few resources there were for families in the same situation. Worse, they saw that there was no social safety net for families living in poverty and trying to deal with disabilities, a situation that often meant children were abandoned on the streets of Santo Domingo.

Most of the children at Casa de Luz came from terrible situations. Some were left to manage for themselves on the streets. Some had been mistreated and abused. And because some suffered from seizures or other symptoms, many people considered them

## WHAT YOU CAN DO

### ANTI-SEIZURE MEDICATIONS

Children with disabilities often require anti-seizure medications that are too costly for families living in poverty and not readily available in many countries. MAP International has partnered with major pharmaceutical companies to provide anti-seizure medications free of charge or at a greatly reduced cost to those in greatest need. Donors cover the cost of shipping and handling so the medications can be delivered to places like Casa de Luz. To help make these lifesaving drugs available, go to map.org/catalog.

possessed or dangerous. Even families who wanted to care for their children couldn't afford the staggering cost of anti-seizure medications and other medical needs.

For the forty children living at Casa de Luz, life has improved tremendously. They receive medical attention and lifesaving medicine as well as healthy meals. Loving caregivers meet their physical and emotional needs. Children who are able attend the local school, while others receive their education in a bright classroom within the facility. It is a wonderful, uplifting place, and visiting it was one of the highlights of our trip. In fact, some of the members of our church have returned just to spend time there.

*It's estimated that one billion people in the world are living with disabilities, and of those, 80 percent live in developing countries.*

But sadly, Casa de Luz is an exception to what most disabled people in resource-poor countries experience. It's estimated that one billion people in the world are living with disabilities, and of those, 80 percent live in developing countries.[2] Not only do most of those countries lack resources to support families with disabled children, many lack even legal protections to save these children from discrimination, neglect, or harm.

A recent study by UNICEF estimates there are 240 million children with disabilities in the world.[3]

## DOUBLE DISCRIMINATION

According to the March of Dimes, each year an estimated eight million children are born with a serious birth defect of genetic or partially genetic origin. Hundreds of thousands more are born with birth defects due to maternal exposure to environmental agents. At least 3.3 million children less than five years of age

## WHAT YOU CAN DO

### THE MARCH OF DIMES

The March of Dimes Foundation was established in 1938 to help eradicate polio. Today the organization aims to improve infant health by preventing birth defects, premature birth, and infant mortality. Working on four continents, it carries out its mission through research, community services, education, and advocacy.

The March of Dimes offers several ways to volunteer, including creating a gratitude gift pack for health-care workers and therapists, a personal care kit for families with premature babies, or hosting a March Your Way event. To learn more or to donate, go to marchofdimes.org.

die annually because of serious birth defects.[4] A fact sheet from UNICEF reports,

"Like every child in the world, children with disabilities have the right to be nurtured through responsive care, supported in education, and provided with adequate nutrition and social protection, including in humanitarian situations. But all too often, such rights are denied," said Rosangela Berman-Bieler, UNICEF Global Lead on Disability. "We can and must do more to ensure the nearly quarter of a billion children with disabilities worldwide are able to realize their rights. We must provide children with disabilities with equal opportunities by ensuring community support and services are inclusive and accessible, stigma and discrimination are eradicated, and that they are protected from violence, abuse and neglect.

There is a story behind every statistic—a child with hopes, fears, potential and ambitions."[5]

Being born with an obvious disability or birth defect is especially perilous for girls. A woman who gives birth to an impaired child is often considered cursed, and her family is stigmatized. These baby girls may be abandoned or even killed.

According to USAID, women and girls with disabilities often face "double discrimination," experiencing high rates of sexual abuse, neglect, maltreatment, and exploitation. Studies show these women and girls are twice as likely to undergo gender-based violence.

> *Being born with an obvious disability or birth defect is especially perilous for girls.*

The exclusion and violence against women and girls with disabilities in any country carries heavy financial and social consequences. Discrimination against persons with disabilities hinders economic development, limits democracy, and erodes societies.[6]

## FUELED BY SUPERSTITION

A BBC report citing a study done in Kenya by Disability Rights International found,

> Most mothers of disabled children in the developing world said their children were considered "cursed, bewitched and possessed" and that a belief prevailed that the mothers were being punished for their sins, including being "unfaithful to their husbands." . . .
>
> An elderly traditional birth attendant . . . told the BBC

that according to her culture, babies with disabilities were killed out of love. . . . "The child would otherwise suffer if it was allowed to live."[7]

## WHAT YOU CAN DO

### SURGERY TO CORRECT DISABILITIES

CURE International operates a global network of children's hospitals in resource-poor countries dedicated to providing excellent care to children living with disabilities. Treating such conditions as hydrocephalus, spina bifida, clubfoot, and other treatable limb deformities, CURE hospitals offer comprehensive care free of charge to children and their families. Often world-renowned surgeons volunteer their time, and the hospitals help thousands of children live full, healthy lives. To learn more or to support CURE International, go to cure.org.

While I was working in Zambia, a woman I met told me the story of her sister who gave birth to a baby girl with a deformity. The newborn was quickly taken away after birth by her mother-in-law to be treated by a traditional healer (she called him a "witch doctor"), and a week later the family quietly buried the baby. The family never knew if the baby died from her condition, her "treatment," or simply neglect. Because of the superstitions surrounding a baby born with a deformity or sometimes even a birthmark, a father or family elder may try to save the family from shame by taking the baby away from the mother soon after birth. Since most women give birth at home in the developing world, live births are not always recorded, and the baby just disappears and is treated as a stillbirth.

Those babies who simply look different in the developing world are often treated as if they are possessed or are rumored to have special powers. This has led to beliefs and actions that are often tragic, such as killing of people with albinism, a genetic disorder that results in lack of pigmentation in the skin and hair and also impaired vision. While it is a relatively rare condition in the developed world, it is one of the genetic conditions much more common in sub-Saharan Africa because of intermarriage among close relatives.

In 2015 the BBC reported, "More than 200 witchdoctors and traditional healers have been arrested in Tanzania in a crackdown on the murder of albino people. The killings have been driven by the belief—advanced by some witchdoctors—that the body parts have properties that confer wealth and good luck."[8]

Girls with disabilities are often hidden at home because their families are either ashamed of them or are overly protective. "Families in Zambia often hide their daughters who have intellectual disabilities—sometimes out of shame, but also out of fear," said Laura Menenberg of Special Hope Network, a nonprofit organization in Zambia focused on improving the lives of children with intellectual disabilities. "The myth that having sex with a virgin will cure you of AIDS makes girls with disabilities especially vulnerable because they are viewed as 'perpetual virgins' by society."[9]

> *Girls with disabilities are often hidden at home because their families are either ashamed of them or are overly protective.*

Children with physical disabilities are too often assumed to be mentally disabled as well, so they are not sent to school. And schools in resource-poor countries can rarely accommodate children with special needs.

## WHAT YOU CAN DO

### WHEELCHAIRS FOR MOBILITY

In the developing world, disability, age, and illness all create mobility issues. It is not uncommon to see disabled children and adults dragging themselves around through the dirt or struggling with makeshift crutches. Without the ability to move freely, people with mobility issues cannot easily access water and sanitation facilities, attend school, go to work, or gather food. Girls and women become extremely vulnerable to sexual assault when they are not mobile. According to the Wheelchair Foundation, it is estimated that at least 100 million children, teens, and adults worldwide need a wheelchair but cannot afford one.[10]

Groups like Chariots of Love, Joni and Friends (Wheels for the World), MedShare, and others provide wheelchairs to those in need. Most are wheelchairs that are donated, refurbished, and sometimes retrofitted to meet the unique needs of people in countries where sidewalks are not common. To support these efforts, go to the individual websites: chariots oflove.org; joniandfriends.org; medshare.org; and wheelchair foundation.org.

## LACK OF CARE

Globally, 150,000 to 200,000 babies are born with clubfoot each year, 80 percent in low- and middle-income countries. Most of these babies will not receive effective treatment and will grow up with a severe disability. Because children with disabilities like clubfoot are stigmatized, they are less likely to attend school, marry, or get a job. Families of children with clubfoot may experience prejudice since some cultures believe that it is caused by a curse or evil spirits. Mothers of children born with clubfoot may be blamed, leading to conflict, separation, and even divorce. All of this because of a condition that is easily treated in the developed world.[11]

Another common—and very treatable—condition is cleft lip or cleft palate, an abnormality resulting in openings in the roof of the mouth or in the upper lip, often resulting in facial deformities. Caused by both heredity and conditions surrounding the mother's health, a child born with one or both of these conditions often has difficulty nursing and eating, leading to malnutrition and other health challenges. Because of the deformity, a child with a cleft lip or palate is often stigmatized and assumed to be mentally disabled.

## INNOVATIONS THAT MAKE A DIFFERENCE

### DO-IT-YOURSELF WHEELCHAIRS

A unique mobility solution is the SafariSeat, an all-terrain, low-cost wheelchair with hand pedals and puncture-proof tires. The wheelchairs are made using local materials with the blueprints for constructing them available free of charge. Made to be durable and easily repaired, the unique design was first funded by a Kickstarter campaign.[12] For more information, go to safariseat.org.

Because uninformed parents often believe the worst about a child with disabilities, they may not expect them to learn, so the parents don't provide stimulation. Said Menenberg, "Sometimes parents don't know that they can read a book to their disabled child, and she will respond."[13]

According to the latest data, compared to children without disabilities, children with disabilities are:

- **24 percent less likely to receive early stimulation and responsive care.** Children with disabilities risk missing out on the care and stimulation they need in the early years due to increased exposure to factors that make them more vulnerable. These include poverty, stigma and discrimination, exclusion from early learning opportunities, institutionalization, violence, abuse and neglect.

- **42 percent less likely to have foundational reading and numeracy skills.** Children with disabilities typically face additional barriers that place them at higher risk of experiencing less than optimal educational trajectories. When families do search for educational opportunities for their children, they often find schools and classrooms that are not accessible, either physically or due to the lack of appropriate learning materials.

- **49 percent more likely to have never attended school.** The likelihood of a child never attending school can depend on her or his functional difficulty or economic background. For example, children with disabilities from the poorest households are substantially more likely to have never attended school than their peers from the richest households.

- **25 percent more likely to be wasted and 34 percent more likely to be stunted.** Children with disabilities frequently experience higher rates of underweight, stunting, and wasting than their peers without disabilities. This is especially true among children with difficulties seeing, playing, and walking as well as those from the poorest households.

- **53 percent more likely to have symptoms of acute respiratory infection.** Children with disabilities, especially those in the poorest and rural households, are at elevated risk of experiencing diarrhea, fever, and symptoms of acute respiratory infection. Children with disabilities who develop an illness or infection, including an ARI [acute respiratory infection], are more susceptible to severe illness, poorer health outcomes, and hospitalization than children without disabilities.

- **51 percent more likely to feel unhappy and 41 percent more likely to feel discriminated against.** How individuals perceive their own well-being is based on a wide array of factors. However, many children with disabilities experience discrimination because of their impairments. Since discrimination can raise barriers in accessing services that these children need to realize their rights, it is likely that it negatively affects their subjective well-being.[14]

## WHAT YOU CAN DO

### SURGERY FOR CLEFT LIPS AND PALATES

When a child is born with a cleft lip or palate, it's important to treat it surgically as soon as possible. The life-changing surgery can take as little as forty-five minutes and cost just $240.

Operation Smile and Smile Train are just two organizations working in resource-poor countries that offer free surgeries to children suffering with these conditions. Performed by both volunteer surgeons and local professionals, the surgery has changed the lives of thousands of children. For more information, go to operationsmile.org and smiletrain.org.

In wealthier countries children are monitored by parents and pediatricians for early signs of developmental delays (including eyesight and hearing issues) that can be treated or corrected early, helping children lead a full life. But in developing countries, parents and caregivers have few resources for evaluating young children. A child with developmental delays may simply be ignored. A child with hearing or sight impairment is often assumed to be mentally disabled.

According to the Borgen Project,

> Children with any disability tend to be the most stigmatized population in many countries. Some cultures shun those with them, believing the ailment is a result of sin or bad luck, or that a disability can be contagious. This leads to the discrimination of disabled children. Additionally, these children are often excluded from programs, education, healthcare, society and family because of the lack of resources and the inability of poor societies to accommodate them.[15]

The entire family feels the impact of a child with special needs. Usually, the burden falls on the mother to care for the child, adding to whatever other work she has. If she has previously worked outside the home, that income may be lost. And if there is an older daughter in the home, she may have to leave school to care for her disabled sibling. The cost of wheelchairs, crutches, glasses, hearing aids, anti-seizure drugs, or other medical interventions must be borne by the family since health insurance either doesn't exist or is too costly for families living in

*The entire family feels the impact of a child with special needs.*

poverty. As a result, some families resort to using their disabled child to beg for money.

Disabled children are also sometimes abducted by criminals or gangs who consider them to be more effective at begging for money.[16]

Again, the Borden Project reports,

Children with disabilities in developing countries have a higher mortality rate due to lack of basic healthcare. While many medical advances have been made, they are mostly seen in wealthier nations. These nations have seen reductions in disability mortality; however, in developing nations, wealthy families can afford treatment and much of the poor cannot afford assistive devices or treatment needed. There is also little literature on care specific to the disabled population.[17]

Families often have low expectations of a disabled child, so she isn't enrolled in school. Schools may be unable to accommodate a disabled child who is unable to see the blackboard or access the bathroom. Reasons like these too often prevent children from finishing or attending school.

According to a UNICEF report,

Despite widespread agreement on the importance of education, children with disabilities are still falling behind. They are more likely to never attend school or to drop out due to multiple barriers, including stigma, lack of trained teachers, inadequate learning materials and inaccessible facilities. . . . The impact of excluding children with disabilities from education goes far beyond diminished educational outcomes. They are also more likely to miss

**DID YOU KNOW?**

**UNDERSTANDING DISABILITY TERMINOLOGY**
A person who has one or more physical or mental impairments that make it difficult to fully participate in society is often referred to as disabled. Disabilities may be congenital, such as Down syndrome or autism, or occur later in life following an accident, illness, or simply from aging. Mental disabilities may not be as obvious as physical disabilities, but people with physical disabilities often have no mental impairments yet report that others often treat them as if they do. Congenital disabilities are sometimes referred to as "birth defects."

out on school-based health and nutrition programmes, such as school meals and immunization campaigns, and face increased vulnerability to violence and exploitation while not at school.[18]

## CAUSES OF DISABILITIES

Mental and physical disabilities at birth occur more often in poor countries where pregnant women lack both prenatal medical care

> *Mental and physical disabilities at birth occur more often in poor countries where pregnant women lack both prenatal medical care and proper nutrition.*

and proper nutrition. Likely malnourished themselves, women living in poverty who become pregnant also lack access to prenatal vitamins or resources that can help them supplement their diets. As we discussed in chapter 2, vitamins and minerals such as folic acid, zinc, and vitamin D have a direct impact on the health and development of a baby, and lack of nutrients can lead to specific conditions or premature birth. In addition, many people living in poverty have homes near toxic sites, drink tainted water, or rely on crops with little nutritional value that leave them anemic or malnourished. Women in the developing world also continue to have babies later in life, or with much older men, both of which are factors in certain mental health issues.[19]

Pregnant women in resource-poor countries are expected to

## WHAT YOU CAN DO

### HELPING CHILDREN WITH IMPAIRED VISION

Millions of children around the world need reading glasses to learn effectively. But in many countries, children with impaired vision are simply assumed to be mentally impaired and unable to stay in school. For lack of a pair of glasses, they lose their ability to pursue an education and sometimes even a livelihood. Impaired vision is especially dangerous to children and adults in developing countries.

Lions Clubs International has made collecting and distributing eyeglasses to those in need one of their signature programs. Working with Walmart and Sam's Club, they offer in-store receptacles at many locations for people to donate gently used glasses that are then cleaned, repaired, and sent to those in need. Donate at your local Walmart or Sam's Club or contact the Lions Club near you at lionsclubs.org.

You can mail your gently used glasses to ReSpectacle, a nonprofit that distributes donated glasses. To donate your own glasses or to host a glasses drive, go to respectacle.org.

Costco also has a glasses donation program. You can find donation boxes in the optical centers at most Costco stores.

continue to work until they deliver, often exposing themselves and their unborn child to toxic fumes and workplace hazards. Babies are sometimes born in a field or in unsanitary conditions where the mothers and their newborns could pick up infections. They may contract malaria or other diseases that affect themselves and their baby. And in many cases, once the mothers deliver, they secure their newborns on their backs and go right back to work, once again exposing that child to hazardous conditions.

A relatively recent factor that has been discovered to affect pregnant women in countries with mosquitoes is the Zika virus. According to the WHO, "Zika virus infection during pregnancy is a cause of microcephaly and other congenital abnormalities in the developing fetus and newborn. Zika infection in pregnancy also results in pregnancy complications such as fetal loss, stillbirth, and preterm birth."[20]

> *Genetic birth defects occur at a much higher rate in in the developing world partially because there is a higher degree of marriage between close blood relatives.*

A number of birth defects are caused by genetics. Some of the most common congenital disabilities are heart defects, cleft lip and palate, Down syndrome, abnormal limbs (such as clubfoot), and spina bifida. Genetic birth defects occur at a much higher rate in the developing world partially because there is a higher degree of consanguinity (marriage between close blood relatives), a practice common among certain tribes or cultures, or simply a practice among people living in remote areas or small villages who have few choices of mates.

In some countries, "cousin marriage" is practiced to keep wealth in the family or is believed to be preferable because of shared values and tradition. One study estimated that 20 percent of the world population lives in communities with a preference for consanguineous marriage, and as many as 10 percent of marriages in the world are between first or second cousins, a practice that is illegal in some developed countries because of the increased risk of genetic disorders.[21] Interestingly, first cousin marriage is still legal in some US states, although it is not widely practiced.[22]

"One billion people worldwide live in countries where marriage among relatives is common. Of this billion, one in three is married to a second cousin or closer relative or is the progeny of such a marriage. The frequency of genetic disorders among such children is around twice that in children of non-related parents," according to a study published in the *British Journal of Medicine* (*BMJ*).[23]

Disabilities also occur in childhood due to unsafe conditions in which children live or play and the lack of access to medical services to treat any injuries. Open fires in the home can lead to scarring and even blinding burns. Stepping on a dirty piece of metal or getting cut without being able to properly clean the wound can mean a lost limb for a child who has not received a tetanus shot. Diarrhea can lead to dehydration severe enough to cause kidney or brain damage. A bout with malaria can also cause permanent brain damage. Strep throat, left untreated, can lead to rheumatic fever that can cause a stroke or permanent heart damage. What would be easily treatable childhood accidents or diseases in developed countries can lead to long-term disability or even death in some parts of the world.

The Human Rights Watch organization tell us,

Women are more likely than men to become disabled during their lives, due in part to gender bias in the allocation of scarce resources and in access to services. When ill, girls and women are less likely to receive medical attention than boys and men, particularly in developing

> *Women constitute 75 percent of the disabled people in low-and middle-income countries.*

countries where medical care may be a considerable distance from home. They are also less likely to receive preventive care, such as immunizations.[24]

Sadly, "approximately 300 million women around the world have mental and physical disabilities. Women constitute 75 percent of the disabled people in low- and middle-income countries. Women with disabilities comprise 10 percent of all women worldwide."[25] No one knows how many have conditions that could have been treated as children.

## ADVOCATING FOR THE VULNERABLE

The Convention on the Rights of Persons with Disabilities was adopted in 2006 and formalizes "the movement from viewing persons with disabilities as 'objects' of charity, medical treatment and social protection towards viewing persons with disabilities as 'subjects' with rights, who are capable of claiming those rights and making decisions for their lives based on their free and informed consent as well as being active members of society."[26]

The Convention adopts a broad categorization of persons with disabilities and reaffirms that all persons with all types of disabilities have the right to enjoy all human rights and fundamental freedoms. It clarifies and qualifies how all categories of rights apply to persons with disabilities and identifies areas where adaptations have to be made for persons with disabilities to effectively exercise their rights and areas where their rights have been violated, and where protection of rights must be reinforced.[27]

Countries that sign the convention agree to protect the rights of their disabled populations. But sadly, even when laws exist, cultural practice often lags behind.

Disability is now being seen as a human rights issue. International organizations, such as UNICEF, state that children should not be discriminated against based on disability and that these children have the right to freedom and happiness as others do. Governments are beginning to advocate for the disabled too.

The World Health Organization (WHO) created specific guidelines to include people with disabilities in the Millennium Development Goals. It recognized that those with disabilities are impacted differently and therefore need different resources. For instance, women with disabilities face more severe discrimination, as do mothers of the disabled. The WHO noted that extra supportive programs are needed for these populations. This trend is continuing in the UN's Sustainable Development Goals.[28]

> *Women with disabilities face more severe discrimination, as do mothers of the disabled.*

Many international nonprofit organizations have also made strides in making their programs more inclusive. World Vision, for example, published *Travelling Together: How to Include Disabled People on the Main Road of Development*. In this handbook, the authors note, "Disabled people are in every community. It's an expression of the diversity of the human race. . . . Good development work challenges conditions which exclude the oppressed—disabled people are among the most oppressed."[29]

A widely used resource is *Disabled Village Children: A Guide for Community Health Workers, Rehabilitation Workers and Families*. Published by the Hesperian Organization, the book includes helpful diagrams and photos for people who aren't health-care professionals to not only assess and diagnose disabilities but also know what treatments are available.[30]

In the United States it is common to see accommodations made for people living with disabilities. We expect to see corner cuts in curbs and ramps for wheelchairs in public places. We're used to parking spots reserved for people with disabilities and special seats reserved on public transportation. We are also more likely to work with or attend school with people who have a disability because of accommodations that make it possible to work, study, travel, and otherwise enjoy the same experiences as everyone.

The Americans with Disabilities Act (ADA) prohibits discrimination based on disability. Passed in 1990, it offers some of the same protection against discrimination as the Civil Rights Act of 1964, which made discrimination based on race, religion, sex, national origin, and other characteristics illegal. The ADA also requires employers to provide reasonable accommodations to employees with disabilities, and defined requirements for public accommodations, such as wheelchair ramps.

ADA disabilities include both mental and physical conditions, including deafness, blindness, an intellectual disability (formerly termed mental retardation), partially or completely missing limbs or mobility impairments requiring the use of a wheelchair, autism, cancer, cerebral palsy, diabetes, epilepsy, attention deficit hyperactivity disorder, human immunodeficiency virus (HIV) infection, multiple sclerosis, muscular dystrophy, major depressive disorder, bipolar disorder, post-traumatic stress disorder, obsessive-compulsive disorder, and schizophrenia. Other mental or physical health conditions also may be disabilities, depending on what the individual's symptoms would be in the absence of "mitigating measures" (medication, therapy, assistive devices, or other means of restoring function), during an "active episode" of the condition (if the condition is episodic).[31]

While many other countries have versions of laws that protect people who are disabled physically or mentally, the degree to which those laws are enforced or even understood among most people varies greatly. And the implementation of the necessary accommodations is often left to individuals or nonprofits if government resources are not available.

Cynthia Bauer, an American, was born without her left hand. While a graduate student conducting research in Kenya, she discovered that many Kenyans believed disabilities like hers were caused by curses and, in fact, had she been born in Kenya she might have been killed. During her research, she met Leonard Mbonani, a Kenyan special needs teacher who introduced her to children living with disabilities, many of whom did not have access to medical care or education. Cynthia worked with Leonard to respond to the needs

## WHAT YOU CAN DO

### SUPPORT DISABLED CHILDREN IN SCHOOLS

Kenya provides free primary education for all children, but children with special needs often require additional resources a family can't afford. Kupenda offers a child sponsorship program to cover additional education costs for disabled children in Kenya. It also helps schools hire and train teachers and other staff to support the needs of disabled children, including sign language training. The nonprofit also helps raise funds to equip schools to provide space for medical and therapy services for children with disabilities. Kupenda is one of the special needs organizations in developing countries that are providing much-needed help to disabled children and their families. To learn more and support the work, go to kupenda.org.

of the children and their families, as well as their communities and eventually started an organization called Kupenda for the Children.

Kupenda advocates for disabled children by hosting Disability Awareness Days in villages. The festive occasions include children from special needs schools performing songs, dances, and plays. Speakers help educate the community and offer families information for connecting to educational and medical resources for disabled children. Kupenda also helps educate pastors. "Many people in Kenya, even Christian pastors, believe disabilities are caused by witchcraft or are a punishment from God," according to the Kupenda for the Children website.[32]

In Lusaka, Zambia, Special Hope Network (SHN) is a nonprofit that "empowers parents and caregivers to provide a safe and loving space for their child and educates communities to value

## INNOVATIONS THAT MAKE A DIFFERENCE

### COMMUNITY CARE CENTERS

Families with disabled children often feel stigmatized and lack support. Community care centers offer a place where families who have children with disabilities can bring them to play, receive medical checkups and evaluations, and get valuable guidance for caring for their children. These centers offer families support and a network of resources as well as the opportunity to meet other families who are raising children with disabilities.

One example of this approach is the Special Hope Network in Zambia. To learn more, go to specialhopenetwork.org, where you can donate to support the work, select items from an Amazon wish list to help stock their centers, or volunteer to help in person.

and embrace children who might otherwise be stigmatized or even abandoned."[33] By helping families who have children with disabilities, SHN makes it possible for the children to not only stay in their homes, but also to thrive. In many countries, families hide a disabled child. The child stays at home and doesn't receive an education or even interact with other children. Community care centers (CCCs) are safe spaces for families to bring their children with disabilities and find guidance as well as counseling, training, medical assistance, feeding instructions, and other education. SHN also advocates on behalf of disabled children, training pastors and church leaders as well as teachers and community leaders to value children with special needs.

## THE ERA OF COVID

Because of some underlying health conditions, children with disabilities are at higher risk for becoming infected with COVID-19 and developing severe illness. Many disabled children also have more difficulty receiving medical care or having access to sanitation facilities that would help prevent disease.

The social isolation and distancing that took place during the epidemic also affected the well-being of all children, leading to stress and anxiety. For families with a disabled child this meant being cut off from social services and medical support, creating even more tension within families and more burden on them to care for the special needs of their children. Lack of access to special schooling and therapy means that children with special needs fell further behind.

## CLOSING THOUGHTS

Girls living with disabilities, especially in developing countries, are some of the most victimized and vulnerable girls in the world.

# 9

. . . . . . . . . . . . . . . .

# PROTECTING
# GIRLS' RIGHTS

THE EARLY MORNING SUN shimmered on the rice paddies below us as our Land Rover slowly maneuvered a narrow mountain road. I tried not to look down too often as we rose higher and the road became narrower. As we drove along the rough and rocky path with no guardrail and only inches between us and a sheer drop-off, the International Justice Mission (IJM) staff member who was driving pointed out to me that gripping the dashboard wasn't really helping. So I closed my eyes and tried to breathe deeply.

I was momentarily relieved when we stopped, only to learn that we would be walking a mile from that point to the village—the road was impassable for vehicles. The staff member, who was a good twenty years younger than me, asked if I thought I could do it.

"Of course!" I said with more confidence than I felt as I took the walking sticks he offered. Besides, what choice did I have? We stumbled on a rocky path and eventually arrived at a small mountain village, high above the clouds.

At the time I was serving on the board of IJM and, along with another board member, was visiting the office in Thailand. We both welcomed the chance to see the staff in action, not realizing the extent to which they went to carry out their work.

High in the mountains of northwestern Thailand, near the border with Myanmar (then Burma), IJM was working to protect the rights of the Karen people. Although the secluded ethnic group had lived in the mountains for generations, they were not recognized as citizens of Thailand because they had never registered with the government. This meant they had no access to education, health services, or protection from their own government. Sadly, human traffickers had infiltrated the villages, promising a bright future with schooling and jobs to the girls and boys who went with them to Bangkok.

These innocent children ended up in brothels or as unpaid restaurant workers. If they ran away or were freed, they had no police protection because they lacked identity papers. While IJM was freeing children sold into sex trafficking, the organization also wanted to stop the traffickers. By helping the Karen people obtain identity papers, they gave them access to government services and protection.

International Justice Mission is a global organization with a mission to "protect people in poverty from violence."[1] Founded by attorney and human rights activist Gary Haugen, the organization not only represents individuals who might otherwise never have access to legal aid, it also works to disrupt corruption and help countries enact better laws. In Thailand, the organization not only helped to free young girls from brothels but also worked to stop them from ending up alone in the city in the first place. With no papers, the Karen children were prime targets for the sex traffickers who could claim impunity.

The plight of the Karen people is just one example of how living in poverty often means living without legal protection. "Basic law enforcement systems in the developing world are so broken that global studies now confirm that most poor people live outside the protection of law," Haugen says in his book *The Locust Effect: Why the End of Poverty Requires the End of Violence.*[2]

While freeing girls from brothels is dramatic and often dangerous work, documenting people's identities is tedious and painstaking. In the Karen village, IJM workers who spoke the local dialect questioned each person about his or her age and any details about relatives and approximate dates of birth. They took photos of families standing together, each holding signs with their age. It was mind-boggling to realize that none of these people had birth certificates, driver's licenses, or any written proof of their existence.

All of this information had to be documented on government forms by staff who spoke and wrote Thai. Once the papers were filed with the government, each person over the age of seven would receive a national identity card that would offer him or her the rights of a Thai national. A simple national identity card would change the lives of these people, offering protection and access to education and other services.

For most of us, proving our identity is as simple as opening our wallet and showing a driver's license, credit card, or social security card, or producing a passport. It is how we confirm our legal, educational, and business rights. If someone threatens violence against us or

## WHAT YOU CAN DO

### BECOME A JUSTICE CHAMPION

You don't have to be a lawyer to fight for the legal rights of girls. International Justice Mission has a network of volunteers who advocate on behalf of victims in a variety of ways. Go to ijm.org/get-involved/volunteer to learn more.

tries to block us from our rights, we have many ways to respond. We can call the police, a hotline, or the office of a member of Congress. We can tweet our outrage and enlist support. We expect our rights to be upheld, not only because we can prove our identity but also because we live in a society where the rule of law is upheld for women and girls.

> *In some cases, laws protecting girls and women against discrimination simply don't exist.*

But more than 2.5 billion women and girls around the world have no such recourse. According to UN Women, they are affected in multiple ways by discriminatory laws and the lack of legal protections.[3] In some cases, laws protecting girls and women simply don't exist and reflect an older patriarchal system. In other cases, laws actually codify discrimination. For example, in some countries, women and girls are prevented from inheriting property. And under some legal systems, if a man rapes a woman or girl, he is not prosecuted if he marries her (even against her will). In too many countries, laws exist but are simply ignored or overridden by cultural practices or local customs.

Countries that join the United Nations agree to uphold certain laws and treaties. The rule of law is the political philosophy that all citizens and institutions within a country, state, or community are accountable to the same laws. The expectation is that these laws are widely known, equitably enforced, and judged fairly. But each country has different types of laws. Even in established democracies with elected governments and a well-educated population, the law is not always applied equitably. In countries where little or no democracy exists and citizens have no voice, the rule of law breaks down. Especially for those who have no power or resources, the legal system and police offer no protection.

## CULTURE OVERRIDES LAW

In some countries, even when laws exist, enforcement on behalf of women is non-existent. Laws are too often trumped by cultural norms. A few years ago I spent a week in Jordan, where I met women who held high positions and seemed to have great respect in society. And yet that same week in the local newspaper I read accounts of two "honor killings" of women.

One was a Muslim family who killed their daughter when they learned she was secretly dating a man. Another was a Christian family whose father killed the daughter when she announced her intentions to marry a Muslim man. These extreme punishments shocked me, but the local Jordanians mostly shrugged them off, explaining that honor killings were against the law but still happen. When I asked if the murderers had been punished, I was surprised that even the women explained that the killers weren't really viewed as committing murder.

"Such slayings are viewed with approval by major segments of Jordanian society, where tribal codes often take precedence over the official legal system and conduct considered unchaste can bring a deep sense of shame to the entire family," wrote Nabih Bulos in the *LA Times* after another honor killing was recorded on camera and sparked protests in Jordan. "For decades, the law reflected that stance, allowing killers to get off scot-free. Judges, officials and police officers—the vast majority of them men—often were sympathetic to the perpetrator's views."[4]

In some countries, laws that exist simply aren't known or understood throughout the country. In Burkina Faso, for example, girls must be seventeen years of age to legally marry. But more than half of the fifteen- to seventeen-year-old girls in the country are married.[5]

## INNOVATIONS THAT MAKE A DIFFERENCE

### LISTENING POSTS

We sometimes think of innovations as being technologically advanced. But in Burkina Faso I encountered a very effective program developed by a group of women who had no money to invest but were dedicated to making their country a better place for women and girls.

The women from both Christian and Muslim backgrounds came up with a unique idea. During market day, they set up a booth called a "Listening Post" where women could get free advice and have their questions answered. If there was a question the Listening Post women couldn't answer, they promised to return the next week with a response. The women who were seeking advice didn't have to lie to their husbands or fathers as to where they were going each week—they were just going to market as usual.

The women in the Listening Post heard basic questions about health and family life. But they also heard questions like "My daughter is only thirteen. Does she have to marry?" While the women at the Listening Post could explain the laws and a woman's rights, they also knew it could be dangerous and futile for some of these wives to try to convince their husbands.

So the women from the Listening Post had a regular meeting with the ministers, priests, and imams in the area, who were also dedicated to helping improve the lives of women in their congregations. When the faith leaders heard what the women were asking, they began to incorporate lessons in their messages that addressed the issues. The women I met told me proudly that child marriage was dropping in their region, thanks to their work and the messages of the faith leaders to the men.

Because more than 2.5 billion girls and women are facing either discrimination or lack of legal protection, UN Women as well as the African Union and several other groups have jointly issued a call for "Equality in law for women and girls by 2030."[6] The strategy is aimed at six areas, including nationality rights, personal status, minimum marriage age, and discriminatory rape laws. With a goal to "repeal discriminatory laws that directly impact women and girls in 20 countries," the movement is identifying laws that openly discriminate against women and girls.

## DID YOU KNOW?

**EXAMPLES OF DIFFERENTIAL TREATMENT UNDER THE LAW**
Women cannot undertake the following in the same way or on an equal basis as men:

- Inherit equally as daughters in 39 countries
- Apply for a passport in 37 countries
- Inherit equally as a spouse in 36 countries
- Be head of household or family in 31 countries
- Get a job or pursue a trade or profession without permission in 18 countries
- Travel outside their home in 17 countries
- Obtain a national ID card in 11 countries
- Register a business in 4 countries[7]

# PROTECTING GIRLS

In 1989 world leaders made a historic international legal agreement with the world's children by adopting the United Nations Convention on the Rights of the Child.[8]

Instead of treating children as objects who belong to their

parents, they are viewed as individuals with their own rights, separating childhood from adulthood. The document states that a child under the age of eighteen should be protected and allowed to grow, learn, play, and flourish.

The protection of girls is often discussed as either child protection or the protection of women and girls. There are many experts who believe the girl child needs to be named specifically and data collected separately because of the many ways girls face specific discrimination.

The Girls' Rights Platform, a "global campaign demanding power, freedom, and respect for girls," sums it up this way:

> Girls' rights are human rights. Yet, millions of girls continue
> to struggle to claim their rights. Rarely are girls mentioned as
> a specific demographic in international law and where they
> are, there is a failure to fully reflect the particular barriers
> they face. In order to remedy this, states, UN Agencies,
> and civil society must identify the realization of girls' rights
> as an objective in itself and attach greater importance to
> empowering girls throughout their life-cycles.[9]

## THE RIGHT TO LIFE

Girls' rights to life are not respected as much as those of boys. More boys have been intentionally carried to full-term, and girls die more frequently before the age of five. We have discussed the reality of this in the health chapter, but it is also worth noting that it is a legal right as well.

In *Half the Sky*, authors Nicholas D. Kristof and Sheryl WuDunn document stories: "A woman named Shahnaz poisoned her daughter to avoid being divorced by her husband. Perveen poisoned her daughter after her father-in-law beat her for giving birth to a girl. Yet sometimes women in Pakistan or China kill their newborn daughters simply because daughters are less prestigious than sons. Rehana drowned her daughter because 'girls are unlucky.'"[10]

## THE RIGHT TO IDENTITY

According to UNICEF, as many as one-quarter of all births (166 million) are never officially counted.[11] Birth registration officially records a child's birth, providing legal recognition of that child's identity. Without it, a child—especially a girl—can disappear without a trace.

Birth registration is required for a birth certificate. It establishes where a child was born and who her parents are.

Birth registration is a human right, according to the UN. The Convention on the Rights of the Child includes the following:

The child shall be registered immediately after birth and shall have the right from birth to a name, the right to acquire a nationality.

Not only is birth registration a fundamental human right, it also helps ensure that children's other rights are upheld—like the rights to protection from

> *Birth registration officially records a child's birth, providing legal recognition of that child's identity.*

violence, and essential social services like health care and justice. The information collected from birth registration records helps governments decide where and how to spend money, and what areas to focus on for development programs, such as education and immunization.[12]

**WHAT YOU CAN DO**

**ARTISTS FOR CHANGE**

Are you an author, poet, musician, sculptor, or other artist who wants to share your gift and raise awareness at the same time? Oxfam has a variety of programs to help you put your creativity to work, raising awareness about issues like gender-based violence and the unequal treatment of girls around the world. Go to oxfamamerica.org/take-action/artists-for-oxfam/ to learn how your creativity can be a gift to girls by raising awareness and support.

## THE RIGHT TO PROTECTION AGAINST VIOLENCE

While violence against women and girls occurs in all societies, it is both more pervasive and less likely to be stopped or prosecuted when the victim lives in poverty.

"Thousands of women and girls in the developing world tell my colleagues that they simply don't feel safe and that sexual violence can feel like a threat everywhere, all the time," writes Gary Haugen.[13] "For instance, sexual violence is in the place that is supposed to be safest: the home—with high rates of sexual assault by relatives (and the friends and sexual partners of those relatives) in the often cramped quarters of the poor." Haugen tells the story of Laura, a ten-year-old who, after her mother died, was regularly raped by her own father. When neighbors heard her cries, they failed to intervene or report it because they viewed it as "a family matter."[14]

While visiting Mozambique, I joined colleagues from World Relief who were meeting with young people at a local church. One young woman stood to thank God for "making it through her

Christmas school holiday." Confused by her words, I later asked the pastor to explain what she meant. That's when I learned school holidays are particularly danger-ous for girls because that's when men return home from working in the mines in South Africa. She was grateful for not being raped during that time. But even more shockingly, I was told that girls in the local community—even in the church—were sometimes given by their own families to the mine

> *While violence against women and girls occurs in all societies, it is both more pervasive and less likely to be stopped or prosecuted when the victim lives in poverty.*

workers, in exchange for payment that the family used to buy food. The girl was thanking God for simply not having been violated during her school holiday.

## THE RIGHT TO NATIONALITY

Nationality laws pertain to the rights of citizenship, and the ability to pass citizenship to children and spouses. In most countries, a child's citizenship is determined by that of her parents. (Some countries, like the United States, also have provisions for conferring citizen-ship on anyone born on the country's soil.) However, "twenty-five countries still deny mothers the equal right to confer nationality on their children. Approximately fifty countries maintain other gender-discriminatory provisions in their nationality laws, such as denying women the right to equally confer nationality on spouses, or stripping women of their citizenship on the basis of their marital status," according to the Global Campaign for Equal Nationality Rights. "This coalition includes local, regional, and international NGOs, academics, civil society partners, UN agencies, and govern-ment allies across the globe."[15]

> *If a child does not have the right to her mother's nationality, she is at risk of becoming stateless.*

If a child does not have the right to her mother's nationality, she is at risk of becoming stateless. The UN Refugee Agency estimates that there are more than 10 million stateless individuals worldwide,[16] although other estimates are even higher. This can lead to the following dangers:

- **Domestic Violence:** Gender discrimination in nationality laws means a woman in an abusive marriage may have a very difficult time leaving her husband for fear of losing her own citizenship (if she acquired it through marriage) or being able to maintain custody of her own children, if their nationality is only conferred through the husband.

- **Human Trafficking:** Research has shown that stateless women and girls are at an increased risk of being trafficked. Statelessness is also linked with high poverty rates, marginalization, and exclusion—all factors exploited by traffickers.

- **Child Marriage:** Some families view early marriage as a route to greater security for their daughters, who can access citizenship and legal status through their husbands. But when a marriage is not registered (which often happens when underage marriages are against the law) and the country's laws only confer citizenship through the father, the children of the union can be rendered stateless.

- **Obstacles to Accessing Services:** Women and girls without citizenship often lack access to public healthcare, legal protection, work permits, and the right to public education.[17]

**DID YOU KNOW?**

**NATIONALITY DISCRIMINATION**

Countries that discriminate against mothers in their ability to confer nationality on their children: *Bahamas, Bahrain, Barbados, Brunei, Burundi, Eswatini [Swaziland], Iran, Iraq, Jordan, Kiribati, Kuwait, Lebanon, Liberia, Libya, Malaysia, Mauritania, Nepal, Oman, Qatar, Saudi Arabia, Somalia, Sudan, Syria, Togo, United Arab Emirates.*

Countries with gender-based discrimination pertaining to the conferral of nationality on spouses and/or acquire, change and retain her nationality: *Bahamas, Bahrain, Bangladesh, Barbados, Benin, Brunei, Burundi, Cameroon, Central African Republic, Comoros, Congo (Republic of), Egypt, Eswatini [Swaziland], Guatemala, Iran, Iraq, Jordan, Kiribati, Kuwait, Lebanon, Libya, Madagascar, Malawi, Malaysia, Mauritania, Morocco, Nepal, Nigeria, Oman, Pakistan, Philippines, Qatar, Saint Lucia, Saint Vincent and Grenadines, Saudi Arabia, Sierra Leone, Singapore, Somalia, Sudan, Syria, Tanzania, Thailand, Togo, Tunisia, United Arab Emirates, Yemen.*[18]

# THE RIGHT TO AVOID CHILD MARRIAGE

Child marriage is illegal in many countries because of the potential harm to the girl but also because it is considered harmful to society in general. According to UNICEF, "Marriage before the age of eighteen is a fundamental violation of human rights."[19]

Depending on the country, there are different legal approaches to child marriage. In many countries, child marriage is a crime. Other countries ban marriage below the legal minimum age but don't criminalize violations. And in some countries, child marriage is

> *Child marriage is illegal in many countries because of the potential harm to the girl but also because it is considered harmful to society in general.*

regulated through civil law, criminal law, or family law. Sometimes customary and religious laws are allowed to take precedent over other laws and may be interpreted by religious leaders, tribal leaders, or community tribunals.

Many countries allow exceptions to the legal minimum age of marriage, such as parental consent, authorization of the court, or the authorization of a religious leader.

In over fifty countries, the minimum legal age of marriage is lower for girls than boys.[20]

## LEGAL PROTECTION FROM FGM

The United Nations calls the practice of female genital mutilation (FGM) a violation of human rights of girls and women, and it is illegal in many countries. However, half of all girls at risk of being cut live in three countries: Egypt, Ethiopia, and Nigeria. While these countries have laws against FGM, enforcement is weak and prosecutions are rare. In Chad, Liberia, Mali, Sierra Leone, Somalia, and Sudan there are no laws against FGM.[21]

Many organizations are working to end the practice of FGM, including 28 Too Many, a UK organization so named for the twenty-eight countries where FGM still exists. Its goal is to have "a world where every girl and woman is safe, healthy and lives free from female genital mutilation."[22] It provides research and resources by country to those fighting the practice. Some NGOs are promoting alternative rites of passage (ARP) that use alternative rituals to celebrate a girl's transition to womanhood instead of FGM.

# THE AGE OF MAJORITY

The age of majority is when a minor is recognized legally as an adult and assumes legal control over their actions and decisions. Most countries set the age of majority at eighteen, but some have a higher age and others lower. Those under the age of majority are referred to as minors and may be legally denied certain privileges or rights.

Religions have their own rules as to the age of maturity, when a child is regarded to be an adult, which may influence—and even override—other laws in the case of marriage and other practices.

- Islam: Males who have entered puberty are considered adults. Females are considered adults when they have their first period.[23]
- Judaism: The age of majority is thirteen years for boys (bar mitzvah) and twelve years for girls (bat mitzvah) for religious purposes.[24]
- Roman Catholicism: The church considers eighteen the age of canonical majority, although seven is considered the age of reason and when Communion and confirmation at the earliest age may occur.[25]
- Baha'i Faith: At fifteen a person born into a Baha'i family is considered spiritually mature and old enough to decide for themselves what religion they want to be.[26]

In general, the age of majority[27] brings the rights and obligations to:

- Be considered capable.
- Leave a family home and parental control.
- Enter into contracts.
- Inherit, manage that inheritance, and, in countries where testaments exist, the possibility of testament.

- Receive bank credits and have bank accounts.
- Drive a vehicle.
- Work.
- Leave the country.
- Be sued for not paying debts or other contracts.
- Be charged with a crime as an adult and sentenced as an adult.

## THE RIGHT TO AVOID CONSCRIPTION

According to Human Rights Watch, "thousands of children are conscripted into the military and serve as soldiers in armed conflicts around the world. Boys and girls, some as young as eight years old, serve in both government forces and armed opposition groups. They may fight on the front lines, participate in suicide missions, and act as spies, messengers, or lookouts. Girls may be forced to serve as "wives" of the male soldiers or may simply be forced into sexual slavery."[28]

> *Thousands of children are conscripted into the military and serve as soldiers in armed conflicts around the world.*

Henrietta Fore, former executive director of UNICEF, notes that "Nearly 75 per cent of conflicts today involve recruitment of children, and well over half of these have included girls. The data also tell us that the longer a conflict continues, the more likely girls are to be recruited and exploited by armed actors."[29]

According to Fore, while boys are often recruited, girls are more like to be abducted. "A recent study of 37 active armed forces and groups conducted by Plan International and UNICEF found that half had abducted girls often targeting them because of their perceived submissiveness."[30]

UNICEF reports that girls are being used in conflicts in Afghanistan, Colombia, the Central African Republic, Nigeria, South Sudan, Syria, and Yemen.

## DID YOU KNOW?

**#WEARBLUEDAY**
January 11 is designated as #WearBlueDay, an event to bring attention to human trafficking and help educate the public to recognize and report it. In addition to wearing the color blue and posting photos on social media, the Department of Homeland Security offers resources to help foster discussions and organize events. To learn more: dhs.gov/blue-campaign /how-participate.

## PROTECTION AGAINST TRAFFICKING

The Protocol to Prevent, Suppress and Punish Trafficking in Persons Especially Women and Children, also called the Palermo Protocol, was adopted by the United Nations in 2000 as part of the United Nations Convention against Transnational Organized Crime. It provides the first internationally recognized definition of human trafficking to use as a tool for the identification of victims and for the detection of all forms of exploitation defined as human trafficking. Countries that ratify the treaty must agree to "criminalize human trafficking and develop anti-trafficking laws in line with the Protocol's legal provisions."[31]

In the United States, this led to the Trafficking Victims Protection Act and established an annual report called the Trafficking in Persons (TIP) report. The 2021 report found,

The economic and social distress generated by the pandemic and related mitigation efforts exacerbated risks for vulnerable and marginalized populations. These included women and children, people affected by travel restrictions and stay-at-home orders, communities in areas of food insecurity, and survivors of trafficking, as well as persons directly and indirectly affected by the disruption of economic activities and reduced livelihood options. Due to school closures, some children lacked access to education, shelter, and/or food.[32]

According to the US Department of Homeland Security, "The Blue Campaign is a national public awareness campaign designed to educate the American public to recognize the indicators of human trafficking and learn how to appropriately respond to possible cases."[33]

## CLOSING THOUGHTS

In some parts of the world, girls are still not afforded appropriate legal protection. In other places, laws are in place that are simply not observed or enforced. Cultural norms and societal pressures sometimes override the law and undermine its protections. Girls, especially those living in poverty, lack the voice and stature in society to be heard. It takes advocates, working on their behalf, to change their situation.

# 10

. . . . . . . . . . . . . . . .

# CHANGING THE
# WORLD FOR GIRLS

THE TENT PROVIDED PROTECTION from the blazing sun, but not from the heat that some women tried to beat back with pieces of paper they fanned in front of their faces. Even the local Zambian women were uncomfortable in the extreme heat of the dry season. But they had gathered for a purpose, and none of them seemed inclined to leave.

One woman rose and explained that this was a support group of women living with HIV. It was 2006, and more than a million Zambians had already died from AIDS. The impact on the country was devastating. Everyone seemed to have lost someone, and for many it was someone close. But these women were all receiving ART (antiretroviral treatment) and were here to talk about their experience.

The meeting started with prayer, as most meetings in this overwhelmingly Christian nation did. Then a woman named Mary[1] stood and said simply, "I was dead and now I'm alive." The dramatic words were clearly understood in this setting. People who had wasted away to the point of certain death were now receiving free treatments that literally brought them back from the brink and restored their health in weeks. It was such a miraculous transformation that it was now routinely called "the Lazarus effect,"[2] named after the biblical story of the man who had died and been raised from the dead by Jesus.[3]

Mary looked at me, the only American in the group, and asked me to thank the American people for PEPFAR (the President's Emergency Plan for AIDS Relief).[4] "Without it, we would all be dead," she said, as the other women nodded in agreement. While lifesaving ART had been available to the wealthy, women like Mary could not afford them before the US began funding the program. It was amazing to hear this woman speak in acronyms about a program most Americans wouldn't even recognize.

She then explained that she had lost her husband, sister, two brothers, and one child to AIDS. "I don't know why God spared me, but I'm grateful," she said. And then she went on to thank the neighbors who had brought her food and water when she was too sick to get out of bed and the friends who had carried her in a wheelbarrow to the clinic so she could get her treatment. The clinic was operated by the Centre for Infectious Disease Research in Zambia (CIDRZ), a nonprofit research and treatment group started by Zambian and American doctors responding to the AIDS crisis.[5] I was there representing the CIDRZ Foundation, the American arm that supported the work in Zambia. The neighbors were part of a group of community health-care workers trained by World Vision that checked on their neighbors and provided basic supplies. The support group was part of a program funded by the government of Sweden.

Mary's life—and millions of others—was saved by a combination of vast government programs, targeted NGOs, and individuals who saw needs around them and did what they could. While HIV/AIDS seemed like an insurmountable, overwhelming issue of the 1990s, the turn of the century saw a remarkable response at every level. The hope at the early stages of the crisis was that doctors and researchers would find a way to prevent or treat the disease. Remarkably, even all these years later, no cure has been found. Yet HIV-positive people live full and long lives, thanks to efforts at all levels.

> *Whenever I grow discouraged about what seems like an intractable problem, I think of the AIDS response: thousands of small efforts that saved millions of lives.*

Whenever I grow discouraged about what seems like an intractable problem, including the ways girls are treated in the world, I think of the AIDS response. There was no big solution. But there were thousands of smaller efforts that added up to saving millions of lives. Year by year, person by person, the cumulative efforts made a huge difference.

## HOW CHANGE HAPPENS

During the early years of Mary's disease,[6] most Americans were either unaware of the problem or assumed it was primarily a disease that affected men who were having sex with other men (MSM) or IV drug users. Some ministers called it punishment for sinful behavior, and some even felt money should not be spent on research for a cure.[7]

Rich Stearns was the relatively new president of World Vision in 2000, a time when AIDS had not only killed millions in Africa but had also orphaned an astounding ten million children.[8] Rich had previously run major corporations and was used to large-scale problem-solving, but his introduction to the world of suffering in developing countries tested his limits. On his first visit to Uganda, he was "heartbroken and angry" by the devastation he saw from the AIDS pandemic and wondered why more wasn't being done to help.[9]

I was on the World Vision board at the time and remember Rich coming to us with his conviction that the organization should do more to respond. It was a brave move for a new CEO. As he says in his book, "My staff knew that the evangelical community and the broader population had been more than apathetic about the issue of AIDS: they had been downright hostile toward it. . . . The prevailing view was that if you had AIDS, you deserved it."[10] As a board, we knew that the supporters of the organization at the time would not donate to the cause and, in fact, might stop giving to World Vision altogether if it seemed sympathetic to those living with AIDS. The organization commissioned a survey and found that only 3 percent of evangelical Christians would support work to help people who were infected or orphans.[11]

Rich felt that if Christians only understood the impact of AIDS on women and children, they would have compassion. In 2003, World Vision started something called "The Hope Tour" to help educate US Christian leaders about the crisis.[12] It was the beginning of World Vision's response and helped establish the organization as one of the leading NGOs responding to HIV/AIDS. In 2005, the organization joined with other NGOs to establish RAPIDS (Reaching HIV/AIDS Affected People with Integrated Development and Support). Other partners were Africare, CARE Zambia, Catholic Relief Services, Expanded Church Response Trust, and the Salvation Army. One of the components of the program was training caregivers who could check on their ill neighbors, like Mary, and the children who had become AIDS orphans. It was a unique program that empowered individuals to care for their own community with simple but effective interventions.

Around the same time, Kay Warren was also beginning to wake up to the crisis. In a talk to those gathered at Saddleback Church in 2008 she told the following story:

> A few years ago I was reading a magazine and saw a story about HIV and AIDS in Africa. Until that moment I didn't care about HIV and AIDS. To be honest I wasn't even sure what it was. But the article said that millions of people were infected with an incurable deadly virus and millions of children were being orphaned because of it.
>
> That day I saw the suffering of those living with HIV and AIDS for the first time. I wondered how it would feel to have my family abandon me because they were afraid they would catch my illness. Or what it would be like to be a child and have my mom and dad die, leaving me to grow up alone. Suddenly their pain became my pain, and it changed me forever.[13]

In 2004, Kay founded the HIV/AIDS Initiative at Saddleback and hosted an annual conference that brought together international leaders, government officials, NGO leaders, pastors, and laypeople. The result was a mobilization of Christians and enormous coordination of resources.

Shayne Moore was a self-described "soccer mom" when she heard U2's Bono speak in her town and became aware of the AIDS crisis. She knew she had to do something. So she took steps to educate herself and eventually played an active role in the ONE campaign and other efforts to fight AIDS. She details her journey in *Global Soccer Mom*.[14]

As someone who had seen the devastation in Africa for more

than a decade, I, too, was frustrated by how little Americans understood about the crisis and astounded by questions like, "Are there really that many gay people in Africa?" I began writing articles about what I had seen and ultimately wrote *The Skeptic's Guide to the Global AIDS Crisis.*[15]

Trying to find a way to raise awareness and connect individuals to the needs, I also started the AIDS Orphan Bracelet project. I hired women in Africa who were widowed or living with HIV to make simple bracelets from wood. Churches, organizations, or individuals in the United States ordered the bracelets, free of charge, from the website. They could then contribute whatever they wanted to a fund for supporting AIDS orphans. Each bracelet came with a card explaining the crisis and the need.

At the time, it seemed like a drop in the bucket. Many evenings I sat in my family room packing parcels of bracelets to ship and wondering if I was making a difference at all. One day as I boarded an airplane for a business trip, I saw a well-dressed woman wearing one of the bracelets. I asked her about it, and she began to tell me about the AIDS orphan crisis and said that the bracelet gave her the opportunity to inform business colleagues about a situation they weren't aware of but needed to know about. "I'm so grateful to know about the issue and be able to help," she said. I had tears in my eyes as I listened, too emotionally overcome to explain my connection with the bracelets. But her comment energized me to keep going with the project.

## YOU CAN CHANGE THE WORLD

In my experience, the seeds of change happen when we as individuals read, hear, see, or experience something that confuses or shocks us. Something that doesn't fit with what we already know. A fact that shakes our belief system and makes us ask, "How can that be?"

Psychologists call it cognitive dissonance.[16] It makes us feel uncomfortable and confused.

For many of us, the awareness that millions of people were dying of AIDS and innocent children were being orphaned while most Americans didn't know or care was shocking. But once

*In my experience, the seeds of change happen when we as individuals read, hear, see, or experience something that confuses or shocks us.*

we were aware, we had to do something—*anything*. As a writer, I responded with the tools I had.

It is the same for the issue of empowering our girls around the world. For me, the birth of my granddaughter has reminded me of all the little girls in the world who will not have the same opportunities as she has. Girls who have as much potential to do great things, but who have been born in the wrong place in the world, without access to clean water, medicine, education, and legal protection. Innocent little girls subjected to the worst of the world. It has made me say, I must do *something*. This book is part of my contribution while I continue to learn about more ways that I can help remove obstacles for girls.

In their very practical book *Impact*,[17] Christen Brandt and Tammy Tibbetts, founders of the organization She's the First, explain how to create a plan for making an impact in the world. The book is full of helpful questions and checklists but also stories that illustrate how good intentions need to be tempered with education, understanding, and an examination of motives. They also demonstrate how we can be misguided in our actions and end up doing more harm than good, propelled forward by our own needs to feel like a hero or savior. It doesn't mean we shouldn't try. But it is a fair and important caution.

Books like *When Helping Hurts*[18] and *More Than Good Intentions*[19] also explain how good works can go wrong and how meaning well isn't good enough. *How to Be Great at Doing Good* is an important look at how we can do a better job of examining the charities we support.[20] All of these resources are important because making a difference in the world takes work and wisdom. None of this is meant to dampen enthusiasm or let anyone off the hook. Everyone has a part to play in making the world more just. But we have to proceed with humility.

## WHAT YOU CAN DO

### FINDING YOUR "NORTH STAR"

In *Impact*, authors Christen Brandt and Tammy Tibbetts challenge readers to find their "North Star"—an end goal or future you want to see. The goal should be something that moves you personally and offers a tangible goal to achieve.

As you read this book, think of something that connected with you. Would you like to see a world in which FGM is outlawed? Do you want to see disabled girls treated with dignity? Do you want to put an end to laws that discriminate against girls? By helping identify a specific issue you want to pursue and an outcome you'd like to see, you begin to develop an action plan that can help you make a real difference in the lives of girls. You can use the Impact Plan Workbook in their book to help you brainstorm and create your own plan.

Reading this book is a first step to educating yourself about the challenges and opportunities facing girls. We all can be part of the solution. Ponder and pray about what you have read and the part you can play in making a difference. Then take the next step.

In *The Blue Sweater*, Jacqueline Novogratz tells the story of meeting a Buddhist monk and seeking his wisdom:

"If you move through the world only with your intellect," he said, in a direct and clear voice, "then you walk on only one leg." With his hands held in prayer, he lifted one leg and slowly and deliberately hopped three times. With the same deliberation and pace, he restored his foot to the floor. After a long breath, he started again.

"If you move through the world only with your compassion," he said, lifting his other leg, "then you walk on only one leg." Again, he hopped three times.

"But if you move through the world with both intellect and compassion, then you have wisdom." He walked slowly and gracefully, taking three long, slow strides.[21]

I'll admit I have been hopping on one foot at times, lacking the wisdom to combine my compassion with intellect. And I have also made the mistake of trying to impose my solutions on others' problems.

Evie's parents—my son and daughter-in-law—are wonderful, loving, and attentive. They adore their daughter and want the very best for her. I often marvel at what wonderful parents they truly are. And yet when I visit, I sometimes ask a question or say something about Evie that sounds a bit "prescriptive." Most days they have the patience and good humor to push back or say something kind but firm, and I realize that I have been doing the stereotypical grandmother meddling. When I look at myself, I see that this inclination grows out of my love for Evie, my own experiences, and my natural tendencies to be a problem solver. If Evie's parents have mentioned a problem and asked for my input, that's one thing. But when I decide to become a problem solver on my own, that is something altogether different. They live with Evie every day. I am a visitor who gets to spoil her and then go home.

When it comes to other girls in the world, as much as I want everything for them that I want for Evie, the same principles apply. I can assume I know what the outcome should be, using my own experience and desire to problem solve, and before I know it, do more harm than good. I can drop in and put a bandage on a problem, only to leave others to clean up the mess I may have caused. It takes time and humility to learn what your place is in helping girls soar.

> *It takes time and humility to learn what your place is in helping girls soar.*

## EDUCATION

Learning more is always the right first step. If in reading this book, certain issues have particularly stirred your soul or upset you, pay attention to that. As a person of faith, I have learned to pray, "Show me what is mine to do." I can easily become overwhelmed with the needs of the world, so I really need divine guidance. If you have been struck by a fact or situation described in this book that created cognitive dissonance, perhaps it is a holy stirring that means you should learn more.

If, for example, you are moved by the subject of human trafficking, there are many helpful books to read, including those I've referenced. There are organizations like International Justice Mission and the Polaris Project working on an international level that have outstanding resources on their websites. By learning more, it may become obvious how you can help. For example, when I began to study the issue of trafficking, I was shocked to find that there were many local organizations combating it in my own region. I had no idea that I lived in an area where girls were actively being recruited. The problem I assumed existed far away was also in my own backyard. Stopping international trafficking continues to be a concern, but now I am more educated about what I can do in my own community and how I can help educate my neighbors about saving girls in our own state. I have found tangible, helpful steps that I didn't even realize I could take.

I have also learned to listen to those who have lived closest to the issues. When I began to research the challenges surrounding education of girls, I didn't know about the obstacles girls faced to remain in school once they started menstruating. I also didn't understand the importance of creating affordable and accessible private schools. Listening to TED Talks by women who had experienced these issues and were creating the solutions themselves was inspiring and helped me understand how to support their efforts, not make up my own solutions out of limited understanding.

When you read about organizations like Casa de Luz, Chikumbuso, the Mekuno Project, and Parfums de Vie that were all started by individuals, it's helpful to remember that these people spent a great deal of time listening and learning before they responded. In fact, when I interviewed each of them, I discovered that they had each originally expected to do something entirely different.

Nicole and Vincent Derieux came to the French Riviera expecting to help start a church for the wealthy of the region. Instead, they ended up working with the children of those who worked for the rich. They came to the region, met people, and listened. They educated themselves about the problems. Once they understood how the children were falling through the cracks, they responded. But even then, their work has evolved as they have learned more about the best ways to help.

One of the strengths of Jacqueline Novogratz's story is how she describes her own failed attempts to respond to needs and how often she was misguided instead of helpful. She shines a light on her missteps but never gives up. Without everything she learned, she never would have founded the Acumen Fund.

There is always more to learn. I have had the privilege of visiting many countries and interacting with many people. While I have been able to write stories from those trips, I'm aware that I sometimes traveled out of my own sense of adventure. My presence took people away from doing their jobs, and my questions were intrusions into the lives of those who were already dealing with enough problems. My quest for knowledge came at their expense, and I regret that I sometimes justified "telling their story," instead of simply listening. It is part of my ongoing education.

Nonprofit organizations often invite donors to go on "vision trips." These organized trips, usually overseas, help donors see the difference their money is making and hopefully inspire them to give more. Some critics view them as a waste of money and suggest that the cost of travel could be better spent as a donation to the organization. Personally, I think vision trips can educate people very effectively and change their perspective in many helpful ways. But it is important to understand that the cost of going and the time spent with staff is a drain on the organization. Generally speaking, do not just show up in a country and expect to see the work of an organization you support. Especially with organizations that work with children, having strangers show up without background checks or prior approval undermines the safety of the children.

> *I think vision trips can educate people very effectively and change their perspective in many helpful ways.*

## WHAT YOU CAN DO

### GO ON A VISION TRIP

If you are offered the chance to go on a trip with an organization you support, ask questions about the purpose, the actual cost, and what is expected from you in return. Do your homework ahead of time about the country you are visiting, the projects you will see, the challenges the organization is facing, and what, if anything, Americans can do to help. Spend your time on the trip listening to people and what they are experiencing, not asking questions that could be found on the internet. Budget time and energy when you return to sharing your experience with your member of Congress, writing a letter to the editor, or speaking to your church missions committee. Consider your trip an investment in your understanding and find ways to pass that experience on to others.

Most organizations charge a fee to help cover the costs of a trip to the organization. They typically also require travelers to obtain travel insurance as well as immunizations required for travel in the region.

# ADVOCACY

Perhaps one of the most effective things Americans can do is advocate for others. We have the power to make our voices heard in numerous ways. Advocacy doesn't necessarily mean a trip to your representative's or senator's office. It can be sharing what you have learned with friends, suggesting a thought-provoking book for your book club, or inviting an expert to speak to your Rotary club, Sunday school, or other group. You can recommend a book to your public library or invite a guest speaker to your home and educate your friends.

When Boko Haram kidnapped the Nigerian schoolgirls in 2014,

*Perhaps one of the most effective things Americans can do is advocate for others.*

parents and others felt the government had been slow and inadequate in their response, but those who protested within the country were shut down and detained. Attention increased when celebrities, including First Lady Michelle Obama, began to tweet #BringBackOurGirls. The media presence brought increased pressure on the Nigerian government, but some said it also made the girls more valuable to Boko Haram, and therefore less likely to be released. But without the advocacy of Americans and others, many believe the girls would have been quickly forgotten except by their families.

We all have spheres of influence. Twitter, Facebook, Instagram, Pinterest, LinkedIn, and other social media platforms give us a voice to the world and a way to help others know what is important to us. Sharing the posts of groups working on issues of concern is a great way to begin expanding the message. For smaller groups, following them and sharing their messages is vitally important to their work.

Letters and emails to the editor of your local paper are more

## WHAT YOU CAN DO

### SIGN UP FOR ADVOCACY ALERTS

Some of the larger NGOs have advocacy departments that not only work with legislators but also keep the organization's supporters involved. CARE has an excellent program. Sign up for information at care.org/our-work/advocacy/connect/. World Vision also provides advocacy tools and updates and engages with a community of volunteers. Find out more at worldvisionadvocacy.org/.

important than most people realize. When I worked in a newsroom, I was surprised by how few people took the time to write and how much the editors listened when we received some correspondence. When readers suggested story ideas, they were often carefully considered by the editor.

Many of the larger nonprofit organizations have advocacy departments that alert followers to an issue before Congress. Because I signed up to receive advocacy alerts, I learn about many issues that I can weigh in on by easily filling out a form and writing to my senators and members of Congress. I can also attend advocacy days in Washington, DC, where I receive more education about the issues and join others in meeting with representatives. The programs are valuable ways to understand how our government works, how we can advocate for resources to help girls (such as the Keeping Girls in School Act), and meet others who are passionate about the same issues.

## WHAT YOU CAN DO

### USE YOUR INFLUENCE

Wondering how to make your voice heard? Wishing you knew how to make social media more effective? Don't know how to contact your member of Congress? Oxfam has a free guide (*How to Take Action Organizing in Your Community*) to help you get started. Download it today and get started taking simple steps to make a difference at s3.amazonaws .com/oxfam-us/www/static/media/files/2018-How_to_Take _Action_Organizer_Guide_toolkit.pdf.

## VOLUNTEER

We've probably all volunteered at a bake sale, church event, or school fair. But there are many opportunities to support worthy organizations near our homes or even abroad. In your own community, mentoring girls is a wonderful way to invest in their future. Many schools have mentoring programs and need adults to encourage girls and help them find a path forward. There are also tutoring programs (both in person and virtual) to help students struggling in school.

In my community, a local church has recognized that many new moms need diapers, formula, clothes, and other items for their babies, so the church created an online wish list and set up a location to drop off items. It's a wonderful program that helps nearby food banks and shelters.

## WHAT YOU CAN DO

### VOLUNTEER OPPORTUNITIES

One of the easiest ways to find volunteer opportunities is to go to VolunteerMatch, a website that consolidates and posts volunteer activities by interest and city. It also includes virtual volunteer opportunities such as making calls, editing and writing materials, online tutoring, and helping with computer programming. Charitable organizations post onetime opportunities and ongoing volunteer positions. Find out more at volunteermatch.org. Idealist also includes volunteer opportunities as well as part- and full-time jobs and internships in the nonprofit sector. Go to idealist.org/en/.

At my church, a volunteer contacts our local food banks and shelters to learn what nonperishable items they need. Then each month our church places a bin in the foyer to collect one particular item for the month. It's easy to pick up an extra item at the grocery store and drop it off on the way to church. It's another program that could be started anywhere. Women's shelters often post a list of needs as well, usually personal care items.

Teaching English to non-native speakers either in the United States or abroad is a wonderful way to help newcomers to the country or those who are struggling to improve their skills. Although teaching English as a foreign language (TEFL) is a certified program offered by many online schools and colleges, many programs simply need volunteers to help with lessons that are often taught in churches and libraries. You can search for refugee services in your area, which are typically managed by one or more nonprofits.

World Relief, Lutheran Immigration and Refugee Services, and Church World Services are just some of the refugee resettlement organizations operating by region.[22] Many need clothing and household goods for settling refugees as well as individuals to help tutor refugee children, teach families the basics of living in a new country, and help them find employment.

## WHAT YOU CAN DO

### VOLUNTEER TO HELP REFUGEES
The International Rescue Committee offers a list of volunteer opportunities (by city) to work with refugees in the United States. Learn more at rescue.org/volunteer.

Some organizations encourage people to go overseas for volunteer experiences. Sometimes called "voluntourism,"[23] they often include some sort of building project or visit to an orphanage to help care for children. Sometimes churches take mission trips. These types of trips have been criticized for spending resources ineffectively. "Money goes far in poor countries. Two thousand dollars can pay for a weeklong trip by an unskilled American volunteer—or it could pay the salary of a village teacher for four months."[24] Some overseas organizations tailor the experience to what they think Americans want to do, whether it's helpful or not. But there are many ways to make these types of trips more effective and meet the needs of the local community.

Local clinics often need medicines that can be carried over by volunteers. International Medical Relief provides a list of medical missions of various lengths of time going to different regions of the world (some domestic) and the expertise needed.[25] Most need medical and nonmedical volunteers to fill various roles.

For example, when I traveled with the Syrian American Medical Society (SAMS) on a weeklong trip to Jordan, I took along a suitcase full of donated medicines from MAP International, took photos, helped get patient information, cared for children while the parents were examined and treated, and provided support for the doctors and nurses who were working nonstop.

On a mission trip to the Dominican Republic, our church supplied over-the-counter medications as well as donated stethoscopes, thermometers, bandages, and vitamins. The church we partnered with in the DR found doctors who offered free checkups and medicine for people in their neighborhood. The church was able to provide a valuable service to its community, where even middle-class people can't afford medical services.

As we've discussed, the foster care system needs more loving families to help give girls, especially, a stable home. If fostering seems like too much of a commitment, short-term or emergency fostering offers a child in need a safe place to stay for a night or a few days.[26] Emergency foster homes are always needed.

> *Volunteering doesn't have to be long-term. But being willing to go just once and help a local organization can be life changing.*

Volunteering doesn't have to be long-term. But being willing to go just once and help a local organization can be life changing.

# DONATIONS

Donating to a charity is probably the way most of us get involved in global issues. Many of the organizations I've mentioned operate on a global level but implement their work through community-level organizations. These nonprofits generally enjoy a tax-exempt status in the United States because they are raising funds to use in charitable work, not aiming to make a profit. Donors to such organizations receive a tax-deduction for their donation. They are sometimes referred to as 501(c)(3)s, an IRS designation that details their purposes.

Charitable organizations can be large (World Vision, UNICEF, CARE, Save the Children) or small (Chikumbuso). Many times the organization that operates in the United States or other developed countries exists to raise funds for the work overseas. This is sometimes called a "friends of" organization or may be organized as a foundation that raises funds to meet the needs of the in-country work. While you don't need to know everything about a charity to give to it, it is important to educate yourself about the group and how it operates.

According to the IRS,

The exempt purposes set forth in section 501(c)(3) are charitable, religious, educational, scientific, literary, testing for public safety, fostering national or international amateur sports competition, and preventing cruelty to children or animals. The term *charitable* is used in its generally accepted legal sense and includes relief of the poor, the distressed, or the underprivileged; advancement of religion; advancement of education or science; erecting or maintaining public buildings, monuments, or works; lessening the burdens of government; lessening neighborhood tensions; eliminating prejudice and discrimination; defending human and civil rights secured by law; and combating community deterioration and juvenile delinquency.[27]

Often the US branch of the organization operates in partnership with offices headquartered in other countries. And some groups, like charity: water, exist to raise funds and bring attention to issues, then fund projects operated by local partners. Some groups primarily offer goods, such as medicine or medical equipment, to partners overseas. These are sometimes referred to as "in kind" or gifts in kind (GIK) organizations. Many large nonprofits have a GIK component in which companies donate needed products to the group that are then sent overseas to be distributed. Donations pay for the handling and shipping costs.

GlobalGiving is a great place to start if you don't know where to give.[28] It offers a wish list of projects from various organizations and allows you to search by interest. When I searched the site for projects benefiting girls, I found 1,144 different programs to support with goals from $10,000 to over $100,000.

## DID YOU KNOW?

### CHARITY INFORMATION

If you are supporting a charitable organization, you should take a few minutes to learn more about it. Go to Charity Navigator (charitynavigator.org/) or GuideStar (guidestar .org/) and look up your charity. You'll find the group rated on a variety of factors, including efficiency. You can even learn how much the top executives are paid and what percentage of donations go to overhead.

Connecting personally through a group like Kiva, where you can choose a person to receive a loan, is another way to feel like you are supporting an individual and can be a great learning tool for the entire family.[29] Another way to connect is through child sponsorship. While child sponsorship has had its critics, most organizations that offer sponsorships have evolved from the days when a child was the only recipient of the aid to a model that offers support to the entire community in which that child lives. So if you sponsor a girl, she will have her school fee covered, but part of the funding will also make sure she and other members of her community get clean water. Our family has sponsored World Vision children for many years, and our sponsored children connected my sons to the rest of the world. My sons helped write letters to the children and picked out small gifts we could send along with our sponsorship. World Vision, Compassion, Food for the Hungry, Plan International, Save the Children, ChildFund, and many others have sponsorship programs.

*If you sponsor a girl through most charitable organizations, she will have her school fee covered, but part of the funding will also make sure she and other members of her community get clean water.*

Donating to a large group doesn't have to feel impersonal. Many of the large charities sponsor local runs or help you use a local run to raise funds. You can find charity runs all over the country at the RunGuides site.[30] Many groups also sponsor walks or other activities that have local components but support the larger program.

Other sports events include golf and bicycling. Golf Fore Africa was established in 2007 by LPGA Hall of Fame golfer Betsy King, who has used her passion for golf to help raise funds that provide clean water to Africa.[31] Now she brings golfers together for tournaments, clinics, and other events that raise money for wells in Africa. Brake the Cycle, an annual event that is part of the Aspen Invitational Bike Ride, raises funds for bicycles and clean water in Zambia.[32]

Donating to organizations that care specifically for the needs of girls is important. As I researched this book, I discovered some smaller charities that I will be including in my future giving. But I also know that giving to such causes as organizations digging wells or stopping trafficking changes the lives of girls as well.

> Donating to organizations that care specifically for the needs of girls is important.

I sometimes donate to specific causes within a larger organization. This is called designated giving and means that my donation must go to the project or specific cause I have requested. Asking to support work with girls is a legitimate request and one that would be honored by most organizations.

## CLOSING THOUGHTS

Writing this book was a way for me to both educate myself and respond to the needs of girls in the world. But it is only a start. We all have power through our voices, time, influence, and resources. Choosing to use that power to help girls can and will make a difference. Learning more, deciding where to concentrate, simply being aware of the needs is a beginning. Thank you for taking this first step with me.

# Acknowledgments

WHEN I BEGAN TO TRAVEL to what is often called the developing world—places where people lived with so much less than I enjoyed—I was in shock. I journeyed with guides who listened to my naive exclamations and simplistic questions with patience and kindness. Some of them were humanitarian workers, some were translators, some were drivers. I wish I had recorded all their names because they deserve credit for helping me make sense of so much. My profound thanks to all of you who took time to share your wisdom and help me understand what I was seeing.

Serving on the boards of international humanitarian organizations has been an incredible privilege, and I am indebted to the staffs of World Vision, Opportunity International, MAP International, and International Justice Mission for offering guidance, explanations, and an ongoing education. The wonderful women who are part of Strong Women Strong World and Oxfam's Sisters on the Planet continue to inspire me.

This book is really the product of so many people who invested in it and gave me the tools to write it. Special thanks to Kathryn Compton, Whitney Groves, Margo Day, Chris Hardy, Emily Nielsen Jones, Jane Sutton-Redner, Joan Mussa, Linda Wilkinson, Jodi Allison, Kristie Urich, Debbie Christian, Karen Piatt, and Martha Holley Newsome. This book would not exist without you.

My agent, Steve Laube, and the Tyndale House team believed in this book from its earliest days. I am especially grateful to Jan Long Harris, who is passionate about its message. Jillian Schlossberg shaped the manuscript when COVID played havoc with our original outline, and she made it a much stronger book in the end. Bonne Steffen did wonders with my often awkward wording, and her team, including Annette Hayward and Stephanie Brockway, checked facts, revised endnotes, and vastly improved what I had given them. If there are still mistakes, they are mine. Designer Lindsey Bergsma brilliantly added visual elements to make the pages more inviting than overwhelming. I'm so grateful that the finished product is more than anything I could have done on my own.

To friends who encouraged me when I was struggling to write, I truly couldn't have done it without your support. Pam Green, Laura Baker, Amy Low, Jennifer Klepper, and Peggy and Robb Cecil were all there for me when I needed them. Thank you.

My first grandchild, Evie, is the inspiration for this book, and I'm grateful that her parents, Mary Brighid and Tyler, allowed me to share details about her with the world. They are amazing parents to her and little Tommy, and I am grateful that they are willing to let us be so involved with our grandchildren. Thanks, too, to Chase and Valerie, for their love and support during the years it took to write this and the years of living through my travels.

Finally, my husband, Tom, has been not only the greatest support on this book, he has encouraged me no matter where in the world I planned to go and believed in every project I've taken on. He has been beyond patient as I've disappeared to write or travel, and he has believed in me when I wasn't sure of myself. I love you and I'm so grateful for you.

And to those of you who have read this book, thank you for being willing to invest in girls by educating yourself. May you be part of making the world a better place.

# Appendix

. . . . . . . . . . . . . . . . . . . . . . . . . . . . . . . . .

# UNITED NATIONS CONVENTION ON THE RIGHTS OF THE CHILD

*The Children's Version*

THIS IS A LEGAL, INTERNATIONALLY BINDING TREATY on the rights of children around the world.[1]

## 1. DEFINITION OF A CHILD
A child is any person under the age of 18.

## 2. NO DISCRIMINATION
All children have all these rights, no matter who they are, where they live, what language they speak, what their religion is, what they think, what they look like, if they are a boy or girl, if they have a disability, if they are rich or poor, and no matter who their parents or families are or what their parents or families believe or do. No child should be treated unfairly for any reason.

## 3. BEST INTERESTS OF THE CHILD
When adults make decisions, they should think about how their decisions will affect children. All adults should do what is best for children. Governments should make sure children are protected and looked after by their parents, or by other people when this is

needed. Governments should make sure that people and places responsible for looking after children are doing a good job.

### 4. MAKING RIGHTS REAL

Governments must do all they can to make sure that every child in their countries can enjoy all the rights in this Convention.

### 5. FAMILY GUIDANCE AS CHILDREN DEVELOP

Governments should let families and communities guide their children so that, as they grow up, they learn to use their rights in the best way. The more children grow, the less guidance they will need.

### 6. LIFE SURVIVAL AND DEVELOPMENT

Every child has the right to be alive. Governments must make sure that children survive and develop in the best possible way.

### 7. NAME AND NATIONALITY

Children must be registered when they are born and given a name which is officially recognized by the government. Children must have a nationality (belong to a country). Whenever possible, children should know their parents and be looked after by them.

### 8. IDENTITY

Children have the right to their own identity—an official record of who they are which includes their name, nationality and family relations. No one should take this away from them, but if this happens, governments must help children to quickly get their identity back.

### 9. KEEPING FAMILIES TOGETHER

Children should not be separated from their parents unless they are not being properly looked after—for example, if a parent hurts or does not take care of a child. Children whose parents don't live together should stay in contact with both parents unless this might harm the child.

## 10. CONTACT WITH PARENTS ACROSS COUNTRIES

If a child lives in a different country than their parents, governments must let the child and parents travel so that they can stay in contact and be together.

## 11. PROTECTION FROM KIDNAPPING

Governments must stop children being taken out of the country when this is against the law—for example, being kidnapped by someone or held abroad by a parent when the other parent does not agree.

## 12. RESPECT FOR CHILDREN'S VIEWS

Children have the right to give their opinions freely on issues that affect them. Adults should listen and take children seriously.

## 13. SHARING THOUGHTS FREELY

Children have the right to share freely with others what they learn, think and feel, by talking, drawing, writing or in any other way unless it harms other people.

## 14. FREEDOM OF THOUGHT AND RELIGION

Children can choose their own thoughts, opinions and religion, but this should not stop other people from enjoying their rights. Parents can guide children so that as they grow up, they learn to properly use this right.

## 15. SETTING UP OR JOINING GROUPS

Children can join or set up groups or organisations, and they can meet with others, as long as this does not harm other people.

## 16. PROTECTION OF PRIVACY

Every child has the right to privacy. The law must protect children's privacy, family, home, communications and reputation (or good name) from any attack.

## 17. ACCESS TO INFORMATION

Children have the right to get information from the Internet, radio, television, newspapers, books and other sources. Adults should make sure the information they are getting is not harmful. Governments should encourage the media to share information from lots of different sources, in languages that all children can understand.

## 18. RESPONSIBILITY OF PARENTS

Parents are the main people responsible for bringing up a child. When the child does not have any parents, another adult will have this responsibility and they are called a "guardian". Parents and guardians should always consider what is best for that child. Governments should help them. Where a child has both parents, both of them should be responsible for bringing up the child.

## 19. PROTECTION FROM VIOLENCE

Governments must protect children from violence, abuse and being neglected by anyone who looks after them.

## 20. CHILDREN WITHOUT FAMILIES

Every child who cannot be looked after by their own family has the right to be looked after properly by people who respect the child's religion, culture, language and other aspects of their life.

## 21. CHILDREN WHO ARE ADOPTED

When children are adopted, the most important thing is to do what is best for them. If a child cannot be properly looked after in their own country—for example by living with another family—then they might be adopted in another country.

## 22. REFUGEE CHILDREN

Children who move from their home country to another country as refugees (because it was not safe for them to stay there) should get help and protection and have the same rights as children born in that country.

## 23. CHILDREN WITH DISABILITIES

Every child with a disability should enjoy the best possible life in society. Governments should remove all obstacles for children with disabilities to become independent and to participate actively in the community.

## 24. HEALTH, WATER, FOOD, ENVIRONMENT

Children have the right to the best health care possible, clean water to drink, healthy food and a clean and safe environment to live in. All adults and children should have information about how to stay safe and healthy.

## 25. REVIEW OF A CHILD'S PLACEMENT

Every child who has been placed somewhere away from home— for their care, protection or health—should have their situation checked regularly to see if everything is going well and if this is still the best place for the child to be.

## 26. SOCIAL AND ECONOMIC HELP

Governments should provide money or other support to help children from poor families.

## 27. FOOD, CLOTHING, A SAFE HOME

Children have the right to food, clothing and a safe place to live so they can develop in the best possible way. The government should help families and children who cannot afford this.

## 28. ACCESS TO EDUCATION

Every child has the right to an education. Primary education should be free. Secondary and higher education should be available to every child. Children should be encouraged to go to school to the highest level possible. Discipline in schools should respect children's rights and never use violence.

## 29. AIMS OF EDUCATION

Children's education should help them fully develop their personalities, talents and abilities. It should teach them to understand their own rights, and to respect other people's rights, cultures and differences. It should help them to live peacefully and protect the environment.

## 30. MINORITY CULTURE, LANGUAGE AND RELIGION

Children have the right to use their own language, culture and religion—even if these are not shared by most people in the country where they live.

## 31. REST, PLAY, CULTURE, ARTS

Every child has the right to rest, relax, play and to take part in cultural and creative activities.

## 32. PROTECTION FROM HARMFUL WORK

Children have the right to be protected from doing work that is dangerous or bad for their education, health or development. If children work, they have the right to be safe and paid fairly.

## 33. PROTECTION FROM HARMFUL DRUGS

Governments must protect children from taking, making, carrying or selling harmful drugs.

## 34. PROTECTION FROM SEXUAL ABUSE

The government should protect children from sexual exploitation (being taken advantage of) and sexual abuse, including by people forcing children to have sex for money, or making sexual pictures or films of them.

## 35. PREVENTION OF SALE AND TRAFFICKING

Governments must make sure that children are not kidnapped or sold, or taken to other countries or places to be exploited (taken advantage of).

## 36. PROTECTION FROM EXPLOITATION

Children have the right to be protected from all other kinds of exploitation (being taken advantage of), even if these are not specifically mentioned in this Convention.

## 37. CHILDREN IN DETENTION

Children who are accused of breaking the law should not be killed, tortured, treated cruelly, put in prison forever, or put in prison with adults. Prison should always be the last choice and only for the shortest possible time. Children in prison should have legal help and be able to stay in contact with their family.

## 38. PROTECTION IN WAR

Children have the right to be protected during war. No child under 15 can join the army or take part in war.

## 39. RECOVERY AND REINTEGRATION

Children have the right to get help if they have been hurt, neglected, treated badly or affected by war, so they can get back their health and dignity.

## 40. CHILDREN WHO BREAK THE LAW

Children accused of breaking the law have the right to legal help and fair treatment. There should be lots of solutions to help these children become good members of their communities. Prison should only be the last choice.

### 41. BEST LAW FOR CHILDREN APPLIES

If the laws of a country protect children's rights better than this Convention, then those laws should be used.

### 42. EVERYONE MUST KNOW CHILDREN'S RIGHTS

Governments should actively tell children and adults about this Convention so that everyone knows about children's rights.

### 43 TO 54. HOW THE CONVENTION WORKS

These articles explain how governments, the United Nations—including the Committee on the Rights of the Child and UNICEF—and other organisations work to make sure all children enjoy all their rights.

# Notes

**INTRODUCTION: IT'S PERSONAL**

1. Leslie Stahl, *Becoming Grandma: The Joys and Science of the New Grandparenting* (New York: Blue Rider Press, 2016), 1.
2. "How Many Babies Are Born Each Day?," The World Counts, accessed October 14, 2022, https://www.theworldcounts.com/stories/how-many-babies-are-born-each-day.
3. "Under-Five Mortality," UNICEF, last updated December 2021, https://data.unicef.org/topic/child-survival/under-five-mortality/.
4. Bill and Melinda Gates Foundation, *The Goalkeepers Report 2019: Examining Inequality* (Seattle: Bill and Melinda Gates Foundation, 2019), 14, https://www.gatesfoundation.org/goalkeepers/report/2019-report.
5. "7 Ways to Empower Women and Girls," World Vision, "#EndChildMarriage: 10-Year-Old Shemema's Poem," video, 1:21, https://www.worldvision.org/gender-equality-news-stories/seven-ways-empower-women-girls.
6. Child marriage (under eighteen) is illegal in Ghana but is still too common in some rural areas.
7. Musimbi Kanyoro, "To Solve the World's Biggest Problems, Invest in Women and Girls," TEDWomen, New Orleans, November 2017, video, 14:21, https://www.ted.com/talks/musimbi_kanyoro_to_solve_the_world_s_biggest_problems_invest_in_women_and_girls/.
8. Peter Dizikes, "The Meaning of the Butterfly," Boston.com, June 8, 2008, http://archive.boston.com/bostonglobe/ideas/articles/2008/06/08/the_meaning_of_the_butterfly/.
9. See The World Counts, accessed January 17, 2023, https://www.theworldcounts.com/challenges/toxic-exposures/polluted-bodies/how-many-babies-are-born-a-day.
10. The number of children under five who died from preventable causes in 1985.
11. Richard Stearns, *The Hole in Our Gospel* (Nashville: Thomas Nelson, 2009), 251.
12. Used in a speech by Chris Crane, then-president of Opportunity International; attributed to various sources, also using "Snakes and Ladders."
13. Gina Wright Buser: Advocate for Women," World Vision, accessed October 15, 2022, https://www.worldvisionphilanthropy.org/hubfs/All%20Newsletters/EE%20Newsletter/Gina%20Buser%20-%20Advocate%20for%20Women.pdf.

**CHAPTER 1: HELPING GIRLS SOAR**

1. Shekhar Mehta, "Leave No Girl Behind," speech, Rotary International virtual convention, June 2021, https://www.rotary.org/en/leave-no-girl-behind.

2. Jenni Lee, "5 Reasons Why Empowering Girls Matters," *Girls and Women* (blog), United Nations Foundation, October 7, 2015, https://unfoundation.org/blog/post/5-reasons-why-empowering-girls-matters/.

3. "Girls' Education," World Bank, last updated February 10, 2022, https://www.worldbank.org/en/topic/girlseducation.

4. Maria Eitel, "The Nike Foundation on Unleashing the 'Girl Effect,'" interview by Rahim Kanani, HuffPost, April 20, 2011, https://www.huffpost.com/entry/nike-foundation-girl-effect_b_850551.

5. The Girl Effect is now an independent nonprofit organization. To learn more, see https://www.girleffect.org/.

6. Eitel, "Nike Foundation."

7. "Elaborate Airplane 'Gender Reveal' Stunt," SWNS, July 18, 2018, video, 1:14, https://www.youtube.com/watch?v=R6yqA8sVW34.

8. Stevan Harrell, "Patriliny, Patriarchy, Patrimony: Surface Features and Deep Structures in the Chinese Family System," University of Washington (faculty web server), accessed October 15, 2022, https://faculty.washington.edu/stevehar/PPP.html.

9. Joseph Chamie, "Gender Imbalances: Missing Girls and Vanishing Men," PassBlue, March 31, 2020, https://www.passblue.com/2020/03/31/gender-imbalances-missing-girls-and-vanishing-men/.

10. John Feng, "China Has Nearly 35 Million More Single Men than Women," *Newsweek*, May 18, 2021, https://www.newsweek.com/china-has-nearly-35-million-more-single-men-women-1592486.

11. Jackie Ogega, *Home Is Us: A Story about Hope and Resilience* (self-pub., 2022). Today Dr. Jackie Ogega is the senior director of Gender Equality and Social Inclusion at World Vision.

12. Robin N. Haarr, "The Girl Child," in "Rights of the Girl Child," in *Global Women's Issues: Women in the World Today*, extended version (British Columbia Open Textbook Collection, 2012, chap. 12, https://opentextbc.ca/womenintheworld/chapter/chapter-12-rights-of-the-girl-child/.

13. Nicholas D. Kristof and Sheryl WuDunn, *Half the Sky: Turning Oppression into Opportunity for Women Worldwide* (New York: Vintage Books, 2010), xvii.

14. "International Day of the Girl Child: October 11," United Nations, accessed October 16, 2022, https://www.un.org/en/observances/girl-child-day.

15. Natalia López, "Girls: Victims of Double Discrimination," trans. Holly-Anne Whyte, Humanium, accessed October 16, 2022, https://www.humanium.org/en/girls-rights/.

16. "Always #LikeAGirl Campaign Ad: 'Super Bowl XLIX,'" Cause Marketing, October 8, 2016, video, 1:14, https://www.youtube.com/watch?v=joRjb5WOmbM.

17. "Our Epic Battle #LikeAGirl," Always, Procter & Gamble, accessed October 16, 2022, https://always.com/en-us/about-us/our-epic-battle-like-a-girl.

18. Anna Coscia, *Always #LikeAGirl: Changing the Meaning of Words to Make Girls Proud to Be Girls* (London: Leo Burnett, 2015), https://www.marketingsociety.com /sites/default/files/thelibrary/P&G%20Always%20like%20a%20girl_0.pdf.

19. Edgar Sandoval, speech, the World Vision Strong Woman, Strong World virtual event, October 8, 2020.

20. Margo Day, interview by author, December 6, 2019.

21. The organizations mentioned in this book are just a small number of those working to help girls and overcome poverty in the world.

22. "UN Documentation: Development," Dag Hammarskjöld Library website of the United Nations, accessed November 3, 2022, https://research.un.org/en/docs/dev /2000-2015.

23. "#Envision2030: 17 Goals to Transform the World for Persons with Disabilities," United Nations Department of Economic and Social Affairs—Disability, accessed November 3, 2022, https://www.un.org/development/desa/disabilities/envision 2030.html.

## CHAPTER 2: KEEPING GIRLS HEALTHY

1. "Child Survival: Key Facts and Figures" in Levels & Trends in Child Mortality, Report 202, accessed November 3, 2020, https://www.unicef.org/media/79371 /file/UN-IGME-child-mortality-report-2020.pdf.pdf.

2. "Child Mortality (Under 5 Years)," World Health Organization, January 28, 2022, https://www.who.int/news-room/fact-sheets/detail/levels-and-trends-in-child-under -5-mortality-in-2020.

3. United Nations Population Fund, *Sex Imbalances at Birth: Current Trends, Consequences, and Policy Implications* (Bangkok: UNFPA Asia and the Pacific Regional Office, 2012). https://www.unfpa.org/sites/default/files/pub-pdf/Sex%20Imbalances%20at %20Birth.%20PDF%20UNFPA%20APRO%20publication%202012.pdf.

4. Ranjani Iyer Mohanty, "Trash Bin Babies: India's Female Infanticide Crisis," *Atlantic*, May 25, 2012, https://www.theatlantic.com/international/archive/2012/05/trash-bin -babies-indias-female-infanticide-crisis/257672/.

5. "Every Child Alive: The Urgent Need to End Newborn Deaths," highlights of 2018 report, UNICEF, accessed October 20, 2022, emphasis added, https://www.unicef .org/eap/reports/every-child-alive.

6. "Investing in Women and Girls," Center for Global Health and Development, accessed October 20, 2022, https://cghd.org/index.php/publication/global-health -challenges/investing-in-women-and-girls.

7. Story used by permission of Medical Teams International, Karen Piatt, communications manager, email message to author, April 11, 2022.

8. Story used by permission of Medical Teams International.

9. "National Day for Prevention of Iodine Deficiency Disorders: Celebrating Universal Salt Iodisation," UNICEF, press release, May 15, 2015, https://www .unicef.cn/en/press-releases/national-day-prevention-iodine-deficiency-disorders.

10. "Vitamin A Deficiency Puts 140 Million Children at Risk of Illness and Death— UNICEF," UN News, May 2, 2018, https://news.un.org/en/story/2018/05 /1008782.

11. Tianan Jiang et al., "Micronutrient Deficiencies in Early Pregnancy Are Common, Concurrent, and Vary by Season among Rural Nepali Pregnant Women," *Journal of Nutrition* 135, no. 5 (May 2005): 1106–1112, https://academic.oup.com/jn/article/135/5/1106/4663907.

12. "Maternal Nutrition: Preventing Malnutrition in Pregnant and Breastfeeding Women," UNICEF, accessed October 21, 2022, https://www.unicef.org/nutrition/maternal.

13. Centers for Disease Control and Prevention (CDC), *Diarrhea: Common Illness, Global Killer* (CDC, 2012), https://www.cdc.gov/healthywater/pdf/global/programs/globaldiarrhea508c.pdf.

14. Bernadeta Dadonaite, "Oral Rehydration Therapy: A Low-Tech Solution That Has Saved Millions of Lives," Our World in Data, August 27, 2019, https://ourworldindata.org/oral-rehydration-therapy. https://orders.map.org/products/gift-catalog-oral-rehydration-salts.

15. "Over-the-Counter Packs," MAP International, October 21, 2022, https://www.map.org/over-the-counter-packs; "Oral Rehydration Salts," MAP International, accessed October 21, 2022, https://orders.map.org/products/gift-catalog-oral-rehydration-salts.

16. "Plumpy'Nut," Nutriset, accessed October 23, 2022, https://www.nutriset.fr/products/en/plumpy-nut. https://www.nutriset.fr/products/en/plumpy-nut.

17. "Plumpy-Nut and the CMAM Model: How Nutriset's R&D Helped Transform the Treatment of Severe Acute Malnutrition," Nutriset, October 1, 2012, https://www.nutriset.fr/articles/en/plumpy-nut-and-the-cmam-model-nutriset-research-and-development-contribution.

18. *World Health Organization Model List of Essential Medicines—22nd List (2021)* (Geneva: World Health Organization, 2021), https://www.who.int/publications/i/item/WHO-MHP-HPS-EML-2021.02

19. "TRIORAL Rehydration Electrolyte Powder—WHO Hydration Supplement Salts Formula—100 Drink Mix Packets," Amazon.com, accessed October 23, 2022, https://www.amazon.com/Rehydration-Organization-Poisoning-Electrolyte-Replacement/dp/B00OG8G9UM/ref=sr_1_16?crid=393UFTVMFSF7I.

20. "Bringing Children Health," MAP International, accessed October 23, 2022, https://www.map.org/bch.

21. "Pneumonia," World Health Organization, November 11, 2021, https://www.who.int/news-room/fact-sheets/detail/pneumonia.

22. World Health Organization, *World Malaria Report 2021* (Geneva: World Health Organization), xv, 22–25, https://www.who.int/teams/global-malaria-programme/reports/world-malaria-report-2021.

23. "Malaria," UNICEF, July 2022, https://data.unicef.org/topic/child-health/malaria/.

24. "Malaria," Bill and Melinda Gates Foundation, accessed October 23, 2022, https://www.gatesfoundation.org/our-work/programs/global-health/malaria.

25. Nicholas D. Kristof and Sheryl WuDunn, *Half the Sky: Turning Oppression into Opportunity for Women Worldwide* (New York: Random House Vintage Books, 2010), 171.

26. "Soil-Transmitted Helminth Infections," World Health Organization, January 10, 2022, https://www.who.int/news-room/fact-sheets/detail/soil-transmitted-helminth-infections.

27. "Soil-Transmitted Helminth Infections."

28. World Health Organization, *Health for the World's Adolescents: A Second Chance in the Second Decade* (Geneva: World Health Organization, 2014), 3, https://apps.who.int/adolescent/second-decade/files/1612_MNCAH_HWA_Executive_Summary.

29. UNICEF, *2021 HIV and AIDS Global Snapshot* (New York: UNICEF, 2021), https://www.childrenandaids.org/sites/default/files/2022-01/211209_HIV%20Global%20Snapshot_V15_0.

30. "HIV," World Health Organization, July 27, 2022, https://www.who.int/news-room/fact-sheets/detail/hiv-aids.

31. "Immunization Coverage," World Health Organization, July 14, 2022, https://www.who.int/news-room/fact-sheets/detail/immunization-coverage.

32. "Immunization," World Health Organization, December 5, 2019, https://www.who.int/news-room/facts-in-pictures/detail/immunization.

33. "Immunization Coverage," World Health Organization.

34. Much of this vaccination information is from "Immunization Coverage," World Health Organization.

35. "UN Condemns Brutal Killing of Eight Polio Workers in Afghanistan," United Nations News, February 24, 2022, https://news.un.org/en/story/2022/02/1112612.

36. Jeffrey Kluger and Tara Law, "Polio Makes a Comeback in Ukraine as War Halts Vaccination Campaign," *Time*, March 9, 2022, https://time.com/6155963/polio-ukraine-war/.

37. Kate Causey et al., "Estimating Global and Regional Disruptions to Routine Childhood Vaccine Coverage during the COVID-19 Pandemic in 2020: A Modelling Study," *Lancet* 398, no. 10299 (August 7, 2021): 522–534, https://www.thelancet.com/article/S0140-6736(21)01337-4/fulltext.

38. Kaja Abbas and Vittal Mogasale, "Disruptions to Childhood Immunisation Due to the COVID-19 Pandemic in 2020," *Lancet* 398, no. 10299 (August 7, 2021): 469, https://doi.org/10.1016%2FS0140-6736(21)01418-5.

39. Nicola Davis, "Pregnancy Problems Are Leading Global Killer of Females Aged 15 to 19," *Guardian*, May 16, 2017, https://www.theguardian.com/global-development/2017/may/16/pregnancy-problems-are-leading-global-killer-of-females-aged-15-to-19.

40. "Adolescent Pregnancy," World Health Organization, September 15, 2022, https://www.who.int/news-room/fact-sheets/detail/adolescent-pregnancy.

41. "Child Marriage," United Nations Population Fund (UNFPA), accessed October 29, 2022, https://www.unfpa.org/child-marriage.

42. Anita Raj and Ulrike Boehmer, "Girl Child Marriage and Its Association with National Rates of HIV, Maternal Health, and Infant Mortality across 97 Countries," *Violence against Women* 19, no. 4 (April 2013): 536–551, https://pubmed.ncbi.nlm.nih.gov/23698937/.

43. Quoted in Stephanie Nolen, "What Pregnancy and Childbirth Do to the Bodies of Young Girls," *New York Times*, July 18, 2022, https://www.nytimes.com/2022/07/18/health/young-girls-pregnancy-childbirth.html.
44. "Obstetric Fistula," World Health Organization, February 19, 2018, https://www.who.int/news-room/facts-in-pictures/detail/10-facts-on-obstetric-fistula.
45. "Adolescent Pregnancy," World Health Organization.
46. "Female Genital Mutilation," World Health Organization, January 21, 2022, https://www.who.int/news-room/fact-sheets/detail/female-genital-mutilation.
47. "Female Genital Mutilation," WHO.

## CHAPTER 3: CLEAN WATER, SANITATION, AND HYGIENE FOR GIRLS

1. "Clean Water and Sanitation: Why It Matters," UN Sustainable Development Goals, accessed October 29, 2022, https://www.un.org/sustainabledevelopment/wp-content/uploads/2016/08/6_Why-It-Matters-2020.pdf; "1 in 3 People Globally Do Not Have Access to Safe Drinking Water—UNICEF, WHO," World Health Organization, June 18, 2019, https://www.who.int/news-room/detail/18-06-2019-1-in-3-people-globally-do-not-have-access-to-safe-drinking-water-unicef-who.
2. "The Water Burden," UNICEF, accessed October 29, 2022, https://www.unicefusa.org/mission/survival/water/water-burden.
3. "Water, Sanitation and Hygiene," Bill and Melinda Gates Foundation, accessed October 29, 2022, https://www.gatesfoundation.org/our-work/programs/global-growth-and-opportunity/water-sanitation-and-hygiene.
4. "Clean Water and Sanitation: Why It Matters," UN Sustainable Development Goals, accessed October 29, 2022, https://www.un.org/sustainabledevelopment/wp-content/uploads/2016/08/6_Why-It-Matters-2020.pdf.
5. W. H. Auden, "First Things First," in *Collected Poems*, ed. Edward Mendelson, 1st Vintage International ed. (New York: Vintage Books, 1991).
6. "UNICEF: Collecting Water Is Often a Colossal Waste of Time for Women and Girls," UNICEF, press release, August 29, 2016, https://www.unicef.org/press-releases/unicef-collecting-water-often-colossal-waste-time-women-and-girls.
7. "Drinking-Water," World Health Organization, March 21, 2022, https://www.who.int/news-room/fact-sheets/detail/drinking-water.
8. "Water Purification: How Much Bleach to Purify Water for Drinking?" Clorox, accessed October 30, 2022, https://www.clorox.com/learn/water-purification-how-much-bleach-purify-water-for-drinking/.
9. John A. Dracup, *Clean Water for Developing Countries* (Santa Monica: Clean Water Press, 2020), 73.
10. "Solar Cooking Builds a Foundation for Our Future," Solar Cookers International (SCI), accessed October 30, 2022, https://www.solarcookers.org/.
11. For example, the Centre for Affordable Water and Sanitation Technology (CAWST), https://www.cawst.org/.
12. "The World of Difference We Create Together," Sawyer, accessed October 30, 2022, https://www.sawyer.com/international#get-involved https://www.sawyer.com/.

13. See *Impact Stories* (blog), Sawyer, https://www.sawyer.com/blog-categories/impact -stories.

14. Chris Huber, "5 Ways World Vision's Water Work Makes a Splash," World Vision, April 16, 2021, https://www.worldvision.org/clean-water-news-stories/clean-water -around-world.

15. "The Key to Drilling Wells with Staying Power in the Developing World," World Vision, accessed October 30, 2022, https://www.worldvision.org/about-us/media -center/key-drilling-wells-staying-power-developing-world.

16. John 4:4-30.

17. Gil Zohar, "Jacob's Well: A Historic Greek Orthodox Church in Nablus, West Bank," *Jerusalem Post*, September 22, 2021, https://www.jpost.com/archaeology /jacobs-well-a-historic-greek-orthodox-church-in-nablus-west-bank-680024.

18. "Hand Dug Wells and Other Manual Methods to Dig a Well Have Been in Existence for Thousands of Years," A Layman's Guide to Clean Water, accessed October 30, 2022, http://www.clean-water-for-laymen.com/hand-dug-wells .html.

19. "What Is a Drilled Well?" Well Owner, accessed October 30, 2022, https://wellowner .org/resources/basics/what-is-a-drilled-well/.

20. "How a UNICEF Well Changed One Girl's Life," UNICEF USA, March 30, 2009, https://www.unicefusa.org/stories/how-unicef-well-changed-one-girls-life/6407.

21. "Sanitation," UNICEF, accessed October 31, 2022, https://www.unicef.org/wash /sanitation.

22. "Water, Sanitation and Hygiene," Bill and Melinda Gates Foundation.

23. "Sanitation," UNICEF.

24. Ijeoma Onuoha-Ogwe, "Toilets Help Keep Children, Especially Girls, in School," UNICEF, November 19, 2021, https://www.unicef.org/nigeria/stories/toilets-help -keep-children-especially-girls-school.

25. "Reinvent the Toilet Challenge: A Brief History," Bill and Melinda Gates Foundation, accessed October 31, 2022, https://www.gatesfoundation.org/our-work/programs /global-growth-and-opportunity/water-sanitation-and-hygiene/reinvent-the-toilet -challenge-and-expo.

26. "5 Innovative Toilets for Developing Countries," Borgen, May 28, 2013, https:// www.borgenmagazine.com/5-innovative-toilets-for-developing-countries.

27. "Valuing Toilets," United Nations, October 31, 2022, https://www.un.org/en /observances/toilet-day.

28. "Handwashing," UNICEF, accessed October 31, 2022, https://www.unicef.org /wash/handwashing.

29. "Diarrhoeal Disease," World Health Organization, May 2, 2017, https://www.who .int/news-room/fact-sheets/detail/diarrhoeal-disease.

30. "Sanitation," UNICEF.

31. "Health and Hygiene," Sesame Workshop, accessed October 31, 2022, https://www .sesameworkshop.org/what-we-do/health-and-hygiene.

32. World Vision Zimbabwe team, *WASH UP! Girl Talk Project: Zimbabwe* (World Vision, August 2021), https://www.worldvision.org/wp-content/uploads/2021 /11/Zimbabwe_GESI-Promising-Practice_FINAL.pdf

33. Jennifer J. Sara et al., "Menstrual Health and Hygiene Empowers Women and Girls: How to Ensure We Get It Right," *The Water Blog*, World Bank, May 28, 2021, https://blogs.worldbank.org/water/menstrual-health-and-hygiene-empowers -women-and-girls-how-ensure-we-get-it-right#_ftn1.

34. Caitlin Geng, "What to Know about Period Poverty," Medical News Today, September 16, 2021, https://www.medicalnewstoday.com/articles/period -poverty.

35. *Period. End of Sentence.*, directed by Rayka Zehtabchi, produced by Melissa Berton, premiered on Netflix February 2019, https://www.netflix.com/title/81074663.

36. The Pad Project, accessed November 1, 2022, https://thepadproject.org/.

37. Desmond Tutu, quoted at Jane Hanson, "Desmond Tutu and the Nobel Peace Prize," Jane Hanson (website), February 12, 2020,https://www.janehanson.com /blog/2020/desmondtutujanehanson.

## CHAPTER 4: EDUCATING GIRLS

1. Malala Fund, accessed November 4, 2022, https://malala.org/

2. Malala Yousafzai: Nobel Peace Prize Lecture 2014," Nobel Lecture, Oslo City Hall, Norway, December 10, 2014, video, 28:28, January 10, 2020, https://www.youtube .com/watch?v=c2DHzlkUI6s.

3. Malala Yousafzai, with Christina Lamb, *I Am Malala: The Girl Who Stood Up for Education and Was Shot by the Taliban* (New York: Little, Brown, 2013).

4. "Table 1.2 Compulsory School Attendance Laws, Minimum and Maximum Age Limits for Required Free Education, by State: 2017," State Education Practices, National Center for Education Statistics, accessed November 4, 2022, https:// nces.ed.gov/programs/statereform/tab1_2-2020.asp.

5. "Girls' Education," UNICEF, accessed November 4, 2022, https://www.unicef.org /education/girls-education.

6. Christina Kwauk, Dana Schmidt, and Erin Ganju, "What Do We Know about the Effects of COVID-19 on Girls' Return to School?," Brookings Institution, September 22, 2021, https://www.brookings.edu/blog/education-plus -development/2021/09/22/what-do-we-know-about-the-effects-of-covid-19-on -girls-return-to-school/.

7. World Vision's education model no longer includes building schools.

8. E. Ce Miller, "This New Memoir Is 'Kimmy Schmidt' Meets 'The Glass Castle' and It's a Must-Read," review of *Educated*, by Tara Westover, Bustle, February 20, 2018, https://www.bustle.com/p/educated-by-tara-westover-is-the-account-of-how -one-woman-raised-without-education-made-it-to-cambridge-8258701.

9. "Girls' Education," World Bank, last updated February 10, 2022, https://www .worldbank.org/en/topic/girlseducation.

10. "'To Educate Girls Is to Reduce Poverty' Says Secretary-General in Message to Global Education Campaign Event," United Nations, press release, April 9, 2003, https://www.un.org/press/en/2003/sgsm8662.doc.htm.

11. "Girls' Education," UNICEF.

12. "Girl's Education," World Vision, accessed November 5, 2022, https://www.wvi .org/education/girls-education.

13. Quentin Wodon et al., *Missed Opportunities : The High Cost of Not Educating Girls. The Cost of Not Educating Girls*, The Cost of Not Educating Girls Notes Series (Washington, DC: World Bank, 2018), Open Knowledge Repository, https://openknowledge.worldbank.org/handle/10986/29956.
14. "Girls' Education," UNICEF.
15. "Education," Tirzah International, November 5, 2022, https://tirzah.org/education-1.
16. "Girls' Education," UNICEF.
17. "Shaheen, Murkowski Reintroduce Bipartisan, Bicameral Bill to Improve Girls' 7ccess to Education around the World," Jeanne Shaheen (official website), press release, June 24, 2021, https://www.shaheen.senate.gov/news/press/shaheen-murkowski-reintroduce-bipartisan-bicameral-bill-to-improve-girls-access-to-education-around-the-world.
18. Kakenya Ntaiya, "Empower a Girl, Transform a Community," May 1, 2019, TED video, 12:31, https://www.youtube.com/watch?v=5nM21P8lJ2I.
19. "IGATE: Improving Girls' Access through Transforming Education," World Vision, accessed November 5, 2022, https://www.wvi.org/education-and-life-skills/igate-improving-girls-access-through-transforming-education.
20. Fazelminallah Qazizai and Diaa Hadid, "Taliban Reverses Decision, Barring Afghan Girls from Attending School beyond 6th Grade," *All Things Considered*, NPR, March 23, 2022, https://www.npr.org/2022/03/23/1088202759/taliban-afghanistan-girls-school.
21. "Boko Haram," National Counterterrorism Center, Office of the Director of National Intelligence, accessed November 5, 2022, https://www.dni.gov/nctc/groups/boko_haram.html.
22. "Belita's Journey," World Bicycle Relief, accessed November 5, 2022, https://worldbicyclerelief.org/belitas-journey/.
23. Kakenya Ntaiya, "Empower a Girl, Transform a Community," April 15, 2019, TED Talk video, 12:21, https://www.google.com/search?q=TED+Talk%3A+%22Empower+a+Girl%2C+Transform+a+Community%22&rlz=1C1GCEB_enUS955US956&oq.
24. James Tooley, "The Beautiful Tree: A Personal Journey into How the World's Poorest People Are Educating Themselves" (Washington, DC: CATO Institute, 2009), 41.
25. Edify, accessed November 5, 2022, https://www.edify.org.
26. "Nearly Half the World Lives on Less Than $5.50 a Day," World Bank, press release, October 17, 2018, https://www.worldbank.org/en/news/press-release/2018/10/17/nearly-half-the-world-lives-on-less-than-550-a-day.
27. Meagan Neal, "Small Costs, Big Impact: How a $6 Uniform Can Change a Girl's Future," ONE, November 1, 2017, https://www.one.org/us/blog/uniform-costs-girls-education/.
28. Chris Huber, "Facts about How Child Sponsorship Works," World Vision, March 7, 2019, https://www.worldvision.org/sponsorship-news-stories/facts-about-how-child-sponsorship-works.
29. Pencils of Promise, accessed November 5, 2022, https://pencilsofpromise.org/.
30. Good Shepherd Center—Marka, Facebook page, accessed November 5, 2022, https://www.facebook.com/Good-Shepherd-Center-Marka-2070213919703597/; "Our Work," Marka Church, accessed November 5, 2022, https://www.markachurch.org/our_work.php.

31. Marni Sommer, Christina Kwauk, and Nora Fyles, "Gender Sensitive Sanitation: Opportunities for Girl's Education," Women Deliver, January 28, 2018, https://womendeliver.org/2018/gender-sensitive-sanitation-opportunities-girls-education/.

32. Sommer, Kwauk, and Fyles, "Gender Sensitive Sanitation."

33. The Pad Project, accessed November 5, 2022, https://thepadproject.org.

34. "Refugee Education in Crisis: More Than Half of the World's School-Age Refugee Children Do Not Get an Education," United Nations High Commissioner for Refugees (UNHCR), press release, August 30, 2019, https://www.unhcr.org/en-us/news/press/2019/8/5d67b2f47/refugee-education-crisis-half-worlds-school-age-refugee-children-education.html.

35. "Jordan: Secondary School Gap for Syrian Refugee Kids," Human Rights Watch, June 26, 2020, https://www.hrw.org/news/2020/06/26/jordan-secondary-school-gap-syrian-refugee-kids.

36. "Our Impact: Education," Questscope, accessed November 5, 2022, https://www.questscope.org/en/our-impact/education.

37. Parfums de Vie, accessed November 5, 2022, https://parfumsdevie.com/.

38. Dale Hanson Bourke, "In the French Riviera, Both Arab Immigrants and Their Secular Neighbors Need Jesus," Christianity Today, November 21, 2019, https://www.christianitytoday.com/ct/2019/november-web-only/missionaries-france-immigrants-locals-need-jesus.html.

39. "Child Marriage," Theirworld, accessed November 5, 2022, https://theirworld.org/resources/child-marriage/.

40. "Child Marriage."

41. "Child Marriage."

42. "One Year into COVID-19 Education Disruption: Where Do We Stand?," UNESCO, March 19, 2021, https://en.unesco.org/news/290-million-students-out-school-due-covid-19-unesco-releases-first-global-numbers-and-mobilizes.

43. "Malala Fund Releases Report on Girls' Education and COVID-19," Malala Fund, report updated July 13, 2020, https://malala.org/newsroom/archive/malala-fund-releases-report-girls-education-covid-19.

44. "COVID-19: At Least a Third of the World's Schoolchildren Unable to Access Remote Learning during School Closures, New Report Says," UNICEF, press release, August 26, 2020, https://www.unicef.org/press-releases/covid-19-least-third-worlds-schoolchildren-unable-access-remote-learning-during. https://www.savethechildren.org/us/charity-stories/learning-loss.

45. "4: Ensure Inclusive and Equitable Quality Education and Promote Lifelong Learning Opportunities for All," Targets and Indicators, Sustainable Development, United Nations, accessed November 5, 2022, https://sdgs.un.org/goals/goal4.

46. "COVID-19 Aftershocks: Access Denied: Teenage Pregnancy Threatens to Block a Million Girls across Sub-Saharan African from Returning to School," ReliefWeb information services of OCHA, August 21, 2020, https://reliefweb.int/report/world/covid-19-aftershocks-access-denied-teenage-pregnancy-threatens-block-million-girls.

47. World Vision, *COVID-19 Aftershocks: Access Denied* (World Vision International, 2020), https://www.wvi.org/publications/report/coronavirus-health-crisis/covid-19 -aftershocks-access-denied.

48. "Malala Fund Releases Report on Girls' Education and COVID-19," Malala Fund, April 6, 2020, https://malala.org/newsroom/malala-fund-releases-report-girls -education-covid-19.

49. Elizabeth Nyamayaro, *I Am a Girl from Africa: A Memopir of Empowerment, Community, and Hope* (New York: Scribner, 2021), 252.

## CHAPTER 5: BREAKING CULTURAL STEREOTYPES

1. Vincent Petit and Tamar Naomi Zalk, *Everybody Wants to Belong: A Practical Guide to Tackling and Leveraging Social Norms in Behavior Change Programming* (UNICEF, May 2019), 17, https://www.unicef.org/mena/media/4716/file/MENA-C4DReport -May2019.pdf.

2. United Nations Office of the High Commissioner for Human Rights (OHCHR), *Fact Sheet No. 23, Harmful Traditional Practices Affecting the Health of Women and Children* (OHCHR: August 1995), https://www.refworld.org/docid/479477410 .html.

3. Bill and Melinda Gates Foundation, *The Goalkeepers Report 2019: Examining Inequality* (Seattle: Bill and Melinda Gates Foundation, 2019), https://www .gatesfoundation.org/goalkeepers/report/2019-report/.

4. "About Child Marriage," Girls Not Brides, accessed November 6, 2022, https:// www.girlsnotbrides.org/about-child-marriage/.

5. "About Us," Girls Not Brides, accessed November 6, 2022, https://www.girlsnot brides.org/about-us/.

6. "Child Marriage," Theirworld, accessed November 6, 2022, https://theirworld.org /resources/child-marriage/.

7. "Child Marriage," UNICEF, May 2022, https://data.unicef.org/topic/child -protection/child-marriage/.

8. "Child Marriage and Humanitarian Contexts," Girls Not Brides, accessed November 6, 2022, https://www.girlsnotbrides.org/learning-resources/child -marriage-and-humanitarian-contexts/.

9. While FGM was banned in Kenya in 2011, it is still popular in some parts of the country.

10. Margo Day, interview by author, December 6, 2019. The quotes that follow are from this same interview.

11. Mekuno Project, accessed November 6, 2022, https://www.mekunoproject.org.

12. "Premiere of *Hidden Truths* at the Millennial Empowerment Conference," Advice Project Media, accessed November 6, 2022, https://www.adviceprojectmedia.com /single-post/2016/09/13/premiere-of-hidden-truths-at-the-millennial-empowerment -conference-watch-now-online.

13. *Hidden Truths: Exposing Cultural Practices That Hurt Teen Girls in Cameroon,* produced by Advice Project Media, premiered August 22, 2016, Bamenda, Cameroon, video, 12:35, https://www.youtube.com/watch?v=X4ZyNwnFAt0.

14. Belinda Mallasasime, "The Culture Where Girls Are Force-Fed into Obesity (to Be Sexy)," *The Story in History* (blog), Medium, March 4, 2011, https://medium.com/the-story-in-history/the-culture-where-girls-are-force-fed-into-obesity-to-be-sexy-80215035eaba.

15. Michael Bamidele, "Kusasa Fumbi—The Sexual Rite of Passage," *Life* (blog), *Guardian* (Nigeria), February 2, 2020, https://guardian.ng/life/kusasa-fumbi-the-sexual-rite-of-passage/.

16. "Kenya Widows Fight Sexual 'Cleansing' Practice," BBC News, December 6, 2017, https://www.bbc.com/news/av/world-africa-41999891.

17. Beenish Ahmed, "Confronting a Sexual Rite of Passage in Malawi," *Atlantic*, January 20, 2014, https://www.theatlantic.com/international/archive/2014/01/confronting-a-sexual-rite-of-passage-in-malawi/283196/.

18. Ahmed, "Confronting a Sexual Rite."

19. CARE, *Gender, Power and Justice Primer* (Atlanta: CARE, June 2017), 6, https://www.care.org/wp-content/uploads/2020/09/care-gender-justice-primer-december-17.pdf.

20. "Channels of Hope for Gender," World Vision, accessed November 7, 2022, https://www.wvi.org/church-and-interfaith-engagement/channels-hope-gender.

21. Nicholas D. Kristof and Sheryl WuDunn, "Is Islam Misogynistic?" in *Half the Sky: Turning Oppression into Opportunity for Women Worldwide* (New York: Vintage Books, 2009) 149–151.

22. Kristof and WuDunn, "Is Islam Misogynistic?," 150.

23. "Afghanistan: Taliban Deprive Women of Livelihoods, Identity," Human Rights Watch, January 18, 2022, https://www.hrw.org/news/2022/01/18/afghanistan-taliban-deprive-women-livelihoods-identity#\.

24. "Child Marriage and Humanitarian Contexts," Girls Not Brides, accessed November 7, 2022, https://www.girlsnotbrides.org/learning-resources/child-marriage-and-humanitarian-contexts/.

## CHAPTER 6: PROTECTING VULNERABLE GIRLS

1. "Figures at a Glance," United Nations High Commissioner for Refugees (UNHCR), June 16, 2022, https://www.unhcr.org/en-us/figures-at-a-glance.html.

2. CARE, *Far from Home: The 13 Worst Refugee Crises for Girls* (CARE, 2018), https://care.exposure.co/far-from-home.

3. Jaclyn Diaz, "The 1.5 Million Children Who Fled Ukraine Are at Risk of Human Trafficking," NPR, March 19, 2022, https//:www.npr.org/2022/03/19/1087749861/ukraine-children-unicef-risk-report-human-trafficking.

4. "Syria Refugee Crisis Explained," United Nations High Commissioner for Refugees (UNHCR), July 8, 2022, https://www.unrefugees.org/news/syria-refugee-crisis-explained/.

5. Because they feared identifying themselves as dissidents or citizens who fled Syria, many refugees used a different name when identifying themselves to strangers.

6. UNHCR Handbook for the Protection of Women and Girls, (Office of the United Nations High Commissioner for Refugees, 2008), 7, https://www.unhcr.org/en-us/protection/women/47cfa9fe2/unhcr-handbook-protection-women-girls-first-edition-complete-publication.html.

7. "Worldwide, about 36.5 Million Children Had Been Displaced as Consequence of Conflict and Violence as of the End of 2021," UNICEF, last update June 2022, https://data.unicef.org/topic/child-migration-and-displacement/displacement/.

8. Save the Children, *Education Under Attack in Syria* (Save the Children, September 2015), 5, http://origin-qps.onstreammedia.com/origin/multivu_archive/ENR /267304-Save-the-Children-Education-Under-Attack.pdf.

9. "27 Million Children out of School in Conflict Zones," UNICEF, September 18, 2017, https://www.unicef.org/press-releases/27-million-children-out-school-conflict -zones.

10. Omer Karasapan, "Syrian Refugees in Jordan: A Decade and Counting," Brookings Institution, January 27, 2022, https://www.brookings.edu/blog/future -development/2022/01/27/syrian-refugees-in-jordan-a-decade-and-counting/.

11. Lin Taylor, "Syrian Girls Flee War Only to Become Mothers in Jordan Camp," Reuters, December 15, 2016, https://www.reuters.com/article/jordan-refugees -childmarriage-idINKBN1441FX.

12. "3 Things to Know about Blue Dots," UNICEF, March 21, 2022, https://www .unicef.org/emergencies/3-things-know-about-blue-dots.

13. Lauren Reed, "Child-Friendly Spaces: Safe Places for Children in Need," World Vision, May 16, 2019, https://www.worldvision.org/child-protection-news-stories /child-friendly-spaces-safe-place-children.

14. "What Is Streetism?" Global Village Action, accessed November 7, 2022, https:// www.globalvillageaction.org/phone/what-is-streetism.html; Mohd Ikram, "Street Children—Statistics, Their Lives and Why We Have to Care," Breakthrough, October 25, 2018, https://inbreakthrough.org/street-children-statistics-lives/.

15. Pat Flanagan, "International Missing Children's Day: Eight Million Kids Disappear around the World Every Year," *Irish Mirror*, May 25, 2014, https://www.irishmirror .ie/news/world-news/international-missing-childrens-day-eight-3606225.

16. *Lion*, directed by Garth Davis, screenplay by Luke Davies (2016), adapted from Saroo Brierley, *A Long Way from Home* (New Delhi: Penguin Books India, 2013).

17. UN General Assembly, Guidelines for the Alternative Care of Children, A/RES /64/142 (February 24, 2010), https://www.refworld.org/docid/4c3acd162 .html.

18. "Facts and Figures: HIV/AIDS Is Destroying the Future of Millions of Children," SOS Children's Villages, accessed November 8, 2022, https://www.sos-usa.org /about-us/where-we-work/africa/children-and-aids.

19. Chris Lockhart and Daniel Mulilo Chama, *Walking the Bowl: A True Story of Murder and Survival among the Street Children of Lusaka* (Toronto: Hanover Square Press, 2022), 56.

20. Lockhart and Chama, *Walking the Bowl*, 95.

21. Wendelin Van Draanen, *Runaway* (New York: Laurel Leaf Books, 2008), 187.

22. Sanna J. Thompson et al., "Runaway and Pregnant: Risk Factors Associated with Pregnancy in a National Sample of Runaway/Homeless Female Adolescents," *Journal of Adolescent Health* 43, no. 2 (August 2008): 125–132, https://www.homelesshub .ca/resource/runaway-and-pregnant-risk-factors-associated-pregnancy-national-sample -runawayhomeless.

23. National Runaway Safeline, accessed November 8, 2022, https://www.1800runaway
.org; "Runaway Homeless Youth Statistics," Youth Services System, accessed
November 8, 2022, https://www.youthservicesystem.org/residential-services/runaway
-homeless-youth-statistics/192.
24. M. H. Morton, A. Dworsky, and G. M. Samuels, *Missed Opportunities: Youth
Homelessness in America, National Estimates* (Chicago: Chapin Hall at the University
of Chicago, 2017), https://voicesofyouthcount.org/brief/national-estimates-of
-youth-homelessness/.
25. "Unaccompanied Youth," SchoolHouse Connection, accessed November 8, 2022,
https://schoolhouseconnection.org/learn/unaccompanied-youth/.
26. "Lifting Up Foster Youth Voices to Help Children and Families Thrive," National
Foster Youth Institute, accessed November 8, 2022, https://nfyi.org/mission/.
27. "The Definition of 'Missing,'" Global Missing Children's Center, International
Centre for Missing and Exploited Children, accessed November 8, 2022,
https://www.icmec.org/global-missing-childrens-center/the-definition-of
-missing/.
28. Office to Monitor and Combat Trafficking in Persons, U.S. Department of State,
accessed November 8, 2022, https://www.state.gov/bureaus-offices/under-secretary
-for-civilian-security-democracy-and-human-rights/office-to-monitor-and-combat
-trafficking-in-persons/.
29. David Batstone, *Not for Sale: The Return of the Global Slave Trade—and How We
Can Fight It* (New York: Harper Collins, 2007).
30. "Basic Principles of GAATW," Global Alliance Against Traffic in Women, February 25,
2009, https://gaatw.org/about-us/basic-principles.
31. "40 Million in Modern Slavery and 152 Million in Child Labour around the
World," International Labour Organization (ILO), September 19, 2017, https://
www.ilo.org/global/about-the-ilo/newsroom/news/WCMS_574717/lang--en
/index.htm.
32. "What We Do," Tech Coalition, accessed November 8, 2022, https://www.technology
coalition.org/what-we-do.
33. Naver Corporation, "NAVER Z Joins Tech Coalition to Prevent Sexual Exploitation
and Abuse of Children Online," PR Newswire, September 13, 2022, https://www
.prnewswire.com/news-releases/naver-z-joins-tech-coalition-to-prevent-sexual
-exploitation-and-abuse-of-children-online-301623734.html.
34. "Lord's Resistance Army," Enough Project, accessed November 9, 2022, https://
enoughproject.org/conflicts/lra.
35. "Child Soldiers," Human Rights Watch, accessed November 9, 2022, https://www
.hrw.org/topic/childrens-rights/child-soldiers.
36. UNHCR Handbook for the Protection of Women and Girls, 7.
37. Liz Ford, "Women Freed from Boko Haram Rejected for Bringing 'Bad Blood' Back
Home," *The Guardian*, accessed November 15, 2022, https://www.theguardian.com
/global-development/2016/feb/16/women-freed-boko-haram-rejected-for-bringing
-bad-blood-back-home-nigeria.
38. Ford, "Women Freed from Boko Haram Rejected."

## CHAPTER 7: OFFERING GIRLS ECONOMIC FREEDOM

1. "A Letter from Our Founder," Our Vision, Chikumbuso, accessed November 9, 2022, https://www.chikumbuso.com/our-vision.
2. Susan Olasky, "Picking Up Pieces: What One Christian in Africa Started," *World*, February 23, 2008, https://wng.org/articles/picking-up-pieces-1617335956.
3. Today the bags are made from donated plastic.
4. "Building Community One Bag at a Time," Micro Enterprise, Chikumbuso, accessed November 9, 2022, https://www.chikumbuso.com/microenterprise.
5. "Microinsurance," National Association of Insurance Commissioners (NAIC), last updated May 3, 2022, https://content.naic.org/cipr-topics/microinsurance.
6. Carol Hymowitz, "Third World Entrepreneurs Thrive with Dreams, Focus and Hard Work," *Forbes*, July 6, 2010, https://www.forbes.com/2010/07/06/micro-finance-loans-nonprofits-startups-eradicating-poverty-forbes-woman-entrepreneurs-small-business-funding.html?sh=454d708610f5.
7. Adam Gorlick, "Novel Winner Pushes for Banking with a Conscience," Stanford Report, November 17, 2008, https://news.stanford.edu/news/2008/november19/yunus-111908.html.
8. "Grameen Group Lending Model," Grameen Research, accessed November 9, 2022, http://grameenresearch.org/grameen-group-lending-model/.
9. Mizla Shrestha, "Microcredit: One of the Best Ways of Empowering Women," Borgen Project, September 16, 2020, https://borgenproject.org/microcredit-empower-women-econ/.
10. Convergences, *Microfinance Barometer 2019* (Paris: Convergences, 2018), https://www.convergences.org/wp-content/uploads/2019/09/Microfinance-Barometer-2019_web-1.pdf; Shreya Shrestha, "Technology Impact on Microfinance," Finflux, March 22, 2021, https://finflux.co/blog/technology-impact-on-microfinanceled/.
11. "Trust Groups," Opportunity International, accessed November 9, 2022, https://opportunity.org/what-we-do/micro-banking/support.
12. Kiva, accessed November 9, 2022, https://www.kiva.org.
13. Jacqueline Novogratz, *The Blue Sweater: Bridging the Gap between Rich and Poor in an Interconnected World* (New York: Rodale, 2009), 192.
14. Novogratz, *The Blue Sweater*, 192.
15. Acumen Academy, accessed November 9, 2022, https://acumenacademy.org.
16. Annie Prafcke, "The Future of Microfinance and Mobile Banking," Borgen Magazine, November 20, 2021, https://www.borgenmagazine.com/microfinance/.
17. "FAS: What Is Mobile Money? How Is It Different from Mobile Banking?," International Monetary Fund, accessed November 9, 2022, https://datahelp.imf.org/knowledgebase/articles/1906552-fas-what-is-mobile-money-how-is-it-different-fro.
18. Gautam Ivatury and Mark Pickens, "Mobile Phones for Microfinance," CGAP, April 2006, https://www.cgap.org/research/publication/mobile-phones-microfinance.
19. Dilip Ratha, "Global Remittance Flows in 2021: A Year of Recovery and Surprises," *People Move* (blog), World Bank, November 17, 2021, https://blogs.worldbank.org/peoplemove/global-remittance-flows-2021-year-recovery-and-surprises.

20. UN Women, *Migrant Women and Remittances: Exploring the Data from Selected Countries* (New York: UN Women, 2020), https://www.unwomen.org/en/digital-library/publications/2020/06/policy-brief-migrant-women-and-remittances-exploring-the-data-from-selected-countries.

21. "Sending Money Home for Education?," WorldRemit, August 20, 2021, https://www.worldremit.com/en/blog/community/sending-money-home-for-education/.

22. Laura Reinhardt, "Lives Transformed: Girls Free to Dream of a Brighter Future," World Vision, April 20, 2020, https://www.worldvision.org/child-protection-news-stories/lives-transformed-girls-free-dream-brighter-future.

23. "Empower Girls," Girls Not Brides, accessed November 10, 2022, https://www.girlsnotbrides.org/learning-resources/theory-change/empower-girls/.

24. Kelton Holsen, "TVET in Developing Countries," Borgen Magazine, November 20, 2019, https://www.borgenmagazine.com/tvet-in-developing-countries/ Kelton Holsen.

25. Vocational Training for Youth, Opportunity International, accessed November 10, 2022, https://opportunity.org/what-we-do/innovative-programs/vocational-training-for-youth.

26. Sonia Madhvani and Danielle Robinson, "Social and Cultural Barriers Keep Young Women Out of the Economy. But We Can Change That," *Jobs and Development* (blog), World Bank, July 12, 2019, https://blogs.worldbank.org/jobs/social-and-cultural-barriers-keep-young-women-out-economy-we-can-change.

27. Kate Plourde et al., *The Skills4Girls Learning Agenda* (UNICEF and FHI 360, 2020), 3, https://www.unicef.org/media/83876/file/S4G-Learning-Agenda.pdf.

28. Plourde et al., *Skills4Girls Learning Agenda*, 4.

29. "Digital Jobs Can Help Young Women Overcome Constraints in the Workforce Says Solutions for Youth Employment Annual Report," World Bank, press release, September 5, 2018, https://www.worldbank.org/en/news/press-release/2018/09/05/digital-jobs-can-help-young-women-overcome-constraints-in-the-workforce-says-solutions-for-youth-employment-annual-report.

30. "About KOTO," KOTO, accessed November 11, 2022, https://www.koto.com.au/about-koto.

## CHAPTER 8: CARING FOR DISABLED GIRLS

1. "Casa de Luz," All Children, accessed November 11, 2022, https://allchildren.org/our-work/casa-de-luz/.

2. World Health Organization (WHO), *World Report on Disability* (Geneva, Switzerland: World Health Organization, 2011), https://www.who.int/publications/i/item/9789241564182; "International Day of Persons with Disabilities, December 3," United Nations, accessed November 11, 2022, https://www.un.org/en/observances/day-of-persons-with-disabilities/background.

3. "FACT SHEET: The World's Nearly 240 Million Children Living with Disabilities Are Being Denied Basic Rights—UNICEF," UNICEF, December 2, 2021, https://www.unicef.org/press-releases/fact-sheet-worlds-nearly-240-million-children-living-disabilities-are-being-denied.

4. Arnold Christianson, Christopher P. Howson, and Bernadette Modell, *March of Dimes Global Report on Birth Defects: The Hidden Toll of Dying and Disabled Children* (New York: March of Dimes Birth Defects Foundation, 2006).

5. "FACT SHEET: The World's Nearly 240 Million Children Living with Disabilities," https://www.unicef.org/press-releases/fact-sheet-worlds-nearly-240-million-children-living-disabilities-are-being-denied.

6. "Advancing Women and Girls with Disabilities," USAID, last updated May 7, 2019, https://www.usaid.gov/what-we-do/gender-equality-and-womens-empowerment/women-disabilities.

7. Anne Soy, "Infanticide in Kenya: 'I Was Told to Kill My Disabled Baby,'" BBC News, September 27, 2018, https://www.bbc.com/news/world-africa-45670750.

8. "Tanzania Albino Murders: 'More Than 200 Witchdoctors' Arrested," BBC News, March 12, 2015, https://www.bbc.com/news/world-africa-31849531.

9. Laura Menenberg, Special Hope Network, telephone interview by author, February 15, 2022.

10. "Mission Statement/Frequently Asked Questions," Wheelchair Foundation, accessed November 11, 2022, https://www.wheelchairfoundation.org/about/.

11. "Clubfoot in Low and Middle Income Countries (LMIC)," Global Clubfoot Initiative, accessed November 11, 2022, https://globalclubfoot.com/clubfoot/low-middle-income-countries/.

12. The Accessibility Institute, accessed November 11, 2022, https://tai.ngo/.

13. Laura Menenberg, Special Hope Network.

14. "FACT SHEET: The World's Nearly 240 Million Children Living with Disabilities."

15. Mary Katherine Crowley, "Children with Disabilities in Developing Countries," Borgen Project, September 9, 2017, https://borgenproject.org/children-with-disabilities-in-developing-countries/.

16. John Ray, "China's Disabled Children Are Sold into Slavery as Beggars," *Guardian*, July 21, 2007, https://www.theguardian.com/world/2007/jul/22/china.theobserver.

17. Crowley, "Children with Disabilities in Developing Countries."

18. United Nations Children's Fund (UNICEF), *Seen, Counted, Included: Using Data to Shed Light on the Well-Being of Children with Disabilities* (New York: UNICEF, 2021), 62, https://data.unicef.org/resources/children-with-disabilities-report-2021/.

19. John J. McGrath et al., "A Comprehensive Assessment of Parental Age and Psychiatric Disorders," *JAMA Psychiatry* 71, no. 3 (2014): 301–309, https://jamanetwork.com/journals/jamapsychiatry/fullarticle/1814892.

20. "Zika Virus," World Health Organization, July 20, 2018, https://www.who.int/news-room/fact-sheets/detail/zika-virus.

21. Hanan Hamamy, "Consanguineous Marriages," *Journal of Community Genetics* 3, no. 3 (July 2012): 185–192, https://www.ncbi.nlm.nih.gov/pmc/articles/PMC3419292/; A. H. Bittles and M. L. Black, "Consanguinity, Human Evolution, and Complex Diseases," *PNAS* 107, no. S1 (January 26, 2010): 1779–1786, https://www.pnas.org/doi/10.1073/pnas.0906079106.

22. "Kissing Cousins: The States Where Marrying Your Relative Is Legal," Inside Edition, November 7, 2018, https://www.insideedition.com/gallery/kissing-cousins-states-where-marrying-your-relative-legal-48234/alabama-1695.

23. Martina Merten, "Keeping It in the Family: Consanguineous Marriage and Genetic Disorders, from Islamabad to Bradford," *BMJ* 365 (April 29, 2019): l1851, https://www.bmj.com/content/365/bmj.l1851.

24. "Women and Girls with Disabilities," Women's Human Rights, Human Rights Watch, accessed November 11, 2022, https://www.hrw.org/legacy/women/disabled.html.

25. "Women and Girls with Disabilities."

26. "Convention on the Rights of Persons with Disabilities (CRPD)," Department of Economic and Social Affairs, United Nations, last updated May 6, 2022, https://www.un.org/development/desa/disabilities/convention-on-the-rights-of-persons-with-disabilities.html.

27. "Convention on the Rights."

28. "Sustainable Development Goals (SDGs) and Disability," Department of Economic and Social Affairs, United Nations, accessed November 12, 2022, https://www.un.org/development/desa/disabilities/about-us/sustainable-development-goals-sdgs-and-disability.html.

29. Sue Coe and Lorraine Wapling, *Travelling Together: How to Include Disabled People on the Main Road of Development* (World Vision UK, 2010), 49, https://www.worldvision.org/our-work/disability-inclusion/more-resources.

30. David Werner, *Disabled Village Children: A Guide for Community Health Workers, Rehabilitation Workers, and Families*, updated edition (Berkeley: Hesperian Health Guides, 2022). Available at www.hesperian.org and Amazon.com.

31. "An Overview of the Americans with Disabilities Act," ADA National Network, last updated November 2022, https://adata.org/factsheet/ADA-overview.

32. "Pastors and Religious Leaders," Kupenda for the Children, accessed November 12, 2022, https://kupenda.org/portfolio/pastors-and-religious-leaders/.

33. Special Hope Network, accessed November 12, 2022, https://specialhopenetwork.org/.

## CHAPTER 9: PROTECTING GIRLS' RIGHTS

1. International Justice Mission (IJM), "About IJM," accessed November 12, 2022, https://www.ijm.org/about-ijm.

2. Gary A. Haugen and Victor Boutros, *The Locust Effect: Why the End of Poverty Requires the End of Violence* (New York: Oxford University Press, 2014) xiii–xiv.

3. UN Women et al., *Equality in Law for Women and Girls by 2030: A Multistakeholder Strategy for Accelerated Action* (New York: UN Women, 2019), https://www.unwomen.org/en/digital-library/publications/2019/03/equality-in-law-for-women-and-girls-by-2030.

4. Nabih Bulos, "After Woman's Brutal Killing by Her Father, Jordan Asks at What Price 'Honor'?," *Los Angeles Times*, July 28, 2020, https://www.latimes.com/world-nation/story/2020-07-28/jordan-honor-killing-protests-violence-against-women.

5. "Girls in Burkina Faso Forced out of School and into Early Marriage," Theirworld, April 29, 2016, https://theirworld.org/news/girls-in-burkina-faso-forced-out-of-school-and-into-early-marriage/.

6. UN Women et al., *Equality in Law for Women and Girls by 2030*.

7. World Bank Group, *Women, Business and the Law* (Washington, DC: World Bank, 2018).

8. UN General Assembly, Convention on the Rights of the Child (November 20, 1989), United Nations, https://www.refworld.org/docid/3ae6b38f0.html.

9. "What Are Girls' Rights?," Girls' Rights Platform factsheet, Plan International (2018), https://girlsrightsplatform.org/assets/16214537547836hmhm4ljxct.pdf.

10. Nicholas D. Kristof and Sheryl WuDunn, *Half the Sky: Turning Oppression into Opportunity for Women Worldwide* (New York: Vintage Books, 2010), 68.

11. Leah Selim, "What Is Birth Registration and Why Does It Matter?," UNICEF, December 10, 2019, https://www.unicef.org/stories/what-birth-registration-and-why-does-it-matter.

12. Selim, "What Is Birth Registration and Why Does It Matter?"

13. Haugen and Boutros, *Locust Effect*, 55.

14. Haugen and Boutros, *Locust Effect*, 32.

15. "About Us," Global Campaign for Equal Nationality Rights, accessed November 12, 2022, https://equalnationalityrights.org/about-us.

16. "Statelessness around the World," United Nations High Commissioner for Refugees (UNHCR), accessed November 12, 2022, https://www.unhcr.org/ibelong/statelessness-around-the-world/.

17. "The Violence of Gender Discrimination in Nationality Laws," Global Campaign for Equal Nationality Rights, accessed November 12, 2022, https://equalnationalityrights.org/news/76-gender-violence-discrimination-nationality-laws.

18. "The Problem," Global Campaign for Equal Nationality Rights, accessed November 12, 2022, https://equalnationalityrights.org/the-issue/the-problem.

19. "Child Marriage," UNICEF, May 2022, https://data.unicef.org/topic/child-protection/child-marriage/.

20. "Legal Age for Marriage," United Nations Statistics Division, July 11, 2013, https://data.un.org/documentdata.aspx?id=336.

21. Emma Batha, "Factbox: Female Genital Mutilation around the World: A Fine, Jail or No Crime?," Reuters, September 13, 2018, https://www.reuters.com/article/us-africa-fgm-lawmaking-factbox/factbox-female-genital-mutilation-around-the-world-a-fine-jail-or-no-crime-idUSKCN1LT2OS.

22. "Female Genital Mutilation," 28 Too Many, accessed November 12, 2022, https://www.28toomany.org/.

23. Zakeeya Ali, "Explaining Puberty for a Muslim Child," Zakeeya Ali (website), accessed November 12, 2022, https://zakeeyaali.com/blog/onset-of-puberty-for-muslim-child.

24. Deborah E. Lipstadt, "The Jewish Age of Majority and Its Obligations," My Jewish Learning, accessed November 12, 2022, https://www.myjewishlearning.com/article/the-jewish-age-of-majority-and-its-obligations/.

25. *Code of Canon Law*, book 1, title 6 (1983), https://www.vatican.va/archive/cod-iuris-canonici/eng/documents/cic_lib1-cann96-123_en.html.

26. "Registration—Age of Maturity," Bahá'í Quotes, accessed November 12, 2022, https://bahaiquotes.com/subject/registration-age-maturity.

27. "Age of Majority," Center for Parent Information and Resources, November 2017, https://www.parentcenterhub.org/age-of-majority/.
28. "Child Soldiers," Human Rights Watch, accessed November 12, 2022, https://www.hrw.org/topic/childrens-rights/child-soldiers.
29. Henrietta Fore, "Opinion: Female Child Soldiers Often Go Unseen but Must Not Be Forgotten," Thomson Reuters Foundation, February 12, 2021, https://news.trust.org/item/20210211143359-cpm3z.
30. Henrietta Fore, "Opinion."
31. "The Protocol," Office on Drugs and Crime, United Nations, accessed November 12, 2022, https://www.unodc.org/unodc/en/human-trafficking/protocol.html.
32. Office to Monitor and Combat Trafficking in Persons, *2021 Trafficking in Persons Report* (U.S. Department of State, 2021), 2, https://www.state.gov/reports/2021-trafficking-in-persons-report/.
33. Blue Campaign, U.S. Department of Homeland Security, accessed November 12, 2022, https://www.dhs.gov/blue-campaign.

**CHAPTER 10: CHANGING THE WORLD FOR GIRLS**

1. Mary is not her real name. To protect families of people living with HIV, all names of those in support groups have been changed.
2. Joe DeCapua, "AIDS: The Lazarus Effect," Voice of America (VOA) News, December 8, 2010, https://www.voanews.com/a/decapua-aids-lazarus-effect-9dec10-111605079/157017.html. A documentary was filmed in Zambia and produced in 2010 about the transformation: *The Lazarus Effect*, directed by Lance Bangs, produced by Spike Jonze (HBO Documentary Films, Red, 2010), video, 31:39, https://www.youtube.com/watch?v=l16YH6xCN4c.
3. John 11:1-44.
4. PEPFAR was launched in 2003 by President George W. Bush and provided funding for HIV/AIDS treatment in the hardest hit countries, including Zambia.
5. Centre for Infectious Disease Research in Zambia (CIDRZ), accessed November 12, 2022, https://www.cidrz.org.
6. Progression from initial HIV infection to AIDS occurs somewhere between five and ten years without treatment, but people living in poverty often deal with other health conditions that can shorten this timeline.
7. Albert R. Jonsen and Jeff Stryker, eds., "Religion and Religious Groups," in *National Research Council Panel on Monitoring the Social Impact of AIDS in the United States* (Washington, DC: National Academies Press, 1993), chap. 5, https://www.ncbi.nlm.nih.gov/books/NBK234570/.
8. UNAIDS, *Children and Young People in a World of AIDS* (UNAIDS, 2001), https://www.unaids.org/sites/default/files/media_asset/jc656-child_aids_en_0.pdf.
9. Richard Stearns, *The Hole in Our Gospel* (Nashville: Thomas Nelson, 2009), 194–195.
10. Stearns, *The Hole in Our Gospel*, 195.
11. Sheryl Henderson, "Bono Tells Christians: Don't Neglect Africa," *Christianity Today*, April 22, 2002, https://www.christianitytoday.com/ct/2002/aprilweb-only/14.18.html.

12. Nina Shapiro, "The AIDS Evangelists," *Seattle Weekly*, February 12, 2007, https://www.seattleweekly.com/news/the-aids-evangelists/.

13. "Kay Warren on HIV & AIDS: The Church as the Solution," HIV/AIDS Initiative, Saddleback Church, accessed November 12, 2022, http://hivaidsinitiative.com/blogs/main/kay-warren-on-hivaids-the-church-is-the-solution/.

14. Shayne Moore, *Global Soccer Mom: Changing the World Is Easier Than You Think* (Grand Rapids, MI: Zondervan, 2011).

15. Dale Hanson Bourke, *The Skeptic's Guide to the Global AIDS Crisis: Tough Questions, Direct Answers* (Colorado Springs: Authentic, 2004).

16. Kendra Cherry, "What Is Cognitive Dissonance?," Verywell Mind, November 7, 2022, https://www.verywellmind.com/what-is-cognitive-dissonance-2795012.

17. Christen Brandt and Tammy Tibbetts, *Impact: A Step-by-Step Plan to Create the World You Want to Live In* (New York: Public Affairs, 2020).

18. Steve Corbett and Brian Fikkert, *When Helping Hurts: How to Alleviate Poverty without Hurting the Poor . . . and Yourself* (Chicago: Moody, 2009).

19. Dean Karlan and Jacob Appel, *More Than Good Intentions: How a New Economics Is Helping to Solve Global Poverty* (New York: Dutton, 2011).

20. Nick Cooney, *How to Be Great at Doing Good: Why Results Are What Count and How Smart Charity Can Change the World* (New York: Rodale, 2009), 129.

21. Jacqueline Novogratz, *The Blue Sweater: Bridging the Gap between Rich and Poor in an Interconnected World* (New York: Rodale, 2009), 129.

22. See "Refugees and Immigrants Need Your Help Today," World Relief, accessed November 13, 2022, https://worldrelief.org/refugees-immigrants-and-displaced-people/; Lutheran Immigration and Refugee Service, accessed November 13, 2022, https://www.lirs.org/; Church World Service, accessed November 13, 2022, https://cwsglobal.org/.

23. Tina Rosenberg, "The Business of Voluntourism: Do Western Do-Gooders Actually Do Harm?," *Guardian*, September 13, 2018, https://www.theguardian.com/news/2018/sep/13/the-business-of-voluntourism-do-western-do-gooders-actually-do-harm.

24. Rosenberg, "The Business of Voluntourism."

25. International Medical Relief, accessed November 13, 2022, https://internationalmedicalrelief.org/.

26. "When Kids Need a Place to Sleep for the Night, Emergency Foster Homes Offer a Safe Landing," Fostering Great Ideas, February 4, 2020, https://fgi4kids.org/short-term-foster-care/.

27. "Exempt Purposes—Internal Revenue Code Section 501(c)(3)," Internal Revenue Service (IRS), last updated June 17, 2022, https://www.irs.gov/charities-non-profits/charitable-organizations/exempt-purposes-internal-revenue-code-section-501c3.

28. "Learn Library," GlobalGiving, accessed November 13, 2022, https://www.globalgiving.org/learn/.

29. Kiva, accessed November 13, 2022, https://www.kiva.org.

30. RunGuides, accessed November 13, 2022, https://www.runguides.com/north-america/runs/fundraiser/all.

31. Golf Fore Africa, accessed November 13, 2022, https://golfforeafrica.org/our -mission/.
32. "Why We Ride," Brake the Cycle, accessed November 13, 2022, https://www .brakethecycle.net/why.

**APPENDIX: UNITED NATIONS CONVENTION ON THE RIGHTS OF THE CHILD**
1. United Nations Convention on the Rights of the Child—The Children's Version, UNICEF, accessed January 18, 2023, https://www.unicef.org/child-rights -convention/convention-text-childrens-version.

# About the Author

**Dale Hanson Bourke** is an award-winning writer who has traveled to sixty-two countries and has a passion for telling the stories of the people she meets and the issues they face. She has served on the boards of major humanitarian organizations, including World Vision (US and International), International Justice Mission, Opportunity International, and MAP International. She currently serves on the board of World Vision's Strong Women Strong World and is a global ambassador for Oxfam's Sisters on the Planet.

In addition to serving as publisher of Religion News Service, editor of *Today's Christian Woman*, and president of Publishing Directions, Dale has also served as president of the CIDRZ Foundation, supporting health care for women and children in Zambia. For five years she wrote a nationally syndicated column. An author of twelve books and hundreds of articles, Dale has won awards for her writing from the Associated Press, ECPA, EPA, ACP, *Christianity Today*, and InterAction.

A graduate of Wheaton College (IL), she also holds an MBA from the University of Maryland. Dale and her husband live in Annapolis, Maryland, and are the parents of two sons and grandparents of Evie and Tommy. You can find her online at DaleHansonBourke.com or on her Amazon author page.